Thank-you
and Merry Christmas!
love the GAPs 2017
Bree & Emily
xoxo

365

COUNTRY WOMEN'S ASSOCIATION FAVOURITES

MURDOCH BOOKS

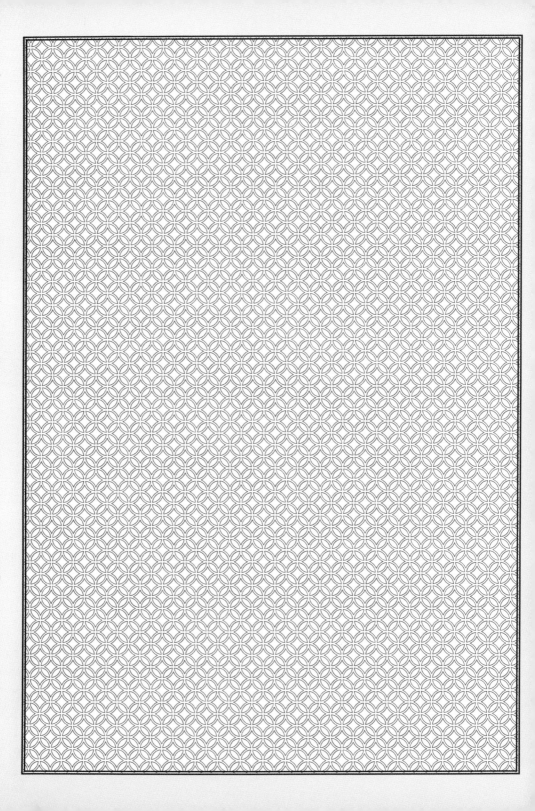

CONTENTS

INTRODUCTION

Over a period of three years in the early 1930s, the Country Women's Association of New South Wales produced three cookbooks. Each took the form of a recipe-a-day calendar and all were filled with recipes contributed by individual members. A huge commercial success, they sold in numbers that would be the envy of any modern-day food author; between October 1930 and April 1933, a staggering 35,000 of the Cakes and Afternoon Tea Delicacies volume alone were purchased for the cover price of 2 shillings. These cookbooks were designed for display on a kitchen wall, handy for everyday reference and use. Each shared the same dimensions and simple layout: narrow, rectangular pages printed on thick paper, bound along the top edge and finished with an arc of string for hanging.

In a CWA Annual Report from the period, it was noted that 'The Cake and Afternoon Tea Delicacies calendar, compiled by Mrs WH Hammond of Wagga Wagga, has been an unqualified success (and) ... has been circulated far and wide.' A Calendar of Puddings was the next to be produced, after which came a collection of Luncheon and Tea Dishes. The latter, it was noted at the time, 'proved most successful'.

The nature of the recipes gives great insight into how women cooked during this era; their dishes are simple, honest and homey. These were Depression years, when money and resources were tight. In a time before access to high-speed information and widespread international travel, culinary influences were few. Accordingly, the various dishes mainly reflect the English, Scottish and Irish cookery traditions that defined early Australian cookery.

Ingredients back then, in comparison to the huge selections we enjoy today, were relatively limited in range. Labour-saving kitchen devices (food processors, electric cake mixers and the like) simply didn't exist. Most cooking was done on a wood- or coal-fired 'range'. Tasks such as creaming butter and sugar – something modern cooks accomplish with ease using electric beaters – involved the manual employment of a wooden spoon. More often than not, even mincing meat was done at home using a hand-cranked mincer; such jobs were laborious yet were part of a cook's everyday routine.

Despite the passage of eight decades, these recipes still hold great appeal for today's cook, especially the tried-and-true cakes, biscuits, puddings and myriad other baking recipes that make up by far the largest category in the original material. For this volume, each of the original recipes chosen has been tested and updated for contemporary use, taking into account modern cookery styles and equipment. The majority of the recipes didn't contain specifics for essentials such as cake tin sizes, baking dish capacities, precise cooking times or even oven temperatures. They carried the tone of recipes shared informally amongst friends, and kitchen-savvy friends at that, who could fill in such gaps in information with ease. Without sacrificing the integrity of the original material, the recipes now include more complete methods, so the modern cook can take them into their own kitchen with confidence and ease.

The spirit of these cookbooks is perhaps best reflected in the words of the CWA of NSW State President during those years, Jessie Sawyer.

'It is in her own home that a good woman is seen at her best. This Cookery Calendar has been compiled by such [a] one to assist her fellow woman. On behalf of all those who need our help – we ask for your support for this venture.'
Jessie Sawyer, 1930
State President
The Country Women's Association of NSW

Gwydir Group
Conference, 1955

From humble beginnings in 1922, the Country Women's Association of New South Wales (including the ACT) is part of the largest female lobby group in Australia, the CWA of Australia. It has approximately 10,000 members belonging to 397 branches, who meet monthly to discuss a variety of initiatives. These range from fundraising for medical research, lobbying for better services for families and helping out in times of emergency, to handicraft and cookery projects.

The CWA of New South Wales is evolving to work in new environments, but still under the same banner of improving conditions and life for women, children and families.

For more information, see our website www.cwaofnsw.org.au or telephone 02 9358 2923.

		1 Sago Snow	2 Yass Savoury	3 Apricot Upside-Down Pudding
4 Cheese Biscuits	5 Genoa Cakes	6 Grapefruit and Walnut Salad	7 Cocoa Cake	8 Oyster Savouries
9 Cream Puffs	10 Tomato, Prune and Cress Salad	11 Cinnamon Sandwich	12 Bengal Canapés	13 Pancakes
14 Carrot Salad	15 Raspberry or Blackberry Jam Tart	16 Tasty Spaghetti	17 Chicken Loaf	18 Iced Chocolate Tart
19 Butterscotch Pie	20 Orange Pudding	21 Banana Snow	22 Oat Biscuits	23 Savoury Toast
24 Sponge Slices	25 Marlborough Tart	26 Currant Cake	27 Coconut Fingers	28 Afternoon Tea Toast
29 Walnut Shortbreads	30 Vanilla Cream Sandwich	31 Lemon Cheese Tarts		

JANUARY

Sago Snow

Mrs Robards, Nevertire Branch

SERVES 4–6
3 lemons
100 g (½ cup) sago
1 litre (4 cups) water
220 g (1 cup) caster sugar
4 egg whites

Custard
600 ml milk
1 vanilla pod, split and
    seeds scraped
4 egg yolks
2 teaspoons cornflour
2 tablespoons caster sugar

Finely grate the zest of one lemon and juice all three lemons. Set the zest and juice aside.

Combine the sago and water in a saucepan and bring to a simmer over medium heat. Reduce heat to low and cook, stirring often to prevent sago catching, for 15–20 minutes, or until the mixture is thick and sago is translucent.

Add the sugar and cook, stirring, for 2–3 minutes, or until sugar is dissolved. Remove from heat and add the zest and juice. Transfer to a bowl and cool slightly.

Using an electric beater, whisk the egg whites in a bowl until firm peaks form. Gently fold the whites into the sago mixture. Chill mixture in the refrigerator.

For the custard, heat the milk with the vanilla pod and scraped seeds until almost simmering, stirring constantly.

Whisk the egg yolks, cornflour and sugar until a smooth paste forms. Pour over the milk mixture and stir to combine well.

Return the mixture to a clean saucepan and cook, stirring constantly with a wooden spoon, over medium–low heat for 10–15 minutes, or until the custard thickens. Do not overheat, or custard may curdle.

Serve the chilled sago with warm custard.

Yass Savoury

Mrs R Connell, Yass Branch

MAKES ABOUT 500 G

170 g (1 cup) sultanas, chopped
200 g finely chopped ham
2½ tablespoons finely
   chopped gherkins
mayonnaise, to bind
lettuce leaves, sandwich bread
   or toast triangles, to serve

Combine sultanas, ham and chopped gherkin in a bowl. Add enough mayonnaise to loosely bind – the mixture should spread easily. Stir to combine well and season to taste with salt and pepper.

Serve in lettuce leaf cups as a light lunch, as a sandwich filling or on toast triangles as a snack.

Apricot Upside-Down Pudding

3 JAN

Mrs L Chapman, Braidwood Branch

SERVES 6–8

1 × 420 g tin apricot halves
   in juice
140 g butter
110 g (½ cup) caster sugar
2 eggs
185 g (1¼ cups) plain flour
2½ teaspoons baking powder
½ teaspoon salt
165 g (¾ cup) brown sugar,
   firmly packed
95 g (1 cup) flaked almonds
whipped cream, to serve

Preheat oven to 180°C. Lightly grease and flour a 20 cm cake tin.

Drain the apricots well, reserving 80 ml (⅓ cup) of the juice.

Using an electric beater, beat 80 g of the butter in a bowl with the caster sugar until light and creamy. Add the eggs one at a time, beating well between each. Sift the flour, baking powder and salt into a bowl. Stir flour into the creamed mixture alternately with the reserved apricot juice.

Heat the remaining butter with the brown sugar in a saucepan over medium–low heat, stirring constantly, until the butter has melted and mixture is smooth. Pour mixture over the base of the cake tin. Arrange the apricot halves over the mixture, cut-side down. Sprinkle over the almonds and pour the batter over the top.

Bake for 40 minutes, or until a skewer inserted in the centre comes out clean. Cool for 5 minutes, then turn the cake out onto a large plate.

🗶 *Apricot Upside-Down Pudding is best served hot, with whipped cream.*

11

Cheese Biscuits

Mrs AF Ross, Glen Innes Branch

4 JAN

MAKES 30

85 g plain flour
¼ teaspoon baking powder
25 g butter, chopped
50 g (½ cup) grated cheddar
    cheese
1 egg yolk

Preheat oven to 180°C. Lightly grease a baking tray.

Sift the flour, baking powder and a pinch of salt into a bowl. Using your fingertips, rub in the butter until mixture resembles breadcrumbs. Stir in the cheese, add the egg yolk and combine by hand to form a coarse dough.

Turn out onto a lightly floured surface and knead briefly until smooth. Roll to 5 mm thickness. Using a 6 cm round pastry cutter, cut rounds from the dough, re-rolling scraps for more rounds. Place on the trays.

Bake for 12–15 minutes, or until light golden.

Genoa Cakes

5 JAN

MAKES 24

4 eggs
220 g (1 cup) caster sugar
300 g (2 cups) plain flour
½ teaspoon salt
2 teaspoons baking powder
125 ml (½ cup) milk
1½ teaspoons vanilla or
    lemon essence, or to taste
250 g (1 cup) butter,
    softened

Preheat oven to 180°C. Line two 12-hole patty cake tins with cupcake cases.

Using an electric beater, beat the eggs and sugar in a bowl until thick and pale. Sift the flour, salt and baking powder into a bowl. Stir the flour mixture and the milk into the creamed mixture, then stir in the essence.

Using an electric beater, beat the butter in another bowl until very soft and creamy. Stir butter into the creamed mixture. Spoon mixture into cases.

Bake for 10–15 minutes, or until a skewer inserted in the centre comes out clean. Turn out the cakes onto a wire rack to cool.

Grapefruit and Walnut Salad

Mrs Frank Dixon, West Maitland Branch

SERVES 4

2 ruby grapefruit, peeled,
  white pith removed
1 butter lettuce, leaves
  separated, washed
  and dried
45 g (⅓ cup) walnut pieces

Dressing
60 ml (¼ cup) white vinegar
90 g (¼ cup) honey

Using a small sharp knife, cut grapefruit along membranes to separate each segment, holding the fruit over a bowl to catch the juices. Squeeze the membrane to extract as much juice as possible, reserving juices.

Tear large lettuce leaves in half and place in a serving bowl. Scatter over the grapefruit and walnuts.

For the dressing, combine the vinegar and honey with the reserved juices and whisk until smooth and well combined.

Drizzle dressing over the salad and serve immediately.

Cocoa Cake

Mrs TR McCracken, Harefield

MAKES ONE 20 CM CAKE

250 g (1 cup) butter,
  softened
250 g caster sugar
4 eggs
2 teaspoons cocoa powder
1 tablespoon hot water
500 g (3⅓ cups) plain flour
1 teaspoon cream of tartar
½ teaspoon bicarbonate
  of soda
whipped cream and chopped
  walnuts, to serve

Preheat oven to 180°C. Lightly grease and flour the base and side of a 20 cm cake tin.

Using an electric beater, beat the butter and sugar in a large bowl until light and creamy. Beating constantly, add the eggs one at a time, beating well between each.

Combine the cocoa with the hot water in a cup. Sift the remaining dry ingredients into a bowl, then stir into the creamed mixture to combine well. Stir in the cocoa mixture, then spoon the batter into the tin.

Bake for 45–50 minutes, or until a skewer inserted in the centre comes out clean. Cool the cake in the tin for 10 minutes, then turn out onto a wire rack to cool completely.

Serve covered with whipped cream and scattered with chopped walnuts.

Oyster Savouries

Miss LM Williams, Maitland Branch

MAKES 12

12 thin slices of brown bread
softened butter, for spreading
1 tablespoon tomato sauce
½ teaspoon Worcestershire
  sauce
60 ml (¼ cup) pouring cream,
  whipped
12 freshly shucked oysters

Using an 8 cm round pastry cutter, cut 12 rounds from the bread. Butter each round and set aside.

Add the tomato and Worcestershire sauces to the cream in a bowl and stir gently to combine. Season with salt and pepper.

Top each bread round with a dollop of cream mixture, then use a teaspoon to create a depression in the middle. Place an oyster on each. Serve immediately.

Cream Puffs

9 JAN

Mrs CA Lamont, Wagga Branch

MAKES ABOUT 12

250 ml (1 cup) water
50 g butter, chopped
150 g (1 cup) plain flour, sifted
3 eggs, beaten
whipped cream, to fill

Preheat oven to 200°C. Line a baking tray with baking paper.

Boil the water with the butter in a saucepan. Reduce heat to medium. Working quickly, add the flour and stir vigorously with a wooden spoon until the mixture forms a thick, smooth paste that leaves the side of the pan. Pour into a bowl and cool slightly.

Beating constantly, add the egg a little at a time, until the mixture has a heavy dropping consistency – you may not need all the egg. Drop tablespoons of the mixture onto the tray, leaving space between each.

Bake for 20 minutes – don't open the oven or puffs may collapse. Transfer to a wire rack to cool.

Slit the cooled puffs open with a knife and fill each with whipped cream.

Tomato, Prune and Cress Salad

Mrs Frank Dixon, Maitland Branch

10 JAN

SERVES 4

16 pitted prunes
16 blanched almonds, roasted
4 large, firm ripe tomatoes
1 large handful watercress sprigs

Dressing
125 ml (½ cup) white vinegar
90 g (¼ cup) honey

Stuff each prune with an almond and set aside. Slice the tomatoes and arrange over the watercress on a platter or in a large bowl. Scatter over the stuffed prunes.

For the dressing, whisk the ingredients together until smooth, season to taste with salt and pepper.

Drizzle dressing over the salad and serve.

Cinnamon Sandwich

Mrs Thompson, Nevertire Branch

11 JAN

MAKES ONE 18 CM CAKE

4 eggs
220 g (1 cup) caster sugar
2 teaspoons vanilla essence
3 teaspoons ground cinnamon
2 teaspoons cocoa powder
1 teaspoon baking power
150 g (1 cup) plain flour
80 ml (⅓ cup) milk
1 tablespoon butter, softened
plum jam, for spreading
whipped cream, to fill
icing sugar, for dusting

Preheat oven to 170°C. Grease and flour the sides of two 18 cm cake tins and line the bases with baking paper.

Using an electric beater, whisk the eggs, sugar and vanilla in a bowl until the mixture is very thick and pale and leaves a trail when the beaters are lifted. Sift the cinnamon, cocoa, baking powder and flour into a bowl.

Combine the milk and butter in a saucepan, bring to the boil then remove from the heat. Gently fold cinnamon and milk mixtures into the egg mixture.

Gently spoon half the batter into each tin, smoothing the tops even. Bake for 20–25 minutes, or until well risen and batter pulls away from the sides of the tins.

Cool the cakes in the tins for 5 minutes, then turn onto wire racks to cool completely.

Spread one cake with jam and cover with whipped cream. Place the other cake on top. Dust with icing sugar to serve.

Bengal Canapés

Miss Minna Sachel, Orange Branch

MAKES 12

6 thin slices of white bread
2 tablespoons butter,
  or as required
75 g ham, very finely chopped
60 ml (¼ cup) pouring cream
30 g very finely grated
  cheddar cheese
chutney, for spreading
cayenne pepper, to taste

Preheat oven to 180°C.

Using a 6 cm round pastry cutter, cut two rounds from each slice of bread. Heat the butter in a large, heavy-based frying pan over medium heat. Add the rounds, in batches, adding more butter as needed. Cook for 2–3 minutes on each side, or until light golden.

Place the ham, cream and cheese in a small bowl and stir to combine well. Season to taste with salt and pepper.

Spread each round with a little chutney, place on a baking tray and top with the ham mixture. Sprinkle with cayenne pepper to taste.

Bake for 10 minutes, or until mixture is bubbling. Serve hot.

Pancakes

Mrs Keith Brougham, Broken Hill Branch

MAKES 12–15

3 eggs, separated
250 ml (1½ cup) milk
75 g (½ cup) plain flour
1½ teaspoons salt
melted butter, for cooking
toppings, as desired, to serve

Place egg yolks and milk in a bowl and whisk to combine well. Sift the flour and salt into a bowl, add to the egg mixture and whisk until smooth.

Using an electric beater, whisk the egg whites in a bowl until soft peaks form. Gently fold into the batter.

Heat a small, heavy-based non-stick frying pan over medium heat. Brush the base lightly with melted butter. Pour 2 tablespoons of the mixture into the pan, swirling to coat the base – the pancake should be thin. Cook for about 3 minutes on each side, or until golden.

Repeat until all the mixture is used.

Pancakes are best served hot with your favourite toppings – sugar and lemon juice is a traditional combination.

Carrot Salad

Mrs Jack Quilter, Gundegai Branch

SERVES 4–6

310 g (2 cups, firmly packed)
   grated carrot
2 large stalks of celery, finely
   chopped
½ teaspoon salt
2½ tablespoons lemon juice
mayonnaise, to bind
lettuce leaves, to serve

Combine the carrot, celery, salt, pepper to taste and lemon juice in a bowl and stir to combine well. Add enough mayonnaise to bind ingredients together.
   Serve salad on lettuce leaves.

Raspberry or Blackberry Jam Tart

Mrs AG Delve, Curlewis Branch

SERVES 6–8

1½ tablespoons butter
1 tablespoon caster sugar
2 eggs
2 tablespoons raspberry
   or blackberry jam
80 ml (⅓ cup) milk

Shortcrust Pastry
90 g self-raising flour
2 tablespoons plain flour
125 g (½ cup) chilled butter,
   chopped
1 egg, lightly beaten

For the pastry, place the flours in a bowl and stir to combine well. Using your fingertips, rub in the butter until mixture resembles breadcrumbs. Make a well in the centre, add the egg and combine by hand to form a coarse dough.
   Turn the dough out onto a lightly floured surface and knead briefly until smooth – do not overwork or the pastry will be tough. Wrap in plastic wrap and refrigerate for 30 minutes.
   Preheat oven to 180°C.
   Roll the pastry out to fit a 20 cm tart tin. Line the tin with the pastry, trimming edges even. Refrigerate.
   For the filling, using an electric beater, beat the butter and sugar in a bowl until light and creamy. Add the eggs one at a time, beating well between each. Add the jam and milk and stir to combine well. Pour into the pastry shell.
   Bake for 20–30 minutes, or until the pastry is golden and the filling is set.

Tasty Spaghetti

Mrs J Neale Taylor, Ilford Beach

SERVES 4

60 g (¼ cup) butter

2 large onions, peeled and
    finely chopped

6 sprigs of thyme

800 g ripe tomatoes, trimmed
    and finely chopped

1 tablespoon olive oil

400 g pork or beef mince

400 g dried spaghetti

100 g (1 cup) grated cheddar
    cheese, or to taste

Heat the butter in a large saucepan over medium heat. Add the onions and thyme and cook, stirring, for 8 minutes, or until onions are soft. Add the tomatoes and bring mixture to a simmer. Cook, stirring, for 10 minutes, or until liquid has evaporated slightly and tomato is very soft.

Heat the oil in a large frying pan over medium–high heat. Add the mince and cook, stirring with a wooden spoon to break mince up, for 5–6 minutes, or until browned. Add to the tomato mixture with any pan juices. Season well with salt and pepper and allow sauce to simmer while the spaghetti cooks.

Cook the spaghetti in boiling water for 7 minutes, or according to packet instructions, until *al dente*. Drain well.

Stir the spaghetti through tomato mixture and the cheese. Serve in heated bowls.

Chicken Loaf

Miss Jenny Bond, Lockhart Branch

SERVES 6

120 g (2 cups, lightly packed)
    fresh breadcrumbs

660 g (4 cups) minced cooked
    chicken

1 small onion, very finely
    chopped

250 ml (1 cup) milk

250 ml (1 cup) chicken stock

1½ teaspoons salt

2 eggs, lightly beaten

Preheat oven to 180°C. Grease a 24 x 12 x 8 cm loaf tin.

Combine all the ingredients in a bowl, season with pepper and mix to combine well. Spoon into the tin, smoothing the top even.

Bake for 1 hour, or until set and golden brown. Serve hot or cold.

Iced Chocolate Tart

Mrs GT Petersen, Manildra Branch

MAKES ONE 24 CM TART

Pastry
280 g plain flour
1 teaspoon baking powder
225 g chilled butter,
    chopped
iced water, to mix

Filling
165 g (½ cup) raspberry jam
35 g butter
35 g caster sugar
2 tablespoons finely chopped
    Amaretti biscuits
1 tablespoon cocoa powder
1 egg, separated
½ teaspoon vanilla essence
12 glacé cherries

Icing
120 g (1 cup) sifted icing sugar
1 tablespoon fresh lemon juice
2 teaspoon grated lemon zest
1 tablespoon milk

For the icing, combine the icing sugar, lemon juice, zest and milk in a bowl and stir to combine well. Spread icing over the cooled tart and top with cherries. Allow the icing to set before serving the Iced Chocolate Tart.

For the pastry, sift the flour, a pinch of salt and the baking powder into a bowl. Divide the butter into 3 equal portions. Using your fingertips, rub one portion of the butter into the flour mixture until it resembles breadcrumbs. Add enough iced water to form a coarse dough.

Turn the dough out onto a lightly floured surface and knead briefly until smooth – take care not to overwork or pastry will be tough. Form the dough into a disc, wrap in plastic wrap and refrigerate for 30 minutes.

Roll the dough into a rectangle about 20 x 24 cm. Using another portion of butter, dot pieces over two-thirds of the dough. Fold the third with no butter over to the middle of the rectangle, then fold the other end over the top of that. Roll the pastry out again to the same sized rectangle as before and repeat the process with the remaining butter, folding the pastry in the same way. Wrap in plastic wrap and refrigerate for 30 minutes.

Roll pastry out on a floured surface to fit over the base and side of a 24 cm tart tin.

Preheat oven to 200°C.

For the filling, spread the jam over the pastry. Using an electric beater, beat the butter and sugar in a bowl until light and creamy. Combine the chopped biscuits and cocoa in a food processor and process until fine crumbs form. Add cocoa mixture to the creamed mixture, then stir in the egg yolk and vanilla.

Whisk the egg white in a bowl until soft peaks form and fold into the cocoa mixture. Spread over the jam and bake for 20 minutes, or until set. Cool tart in the tin.

Butterscotch Pie

Mrs S Warby, Wagga Branch

MAKES ONE 24 CM PIE

Pastry

150 g (1 cup) plain flour

1¼ teaspoons bicarbonate
  of soda

½ teaspoon cream of tartar

75 g chilled butter,
  chopped

2 tablespoons chilled milk,
  as required

Filling

260 g caster sugar

375 ml (1½ cup) boiling
  water

185 g (1 cup) brown sugar,
  lightly packed

1 tablespoon cornflour

60 g (¼ cup) butter

2 eggs, separated

90 g (1 cup) desiccated
  coconut

1 teaspoon vanilla essence

*Serve Butterscotch Pie
hot or at room temperature.*

Preheat oven to 180°C.

For the pastry, combine the flour, soda, tartar and a large pinch of salt in a bowl. Using your fingertips, rub in the butter until mixture resembles breadcrumbs. Stir in the milk until a course dough forms, adding extra if required.

Turn the dough out onto a lightly floured surface and knead briefly – take care not to overwork or pastry will be tough. Form into a disc, wrap in plastic wrap and refrigerate for 30 minutes.

Roll dough out to fit the base and side of a 24 cm tart tin, trimming the side even. Line the tart shell with baking paper and fill with baking beads or dried beans. Bake for 20 minutes.

Place 2 tablespoons of caster sugar in a small saucepan with 1 tablespoon water. Cook over medium heat for 6–7 minutes, or until a dark caramel forms. Remove from the heat and quickly add the boiling water and brown sugar, taking care as mixture will split. Return to the heat and cook, stirring, for 5 minutes.

Combine the cornflour with 1 tablespoon water in a bowl to make a smooth paste. Add to the mixture in the pan and cook until it boils and thickens. Remove from the heat, then stir in the butter. Allow mixture to cool slightly, then stir in the egg yolks, coconut and vanilla.

Pour filling into the tart shell and bake for 20–30 minutes.

Using an electric beater, whisk the egg whites in a bowl until firm peaks form. Gradually add remaining caster sugar and whisk until it is dissolved and mixture is thick and glossy. Spoon whites over the baked tart. Bake for a further 10–15 minutes, or until meringue is golden.

Orange Pudding

Mrs E Allen

SERVES 6–8

6 oranges
1 litre (4 cups) milk
1½ tablespoons cornflour
2 tablespoons water
5 eggs, separated
330 g (1½ cups) caster sugar

Preheat oven to 180°C.

Finely zest three of the oranges and juice all the oranges, mixing together in a bowl or jug.

Bring the milk to a gentle simmer in a saucepan over low heat. Combine the cornflour and water in a small bowl to form a smooth paste. Add the paste to the milk, stirring constantly. Cook, stirring, over medium heat for 2–3 minutes, or until the mixture simmers and thickens. Remove from the heat and cool slightly.

Beat egg yolks in a bowl and pour in a little of the milk mixture, stirring to combine. Pour the egg mixture into the milk mixture, stirring to mix well. Add 220 g (1 cup) of the sugar and three-quarters of the orange mixture, mixing well. Reserve the remaining orange mixture for another use.

Pour the mixture into a 1.5 litre (6 cup) capacity baking dish. Bake for 18–20 minutes, or until set. Remove from the oven.

Reduce oven temperature to 160°C. Using an electric beater, whisk the egg whites in a bowl until soft peaks form. Whisking constantly, slowly add the remaining sugar and whisk until it has dissolved and mixture is glossy. Pile the whites over the pudding.

Return pudding to the oven and bake a further 20 minutes, or until meringue is light golden. Serve warm.

Banana Snow

Mrs R Wearne, Cootamundra Branch

SERVES 4–6

3 very ripe bananas, mashed
juice of ½ lemon
2 tablespoons caster sugar
2 tablespoons strawberry jam
2 egg whites

Place banana, juice, sugar and jam in a bowl and stir to combine well.

Using an electric beater, whisk the egg whites in a bowl until soft peaks form, then gently fold into the banana mixture. Transfer to a serving bowl.

Refrigerate for 30 minutes, or until chilled. Serve cold.

Oat Biscuits

Yass Branch

MAKES 30

190 g (2 cups) rolled oats
75 g (½ cup) plain flour
220 g (1 cup) caster sugar
½ teaspoon baking powder
125 g (½ cup) butter,
   melted
a few tablespoons of boiling
   water, for mixing

Preheat oven to 180°C. Line two baking trays with baking paper.

Combine oats, flour, sugar and baking powder in a bowl. Add the butter and 2 tablespoons boiling water, or enough to form a firm dough.

Place heaped teaspoons of the dough on the prepared tray, leaving room from spreading. Bake for 10–12 minutes, or until golden. Transfer to a wire rack to cool.

Savoury Toast

Mrs J Heckendorf, Lockhart Branch

SERVES 4

4 slices toast bread
60 g (¼ cup) butter,
  softened
2 teaspoons prepared
  mustard, or to taste
125 g (1¼ cups) grated
  cheddar cheese
juice of 1 lemon
2½ tablespoons fresh
  breadcrumbs

Preheat oven to 190°C.

Place bread on a baking tray. Place the butter and mustard in a bowl and beat to combine well.

Spread bread with the mixture. Top with the cheese, drizzle with lemon juice and scatter over the breadcrumbs.

Bake for 10 minutes, or until crisp and bubbling. Cut into fingers and serve hot.

Sponge Slices

MAKES 36

175 g butter, softened
175 g caster sugar
4 eggs
275 g self-raising flour, sifted
1 tablespoon warm water
50 g (½ cup) toasted flaked
  almonds

Orange Icing
60 g (¼ cup) butter, room
  temperature
80 g (½ cup) sifted icing sugar
1 teaspoon finely grated
  orange zest
2 teaspoons fresh orange juice

Preheat oven to 180°C. Lightly grease and flour a 24 × 30 cm slice tin.

Using an electric beater, beat butter and sugar in a bowl until light and creamy. Add the eggs, one at a time, beating well between each. Stir in the flour and warm water.

Spoon the batter into the tin, smoothing the top even. Bake for about 25 minutes, or until golden. Turn out onto a wire rack to cool.

For the orange icing, using an electric beater, beat the butter in a bowl until soft. Gradually add the icing sugar and beat until pale and creamy. Add the orange zest and juice and beat until just combined. Ice cake with orange icing. Using a sharp knife, cut into squares and scatter over the almonds.

Marlborough Tart

Mrs S Alfred Blackman, Tooraweenah Branch

MAKES ONE 24 CM TART

Pastry
150 g (1 cup) plain flour
¼ teaspoon bicarbonate
  of soda
½ teaspoon cream of tartar
75 g chilled butter,
  chopped
2 tablespoons cold milk,
  as required

Filling
75 g butter, softened
75 g (⅓ cup) caster sugar
2 eggs
60 g almond meal
2 tablespoons self-raising
  flour
165 g (½ cup) raspberry jam

For the pastry, combine the flour, soda and tartar in a bowl. Using your fingertips, rub in the butter until mixture resembles breadcrumbs. Add the milk and mix until a dough forms, adding a little more milk if required to form a firm dough.

Turn the dough out onto a lightly floured surface and knead briefly until smooth. Form into a disc, wrap in plastic wrap and refrigerate for 30 minutes.

Preheat oven to 180°C.

Roll pastry out into a circle to fit the base and side of a 24 cm round tart tin, trimming the side even. Line the tart shell with baking paper and fill with baking beads or dried beans. Bake for 20 minutes.

For the filling, using an electric beater, beat the butter and sugar in a bowl until light and creamy. Add the eggs, one at a time, beating well between each. Stir in the almond meal and flour.

Spread the jam over the tart shell and spoon the creamed mixture over the top, covering the jam.

Bake the tart for 20 minutes, then reduce the heat to 170°C – cover the tart with foil if it browns too quickly. Bake for a further 20–30 minutes, or until the filling is set and a skewer inserted in the centre comes out clean.

Marlborough Tart can be served hot or at room temperature.

Currant Cake

26 JAN

Miss Alma Buckley, Mendooran Branch

MAKES ONE 20 CM CAKE
250 g (1 cup) butter,
  softened
220 g (1 cup) caster sugar
2 teaspoons vanilla essence
5 eggs
300 g (2 cups) flour
2 teaspoons baking powder
215 g (1½ cups) currants

Preheat oven to 170°C. Line the base and side of a 20 cm cake tin with baking paper.

Using an electric beater, beat the butter and sugar in a bowl until light and creamy. Add the vanilla and eggs, one at a time, beating well between each. Sift the flour and baking powder into a bowl, then stir into the creamed mixture with the currants.

Spoon batter into the tin, smoothing the top even. Bake for about 1 hour 10 minutes, or until a skewer inserted in the centre comes out clean.

Cool the cake in the tin for 20 minutes, then turn out onto a wire rack to cool completely.

Coconut Fingers

27 JAN

Mrs CL Griffith, Albury Branch

MAKES ABOUT 12
125 g (½ cup) butter,
  softened
50 g (¼ cup) caster sugar
1 egg, separated
200 g (1⅓ cups) plain flour
1 teaspoon baking powder
120 g (1 cup) icing sugar
25 g (¼ cup) desiccated
  coconut, for sprinkling

Preheat oven to 180°C. Grease and flour the sides of a 28 × 18 cm slice tin and line the base with baking paper.

Using an electric beater, beat the butter and sugar in a bowl until light and creamy. Add the egg yolk and beat well. Sift the flour and baking powder into a bowl, then stir into the creamed mixture to form a stiff dough. Press dough evenly over the base of the tin.

Whisk the egg white and icing sugar in a bowl until smooth. Spread mixture over the dough and sprinkle with coconut.

Bake for 15–20 minutes, or until golden.

Afternoon Tea Toast

Mrs Waddell, Merriwa Branch

28 JAN

SERVES 2–4

4 slices toast bread
75 g (⅓ cup) caster sugar
1 tablespoon ground cinnamon
50 g butter

Preheat oven grill to medium and place the bread on a tray. Toast under the grill on one side only. Turn over so toasted side faces down.

Combine the sugar and cinnamon in a bowl and sprinkle evenly over the bread. Dot with butter and return the toast to the grill.

Cook for 3–4 minutes, or until the butter and the sugar mixture are bubbling.

Cut toast into fingers and serve hot.

Walnut Shortbreads

29 JAN

MAKES ABOUT 35

75 g walnuts, chopped
275 g self-raising flour
125 g caster sugar
125 g (½ cup) butter,
    softened
35 walnut halves,
    to decorate

Place the chopped walnuts in a food processor and grind very finely. Transfer to a bowl with the flour and sugar and mix well. Add the butter and work the butter into the mixture by hand until a dough forms.

Line two baking trays with baking paper. On a well-floured surface, roll the dough out to about 6 mm thickness. Using a 5 cm round pastry cutter, cut rounds from the dough. Re-roll scraps and cut rounds from these. Place rounds on the trays, leaving room for spreading. Gently press a walnut half into each. Refrigerate for 30–40 minutes to firm the dough.

Preheat oven to 160°C.

Bake shortbread for 15 minutes, or until light golden. Cool on the trays for 5 minutes, then transfer to wire racks to cool.

Vanilla Cream Sandwich

Mrs Mark Morton, Nowra Branch

MAKES ONE 18 CM CAKE

3 eggs
220 g (1 cup) caster sugar
150 g (1 cup) plain flour
1 teaspoon baking powder
2 tablespoons cold water

Filling
250 ml (1 cup) milk
110 g (½ cup) caster sugar
1 tablespoon butter
1 egg
1 tablespoon cornflour
vanilla essence, to taste

Preheat oven to 170°C. Lightly grease and flour two 18 cm cake tins.

Using an electric beater, whisk the eggs and sugar in a bowl until mixture is thick and pale and holds a trail when the beaters are lifted.

Sift the flour and baking powder into a bowl. Gently fold flour into the egg mixture with the water.

Spoon half the batter into each tin, smoothing the tops even. Bake for 18–20 minutes, or until golden and the cakes spring back slightly when pressed.

Cool the cakes in the tins for 10 minutes, then turn out onto a wire rack to cool completely.

For the filling, combine the milk, sugar and butter in a small saucepan and bring to a simmer, stirring to dissolve sugar.

Combine the egg and cornflour in a bowl and, stirring constantly, pour into the milk mixture. Cook, stirring, over medium–low heat for 5 minutes. Remove from the heat. Add vanilla essence and leave to cool.

Spread filling over one cake, top with the remaining cake and serve.

Lemon Cheese Tarts

Lemon Cheese: Mrs EJ George, Brewarrina Branch
Pastry: Mrs RK Wood, Adelaide Branch

MAKES 24

Lemon Cheese

2 lemon
2 eggs
2 tablespoons butter, chopped
220 g (1 cup) caster sugar

Pastry

225 g (1½ cups) self-raising
  flour
125 g (½ cup) chilled butter,
  chopped
1 egg, lightly beaten
2 tablespoons caster sugar

For the lemon cheese, combine the ingredients in a double boiler over medium–low heat. Cook, stirring constantly, for about 15 minutes, or until the mixture thickens enough to coat the back of a spoon. Pour into a bowl and cool.

For the pastry, place flour in a bowl. Using your fingertips, rub in the butter until mixture resembles breadcrumbs. Stir in egg and sugar and mix by hand until a coarse dough forms.

Turn the dough out onto a lightly floured surface and knead briefly until smooth – do not overwork or pastry will be tough. Form into a disc, wrap in plastic wrap and refrigerate for 30 minutes.

Preheat oven to 180°C.

Roll the pastry out on a lightly floured surface to 2–3 mm thickness. Using a 6 cm round pastry cutter, cut rounds from pastry and line two 12-hole mini tart tins. Fill each tart with lemon cheese.

Bake for 10 minutes, or until pastry is golden and cooked through. Cool the tarts in the tins, then turn out onto a wire rack to cool completely.

Family recipes

	1	2	3
	Savoury Eggs	Sago and Coconut Custard	Oatmeal Biscuits

4	5	6	7	8
American Shortcake	Stuffed Tomato Salad	Coconut Dainties	Waldorf Salad	Orange Sandwich

9	10	11	12	13
Bernardin de Fleurus	Cheese Straws	Lemon Cream Tart	Date Bun	Sunbeams

14	15	16	17	18
Carinda Rice Savoury	Mint Chutney	Creamed Eggs	Savoury Scones	Savouries

19	20	21	22	23
Chocolate Sauce	Fudge Cake	Pikelets	Salmon Loaf	English Seed Cake

24	25	26	27	28
Apple Snow	Egyptian Cake	Countess Pudding	Chocolate Mould	Apricot Jelly

29
Brown Sugar Nut Cake

FEBRUARY

Savoury Eggs

1 FEB

Mrs EM Hamblin, Nevertire Branch

SERVES 6

6 eggs, hard-boiled and peeled
2 tablespoons butter
2–3 finely chopped anchovies
2 teaspoons tomato sauce
2 teaspoons Worcestershire sauce
1 teaspoon mustard powder
cayenne pepper, to taste
2 tablespoons finely chopped parsley

Cut the eggs in half lengthways and, using a teaspoon, carefully remove the yolks. Mash yolks in a bowl with a fork.

Melt butter in small saucepan over low heat. Add anchovies, sauces and mustard and heat through. Combine with yolks, cayenne pepper and parsley, stirring to mix well, and season to taste with salt and pepper.

Fill the halved egg whites and serve.

Sago and Coconut Custard

2 FEB

Mrs Phil Kelly, Junee

SERVES 8

50 g (¼ cup) sago, soaked overnight and drained
1 litre (4 cups) milk
4 eggs, separated
275 g (1¼ cups) caster sugar
25 g (¼ cup) desiccated coconut, plus extra, for sprinkling

Preheat oven to 180°C.

Combine the sago and milk in a saucepan and bring to a simmer over medium heat. Cook for 15–20 minutes, or until sago is translucent, then remove from heat.

Beat the yolks and 220 g (1 cup) of the sugar in a bowl until well combined. Add to the sago mixture with the coconut and pour into a 1.5 litre (6 cup) capacity baking dish. Bake for 10 minutes.

Using an electric beater, whisk the egg whites in a clean bowl until soft peaks form. Gradually add the remaining sugar, whisk until it has dissolved and the mixture is thick and glossy. Spoon the whites over the custard and sprinkle with a little extra coconut.

Bake for a further 20–25 minutes, or until meringue is light golden and custard is set.

Oatmeal Biscuits

3 FEB

Mrs RK Wood, Adelaide

MAKES 20–24
125 g (½ cup) butter,
   melted and cooled
1 egg, lightly beaten
165 g (¾ cup) caster sugar
1 teaspoon vanilla essence
185 g (1¼ cups) self-raising
   flour
145 g (1½ cups) rolled oats

Preheat oven to 180°C. Line two baking trays with baking paper.

Beat the butter, egg, sugar and vanilla in a bowl. Combine the flour and oats in a large bowl and stir to mix well. Add the egg mixture and stir until a soft dough forms.

Drop heaped teaspoons of dough onto prepared trays, leaving space for biscuits to spread.

Bake for 10 minutes, or until golden.

American Shortcake

4 FEB

Mrs EM Haigh, Goulburn Branch

MAKES 12 PIECES
125 g (½ cup) butter,
   softened
330 g (1½ cups) caster
   sugar
2 eggs
250 g (1⅔ cups) self-raising
   flour
85 g (¼ cup) raspberry jam
90 g (1 cup) desiccated
   coconut

Preheat oven to 180°C. Grease and flour the base and sides of a 24 × 12 cm slice tin.

Using an electric beater, beat the butter and sugar in a bowl until light and creamy. Add one egg and beat well. Stir in the flour to form a soft dough.

Press the dough evenly over the base of the tin. Spread the jam over.

In a bowl, beat the remaining egg well, add the coconut and mix well. Spread the coconut mixture over the jam.

Bake for 15–20 minutes. Cool slightly in the tin. Cut into 4 × 2 cm pieces and leave to cool completely in the tin.

Stuffed Tomato Salad

Mrs Waddell, Merriwa Branch

SERVES 6

6 firm ripe tomatoes, about 500 g
½ Lebanese cucumber, peeled and finely chopped
40 g (¼ cup) peas, fresh or frozen, cooked
1 tablespoon capers
50 g (⅓ cup) gherkins, finely chopped
130 g (¾ cup) chicken or turkey, cooked, finely shredded
60 ml (¼ cup) mayonnaise

Cut a small piece off the base of each tomato so it will sit flat. Cut a 1 cm horizontal slice off the top of each tomato.

Using a spoon, scoop out the flesh and separate the seeds. Finely chop half the flesh, reserving the remainder for another purpose. Combine in a bowl with the reserved seeds and remaining ingredients. Mix well and season to taste with salt and pepper.

Fill the tomato shells with the mixture and serve.

Coconut Dainties

Mrs AR Raleigh, Wagga Branch

MAKES ABOUT 15

1 egg white
2 tablespoons caster sugar
30 g (⅓ cup) desiccated coconut

Preheat oven to 180°C. Line a baking tray with baking paper.

Using an electric beater, whisk the egg white in a bowl until soft peaks form. Whisking constantly, add the sugar gradually and whisk until it has dissolved and mixture is thick and glossy. Fold in the coconut.

Drop teaspoons of the mixture onto the tray. Bake for 15 minutes, or until light golden. Transfer to a wire rack to cool.

Waldorf Salad

Mrs JJ Quilter, Gundagai Branch

SERVES 4

2 red delicious or lady
   williams apples
2 desiree or pontiac
   potatoes, cooked
2 stalks of celery, trimmed
80 g (½ cup) walnut pieces
60 ml (¼ cup) mayonnaise

Halve and core the apples, and cut into
1 cm pieces.
   Cut the potatoes into the same size
pieces and thinly slice the celery.
   Combine apple and potato in a bowl with
the walnuts and mayonnaise, seasoning to
taste with salt and pepper. Stir to mix well.
   Serve immediately.

Orange Sandwich

Mrs Douglas Mackellar, Leeton Branch

MAKES ONE 18 CM CAKE

60 g (¼ cup) butter,
   softened
220 g (1 cup) sugar
3 eggs
grated zest of 1 orange
250 ml (1 cup) water
300 g (2 cups) plain flour
2 teaspoons baking powder

Filling
2 eggs, lightly beaten
juice and grated zest of
   1 orange
1 tablespoon caster sugar
1 tablespoon butter

Preheat oven to 180 C. Lightly grease and
flour the base and sides of two 18 cm cake tins.
   Using an electric beater, beat the butter
and sugar in a bowl until light and creamy.
Add the eggs one at a time, beating well
between each, then add the zest and water.
Sift the flour and baking powder into a bowl,
then stir into the butter mixture.
   Spoon half the batter into each tin,
smoothing the tops even. Bake for 30 minutes,
or until a skewer inserted in the centre comes
out clean. Cool cakes for 10 minutes in the
tins, then turn out onto wire racks to cool.
   For the filling, combine all the ingredients in
a bowl and place the bowl over a saucepan of
simmering water. Cook, stirring constantly, for
5 minutes, or until the mixture has thickened.
   Cool the filling. Spread it over one cake and
top with the other to serve.

Bernardin de Fleurus

Miss Elsie Segaert, Manly Branch

MAKES 12–15
100 g (1 cup) almond meal
2 egg whites
185 g (1 cup, lightly packed)
  brown sugar
110 g (½ cup) caster sugar
2 teaspoons ground cinnamon
75 g (½ cup) plain flour
95 g (1 cup) flaked almonds

Preheat oven to 180°C. Line a baking tray with baking paper.

Combine the almond meal and egg whites in a bowl and beat to mix well. Add the remaining ingredients except flaked almonds and mix well to form a firm dough. Leave the dough to stand for 30 minutes.

On a lightly floured surface, roll the dough out to about 2 cm thickness. Cut into strips about 5 cm long and 2 cm wide. Place on prepared tray, gently press flaked almonds on top and sprinkle with sugar.

Bake for about 15 minutes, or until golden and firm.

Cheese Straws

Mrs Ivy Quinton, Maitland Branch

MAKES ABOUT 20
60 g self-raising flour
large pinch cayenne pepper
60 g (¼ cup) butter,
  chopped
60 g grated cheddar cheese
1 egg yolk
lemon juice, to mix

Preheat oven to 180°C. Line a baking tray with baking paper.

Combine flour and cayenne in a bowl. Using your fingertips, rub in the butter until mixture resembles breadcrumbs. Add the cheese, egg yolk and enough lemon juice to mix into a firm dough.

Turn the dough out onto a lightly floured surface and knead briefly until smooth – do not overwork or straws will be tough. Roll the dough out into a 20 cm square and cut into 1 cm-wide strips.

Place straws on tray and bake for 10–12 minutes, or until crisp and golden.

Lemon Cream Tart

Mrs AG Delve, Curlewis Branch

MAKES ONE 22 CM TART

Pastry
2 tablespoons plain flour
95 g self-raising flour
115 g chilled butter,
   chopped
1 egg

Filling
2 tablespoons butter
220 g (1 cup) caster sugar
45 g cornflour
2 eggs, separated
juice of 2 lemons
250 ml (1 cup) milk

Preheat oven to 180°C.

For the pastry, combine the flours in a bowl. Using your fingertips, rub in the butter until mixture resembles breadcrumbs. Add the egg and mix to form a dough.

Turn the dough out onto a lightly floured surface and knead briefly until smooth. Roll it out to a circle large enough to line a 22 cm tart tin, trimming the edges even.

For the filling, using an electric beater, beat the butter and sugar in a bowl until light and creamy. Beat in the cornflour and egg yolks, lemon juice and milk.

Pour filling into the pastry shell and bake for 15–20 minutes, or until nearly set.

Using an electric beater, whisk the egg whites in a bowl until firm peaks form. Spoon whites on top of the filling.

Bake for a further 10 minutes, or until the meringue is light golden. Serve warm.

Date Bun

Mrs Douglas Mackellar, Leeton Branch

SERVES 4

250 g (1⅔ cups) plain flour
1½ teaspoons baking powder
125 g (½ cup) butter,
   chopped, plus extra,
   to serve
1 egg, beaten
60 ml (¼ cup) milk
12 pitted dates
1 egg yolk, beaten
2 tablespoons caster sugar

Preheat oven to 180°C. Line a baking tray with baking paper.

Sift flour and baking powder into a bowl. Using your fingertips, rub in the butter until mixture resembles breadcrumbs. Make a well in the centre of the mixture and add the egg and milk to the well. Using a flat-bladed knife, stir until a coarse dough forms.

Turn the dough out onto a lightly floured surface and knead gently until mixture comes together – do not overwork or bun will be tough. Divide mixture in half and roll one half out to form a circle about 18–20 cm across.

Top the circle evenly with dates, leaving a 1.5 cm border. Roll the remaining dough out to fit over the top. Press the edges to seal and brush the top with egg yolk. Sprinkle over the sugar and transfer to the tray.

Bake for 20–30 minutes, or until golden.

Serve the Date Bun hot or at room temperature, spread with butter.

Sunbeams

Mrs Arthur Raleigh, Wagga Branch

MAKES 24

2 tablespoons butter,
  softened
2 tablespoons caster sugar
2 eggs
225 g (1½ cups) plain flour
60 g (½ cup) cornflour
2 teaspoons baking powder
85 g (¼ cup) raspberry jam

Preheat oven to 180°C. Line a baking tray with baking paper.

Using an electric beater, beat the butter and sugar in a bowl until light and creamy. Add the eggs and beat well. Sift the remaining ingredients into a bowl, then stir into the creamed mixture to form a dough.

Turn the dough out onto a lightly floured surface and knead briefly until smooth. Roll out to a 24 x 18 cm rectangle. Spread with the jam, leaving a 3 cm border around the edges. With a long side facing you, roll up like a swiss roll. Cut the roll into 5 mm thick slices.

Place slices on the tray and bake for 10 minutes. Transfer to a wire rack to cool.

Carinda Rice Savoury

Mrs Wass, Carinda Branch

SERVES 4–6

1½ tablespoons olive oil
2 tablespoons butter
1 large onion, peeled and
  chopped
750 ml (3 cups) chicken
  stock
300 g (1½ cups) white long-
  grain rice, rinsed
1 small handful parsley,
  chopped

Heat the oil and butter in a saucepan over medium heat. Add the onion and cook, stirring, for 5–6 minutes, or until softened. Add the stock and rice and bring to a simmer.

Cover the pan with a tight-fitting lid, reduce the heat to low and cook for 15 minutes, or until the liquid is absorbed.

Remove from the heat and stand, covered, for 5 minutes, or until rice is tender.

Stir in the parsley and season to taste with salt and pepper. Serve hot.

Mint Chutney

Miss Ivy Quinton, Maitland Branch

MAKES 1 CUP
1 large handful mint leaves
85 g (½ cup) sultanas
1 fresh red chilli, chopped
2 tablespoons caster sugar
2 tablespoons red wine
  vinegar

Combine all ingredients except the vinegar in a food processor. Using the pulse button, process the mixture until a coarse paste forms. Stir in the vinegar.

Serve chutney with cold roast meat.

Creamed Eggs

Mrs AE Gall, Pallamallawa Branch

SERVES 4–6
2½ tablespoons butter
1 tablespoon very finely
  chopped onion
2 tablespoons plain flour
600 ml milk
100 g (1 cup) grated cheddar
  cheese
6 eggs, hard-boiled, peeled
  and halved
toast, to serve

Preheat oven to 180°C.

Melt the butter in a saucepan over medium–low heat. Add the onion and cook, stirring often, for 3–4 minutes, or until softened, then add the flour and stir to form a paste. Add the milk, a little at a time, stirring well between each addition and allowing mixture to come to a simmer before adding more.

Cook, stirring, for 5 minutes, then remove from the heat and season to taste. Stir in half the cheese, add the eggs and transfer to a 1.5 litre (6 cup capacity) baking dish. Sprinkle remaining cheese on the top.

Bake for 20 minutes, or until golden and bubbling. Serve hot on toast.

Savoury Scones

Mrs Fred Simmons, Trundle Branch

MAKES ABOUT 12

2 eggs, hard-boiled, peeled
  and finely chopped
1 tablespoon melted butter
4–6 anchovies, finely chopped
2 teaspoons lemon juice

Scones

450 g (3 cups) plain flour
2 teaspoons baking powder
150 ml milk, or as required
150 ml water, or as required

Preheat oven to 220°C. Line a baking tray with baking paper.

Combine the eggs, butter, anchovies and lemon juice in a bowl and stir to mix well.

For the scones, sift flour, baking powder and a pinch of salt into a bowl. Using your fingertips, rub in the butter until mixture resembles breadcrumbs. Using a knife, lightly mix in the milk and water to form a smooth dough – don't add all liquid at once as you may not need it all.

Turn the dough out onto a lightly floured surface and knead gently. Roll out into a rectangle 1.5 cm thick.

Spread egg mixture over the scone dough and roll up like swiss roll. Cut into 2 cm thick slices and place on the tray, just touching.

Bake for 10–15 minutes, or until risen and golden and cooked through. Transfer to a wire rack to cool.

Savouries

Mrs OK Steindl, Glen Innes Branch

MAKES 2 CUPS

250 g (1 cup) celery heart
  (tender inner stalks),
  very finely chopped
90 g grated vintage cheddar
  cheese
250 ml (1 cup) pouring
  cream, whipped
crackers or croutons, to serve
cayenne pepper, to serve

Combine the celery and cheese in a bowl. Add the cream and gently stir to combine. Season to taste with salt and pepper.

Serve spooned onto crackers or croutons, sprinkled with cayenne pepper.

Chocolate Sauce

Mrs George Killen, Erricton, Burren Junction

MAKES ABOUT 250 ML (1 CUP)
1 tablespoon cocoa powder
1 teaspoon cornflour
2½ tablespoons water,
  plus 200 ml extra
2 teaspoons sugar
1 teaspoon vanilla essence
ice cream, to serve

Combine the cocoa and cornflour in a cup with 2½ tablespoons of water to form a smooth paste.

Bring the remaining water to a simmer in a small saucepan and add the sugar. Stirring constantly, add the cocoa paste and cook for 3–4 minutes, or until it boils and thickens. Remove from the heat and stir in the vanilla.

Serve sauce hot or warm over ice cream.

Fudge Cake

Mrs Lamrock, Penrith Branch

MAKES ONE 20 CM CAKE
125 g (½ cup) butter
220 g (1 cup) caster sugar
1 egg, well beaten
1 tablespoon cocoa powder
225 g (1½ cups) self-raising
  flour
125 ml (½ cup) milk
60 ml (¼ cup) hot water

Chocolate Icing
30 g butter, chopped
2 tablespoons cocoa powder
2 tablespoons of hot water
150 g icing sugar, sifted

Preheat oven to 180°C. Lightly grease and flour the base and side of two 20 cm round cake tins.

Using an electric beater, beat the butter and sugar in a bowl until light and creamy. Add the egg and beat well. Sift the cocoa and flour into a bowl, then stir into the creamed mixture with the milk and hot water. Spoon batter into tins, smoothing tops even.

Bake for 30 minutes, or until a skewer inserted in the centre comes out clean. Cool cakes in tins for 10 minutes, then turn out onto wire racks to cool.

For the icing, dissolve the butter and cocoa in the water. Add the icing sugar and stir until smooth.

To join the cakes, spread icing over one cake and top with the other cake.

Pikelets

Aylmerton Branch

MAKES 20–24
150 g (1 cup) plain flour
1 teaspoon cream of tartar
½ teaspoon bicarbonate
   of soda
2 eggs
1 tablespoon caster sugar
80 ml (⅓ cup) milk,
   approximately
butter, for cooking, plus
   extra, to serve.

Sift the flour, tartar, soda and a large pinch of salt into a bowl.

In a separate bowl, beat the eggs, sugar and milk and add to the flour mixture, whisking until smooth.

Heat a little butter in a large, heavy-based frying pan on medium heat. Drop heaped tablespoons of the batter into the pan and cook for 2–3 minutes, or until bubbles form on the surface. Turn and cook for a further 2–3 minutes, or until golden and cooked through.

Transfer pikelets to a plate and cover with a clean tea towel to keep warm. Repeat with remaining batter.

Serve warm, spread with butter.

Salmon Loaf

Miss Helen Sandilands, Uralla Branch

SERVES 4
1 x 415 g tin red salmon,
   drained and flaked
120 g (2 cups, lightly packed)
   fresh breadcrumbs
1 tablespoon butter, melted,
   plus extra, for greasing
1 small handful parsley, finely
   chopped
1 egg, lightly beaten
50 g (½ cup) grated cheddar
   cheese

Preheat oven to 170°C. Lightly grease the base and sides of a 20 x 12 cm loaf tin.

Combine all the ingredients in a bowl and mix well. Season to taste with salt and pepper.

Spoon mixture into the tin, smoothing the top even. Bake for 20–25 minutes.

Serve hot or cold.

English Seed Cake

Mrs Cox, Mudgee Branch

23 FEB

MAKES ONE 20 CM CAKE
525 g (3½ cups) plain flour
1 teaspoon baking powder
125 g (½ cup) butter,
  chopped
220 g (1 cup) caster sugar
2½ tablespoons caraway seeds
3 eggs
300 ml milk

Preheat oven to 160°C. Lightly grease and flour the base and side of a 20 cm cake tin.

Sift the flour and baking powder into a bowl. Using your fingertips, rub in the butter until mixture resembles breadcrumbs. Stir in the sugar and caraway seeds.

Whisk the eggs in a bowl, add the milk and whisk to combine well. Add to the flour mixture and stir until smooth. Spoon batter into the tin, smoothing the top even.

Bake for 1½–2 hours, or until a skewer inserted in the centre comes out clean.

Cool the cake in the tin for 10 minutes, then turn out onto a wire rack to cool.

Apple Snow

Mrs A Howard, Albury Branch

24 FEB

SERVES 4
3 large granny smith apples
2 egg whites
75 g (⅓ cup) caster sugar
whipped cream, to serve

Preheat oven to 180°C.

Place the apples in a baking dish and bake for 15–20 minutes, or until very tender. Remove from the oven, cool to room temperature then remove apple skins. Push the flesh through a sieve, discarding solids.

Using an electric beater, whisk the egg whites in a bowl until firm peaks form. Whisking constantly, gradually add the sugar and whisk until it is dissolved and mixture is thick and glossy. Gently fold the apple purée into the whites.

Spoon into individual serving bowls. Serve topped with whipped cream.

Egyptian Cake

MAKES ONE 18 CM CAKE

125 g (½ cup) butter,
   softened
250 g caster sugar
3 eggs
450 g (3 cups) plain flour
1 teaspoon cream of tartar
½ teaspoon bicarbonate
   of soda
85 g (½ cup) raisins
1 teaspoon treacle
1 teaspoon mixed spice
¼ teaspoon each ground
   cinnamon and nutmeg
80 g (½ cup) mixed peel

Vienna Icing
125 g (½ cup) butter,
   chopped
280 g (2¼ cups) icing sugar
2 tablespoons milk

Preheat oven to 180°C. Grease and flour the base and sides of three 18 cm cake tins.

Using an electric beater, beat the butter and sugar in a bowl until light and creamy. Add the eggs, one at a time, beating well between each. Sift the flour, tartar and soda into a bowl, then stir into the creamed mixture.

Divide the mixture into 3 even portions. Add the raisins, treacle, spices and mixed peel to one portion of mixture. Spoon into a tin, smoothing the top even. Spoon remaining portions into the other two tins, smoothing the tops even.

Bake the plain cakes for 20 minutes, and the spiced cake for 30 minutes, or until a skewer inserted in the centres comes out clean.

Cool cakes for 10 minutes, then turn out of the tins onto wire racks to cool.

For the icing, using an electric beater, beat butter in small bowl until very pale. Gradually add half the sugar and beat well. Add the milk and the remaining sugar, mixing well.

Spread icing over each of the cooled cakes and stack on top of one other, with the spiced layer in the middle.

Countess Pudding

Mrs WG Keith, Crookwell Branch

SERVES 8

150 g (1 cup) plain flour
110 g (½ cup) caster sugar
1 teaspoon baking powder
45 g (¼ cup) raisins or currants
60 g (¼ cup) butter, melted
grated zest of 1 lemon
1 egg
80 ml (⅓ cup) milk
custard, to serve

Preheat oven to 180°C. Lightly grease a 1.5 litre (6 cup) capacity baking dish.

Sift the flour, sugar and baking powder into a bowl, then stir in the currants. Place the remaining ingredients in a bowl and whisk to combine well. Add to the flour mixture and stir to mix well.

Pour batter into the baking dish. Bake for 45 minutes, or until cooked through and golden.

Serve pudding hot with custard.

Chocolate Mould

Mrs Jas. Rawsthorne, Forbes Branch

SERVES 6

1 litre (4 cups) milk
18 g (1½ tablespoons) powdered gelatine
2 tablespoons caster sugar
75 g dark chocolate, finely chopped
1 teaspoon vanilla essence
whipped cream, to serve

Place 125 ml (½ cup) of the milk in a small, heatproof bowl and sprinkle over the gelatine. Stand for 5 minutes or until gelatine softens. Place the bowl in a small saucepan of simmering water coming halfway up the side of the bowl. Heat for 5 minutes, or until the gelatine dissolves.

Combine the remaining milk, sugar and chocolate in a saucepan. Stir over medium–low heat until chocolate has melted. Whisk until smooth, remove from the heat, then stir in the gelatine mixture and the vanilla.

Cool to room temperature. Pour the chocolate mixture into a wet 1.5 litre (6 cup) capacity jelly mould. Refrigerate for 6 hours, or overnight, until set.

To serve, turn the mould out onto a dish.

Whipped cream is a perfect accompaniment to the Chocolate Mould, or use ice cream if preferred.

Apricot Jelly

Mrs George Killen, Erricton, Burren Junction

SERVES 4

155 g (1 cup) dried apricot
   halves
500 ml (2 cups) boiling water
60 g caster sugar
1 tablespoon arrowroot
125 ml (½ cup) cold water
whipped cream, to serve

Place the apricots in a bowl and add the boiling water. Cover and stand for 1 hour, or until apricots are soft.

Transfer apricots to a saucepan and bring to a simmer, then cover and cook over medium heat for about 1 hour, or until very soft. Add sugar and stir to dissolve.

Combine the arrowroot and cold water in a bowl and stir until smooth. Add to the apricot mixture, stirring constantly, until mixture boils and thickens.

Spoon mixture into a 500 ml (2 cup capacity) jelly mould. Cool to room temperature, then refrigerate until firm.

Serve jelly with whipped cream.

Brown Sugar Nut Cake

29 FEB

Mrs Evans, Wagga Branch

MAKES ONE 20 CM CAKE

125 g (½ cup) butter,
   softened
185 g (1 cup, lightly packed)
   brown sugar
2 eggs, separated
200 g (1⅓ cups) plain flour
2 teaspoons baking powder
125 ml (½ cup) milk
1 teaspoon vanilla essence
125 g (1 cup) chopped
   walnuts

Preheat oven to 180°C. Lightly grease and flour a 20 cm round cake tin.

Using an electric beater, beat the butter and sugar in a bowl until light and creamy. Add the egg yolks and beat well. Sift the flour and baking powder into a bowl and add to the creamed mixture alternately with the milk. Stir in the vanilla and walnuts.

Using clean beaters, whisk the egg whites in a bowl until firm peaks form, then stir into the cake batter. Spoon mixture into the tin.

Bake for 30–40 minutes, or until a skewer inserted in the centre comes out clean.

Cool the cake in the tin for 10 minutes, then turn out onto a wire rack to cool completely.

47

Family recipes

❧ Family recipes ❧

_____

_____

_____

_____

_____

_____

_____

_____

_____

_____

_____

_____

_____

_____

_____

_____

_____

_____

		1	2	3
		Fish Baked in Vinegar	Fruit Flummery	Canowindra Salad
4	5	6	7	8
Caramel Custard	Cheese Omelette	Mint and Orange Salad	Tingha Pudding	Beetroot Mould
9	10	11	12	13
Washing Day Pudding	Apple Tart	Date Crackers	Chocolate Cake	Banana Nut Cake
14	15	16	17	18
Hard Times Cake	Aberdeen Sausage	Sponge Pudding	Australian Rice	Baked Fruit Rolls
19	20	21	22	23
Banana Fritters	Baked Apples	Chocolate Meringue	'Curyo' Loaf	Lemon Bread Pudding
24	25	26	27	28
Mysterious Pudding	Cowra Savoury Biscuits	Coffee Cake No 1	Ginger Sandwich	Egg and Tomato Luncheon Dish
29	30	31		
Passionfruit Sandwich	Apple Soufflé	Rhubarb Snow		

MARCH

Fish Baked in Vinegar

Mrs WS Forsyth, Armidale Branch

1 MAR

SERVES 4–6

2 mackerel or other oily fish
about 500 g each
¼ cup salt, as required
1 small bunch of fresh thyme
12 black peppercorns
300 ml white wine vinegar
150 ml water
sprigs of parsley, to decorate

Preheat oven to 150°C.

Wash the fish well and pat dry using paper towels. Rub fish all over with the salt and place in a deep, non-reactive baking dish. Scatter over the thyme and peppercorns, add the vinegar and water.

Cover the dish tightly with foil and bake for 20–30 minutes, or until fish is cooked through. Remove from the oven and stand until cool.

Place fish in a serving dish, straining cooking liquid over. Decorate with parsley and serve.

Fruit Flummery

Mrs AJ Arthur, Binalong Branch

2 MAR

SERVES 4–6

1 tablespoon powdered
gelatine
1 tablespoon plain flour
375 ml (1½ cup) water
220 g (1 cup) caster sugar
juice of 2 lemons
pulp of 6 passionfruit
pitted cherries, to serve

Stir the gelatine and flour together in a bowl and whisk in 125 ml (½ cup) of water until smooth. Add the remaining water and stir to mix well.

Combine in a saucepan with the sugar and, stirring constantly, bring the mixture to a boil. Cook over medium heat, stirring to prevent lumps forming, for 3 minutes, or until the mixture has thickened. Transfer to a bowl to cool.

Add the juice and passionfruit and beat with a wooden spoon until thick and creamy.

Spoon into a serving bowl and refrigerate for about 1 hour.

Serve Fruit Flummery decorated with cherries.

Canowindra Salad

Mrs A Patterson, Canowindra Branch

SERVES 6

1 iceberg lettuce, outer leaves
  removed
iced water, as required
250 ml (1 cup) sour cream
1 teaspoon salt
pinch cayenne pepper
55 g (¼ cup) caster sugar
60 ml (¼ cup) malt vinegar
2 tablespoons finely chopped
  parsley

Using a large, sharp knife, cut the lettuce into quarters and trim core. Finely slice the lettuce and plunge it into a bowl of iced water to crisp. Drain well and arrange on a serving platter or in a large bowl.

Combine the remaining ingredients except the parsley in another bowl, add 1 tablespoon of cold water and whisk until smooth. Season to taste with black pepper.

Pour the dressing over the lettuce, scatter over the parsley and serve immediately.

Caramel Custard

Mrs DA Thompson, Albury Branch

SERVES 6

110 g (½ cup) caster sugar,
  plus 1 tablespoon extra
80 ml (⅓ cup) of water
4 eggs, beaten well
600 ml milk
boiling water, for baking

Preheat oven to 150°C. Generously grease a 22 x 4 cm (4 cup capacity) pie dish with butter.

Combine the sugar and 80 ml water in a small saucepan and slowly bring to a simmer. Cook over medium for about 6–7 minutes, or until it turns a deep caramel colour. Working quickly and taking care as the mixture is very hot, pour the caramel over the base of the greased dish.

In a bowl, stir together the eggs, milk and the remaining 1 tablespoon of sugar, then pour over the caramel in the dish. Place the custard dish in a larger baking dish filled with enough boiling water to come halfway up the side.

Bake for 60 minutes, or until just set. Cool to room temperature, then refrigerate.

To serve, loosen edges carefully using a flat-bladed knife and turn out onto a plate.

Cheese Omelette

Mrs P Styles, Yass Branch

SERVES 1

2 eggs, separated

2 tablespoons grated cheddar
cheese

3 teaspoons butter

Preheat oven grill to medium–high.

Beat egg yolks in a bowl, then add the cheese and stir to mix well. Using an electric beater, whisk the egg whites in a bowl with a pinch of salt until firm peaks form. Gently fold the whites into the yolk mixture.

Heat the butter over medium–high heat in a 20 cm heavy-based pan with a heatproof handle. Add the egg mixture and cook for about 1–2 minutes, or until the edges begin to set. Using a spatula, draw the edges of the omelette into the centre of the pan, allowing uncooked mixture to run to the edges of the pan. Continue to cook for about 5 seconds.

Place the pan under the grill and cook for 4–5 minutes, until omelette is golden and puffy. Turn out onto a plate and serve immediately.

Mint and Orange Salad

6 MAR

Mrs SA Ripper, Narrabri Branch

SERVES 6

6 oranges

1 handful of mint leaves,
finely chopped

juice of ½ lemon

2 teaspoons caster sugar

1 iceberg lettuce, outer
leaves removed

Using a sharp knife, peel the oranges, removing all the white pith. Cut oranges along membranes to separate each segment, holding the fruit over a bowl to catch the juices.

Combine segments and juice in the bowl with mint, lemon juice and sugar.

Wash lettuce leaves and tear into large pieces. Toss lettuce with the orange mixture in a serving bowl.

Season salad with salt and pepper and serve.

Tingha Pudding

Mrs B Thurling, Tingha Branch

SERVES 8

2 eggs, separated
90 g (¾ cup) cornflour
875 ml (3½ cups) milk
60 g (¼ cup) butter,
    chopped
100 g caster sugar, plus
    2 tablespoons extra
85 g (¼ cup) raspberry jam,
    warmed
1 teaspoon lemon juice

Preheat oven to 160°C. Grease a 1.5 litre (6 cup) capacity baking dish with butter.

Combine the egg yolks and cornflour in a bowl with just enough of the milk to make a smooth paste.

In a small saucepan, heat the remaining milk until nearly simmering. Stirring constantly, add the butter, 80 g of the sugar and the cornflour mixture. Bring to a simmer, stirring to prevent lumps forming and cook until the mixture boils and thickens. Pour into the dish and spread over the warm jam.

Using an electric beater, whisk the egg whites in a bowl until firm peaks form. Gradually add the remaining sugar and whisk until it is dissolved and mixture is thick and glossy. Spread the whites over the jam.

Bake the pudding for 50–60 minutes, or until golden. Serve hot.

Beetroot Mould

Mrs EM Hamblin, Nevertire Branch

SERVES 4–6

2 large beetroot, trimmed
and scrubbed clean
12 g (1 tablespoon) powdered
gelatine
375 ml (1½ cup) water
125 ml (½ cup) malt vinegar
shredded lettuce and sliced
tomatoes, to serve

Cook the beetroot in boiling water until tender, then drain well. When completely cooled, peel the beetroot and slice thinly into rounds. Layer the slices in a 1 litre (4 cup) capacity mould or bowl.

Sprinkle gelatine over 125 ml (½ cup) of water in a small heatproof cup and stand until softened. Place the cup in a small saucepan of gently simmering water coming half way up the side of the cup. Heat for 4–5 minutes, or until gelatine has dissolved.

Combine gelatine with the vinegar and remaining water in a bowl and stir. Pour gelatine mixture over the beetroot in the mould and cool to room temperature.

Refrigerate overnight until firmly set. To serve, dip mould briefly in hot water to loosen, then turn out onto a large plate. Serve with lettuce and tomatoes.

Washing Day Pudding

Mrs B Bromley, Bowral Branch

SERVES 4

1 pineapple, peeled and
cored
1 tablespoon whisky or
brandy, or to taste
2 large, firm, ripe bananas,
sliced
whipped cream, to serve

Grate the pineapple using the coarsest side of a box grater.

Combine pineapple in a bowl with the whisky and bananas, stirring gently to mix.

Spoon pudding into bowls and serve with whipped cream.

Apple Tart

Miss A Travis, Gilgandra Branch

SERVES 8

60 g caster sugar, plus
   2 tablespoons, for sprinkling
115 g butter, softened
1 egg
250 g (1⅔ cups) self-raising
   flour
2 large granny smith apples,
   peeled and finely chopped

Preheat oven to 180°C. Lightly grease a
23 cm tart tin.

Using an electric beater, beat 60 g of the
sugar with butter in a bowl until light and
creamy. Add the egg and beat well. Add the
flour and stir to form a soft dough. Wrap in
plastic wrap and refrigerate for 30 minutes.

Divide the dough in two pieces, with one
piece slightly larger than the other. Using your
hands, press the larger piece over the base
and side of the tart tin. Scatter apples and
remaining sugar over pastry.

Press the remaining pastry out on a lightly
floured surface into a round large enough
to cover the tart. Place pastry round over
the apples and press edges together to seal.
Sprinkle top with extra sugar.

Bake for 40 minutes, or until pastry is
golden and cooked through and filling
is bubbling.

Date Crackers

Mrs Tom Gaffney, Tamworth Branch

MAKES ABOUT 15

220 g (1 cup, firmly packed)
  brown sugar
250 g (1 cup) butter
240 g (2½ cups) rolled oats
375 g (2½ cups) plain flour
1 teaspoon bicarbonate
  of soda
125 ml (½ cup) warm water

Filling

400 g (2½ cups) dates,
  pitted, chopped
220 g (1 cup) caster sugar
125 ml (½ cup) water

For the filling, combine the dates and sugar with the water in a saucepan. Cover and bring to a simmer. Cook for 10–15 minutes, or until dates are tender. Stand until cool.

Preheat oven to 180°C. Line a 40 x 27 cm baking tray with baking paper.

Using an electric beater, beat the butter and brown sugar in a bowl until light and creamy. Stir in the rolled oats and flour to form a dough. Mix the soda with the warm water and stir into the dough.

Turn the dough out onto a lightly floured surface and divide it into four even-sized pieces. Working with one piece at a time, roll dough out into a rectangle about 15 x 10 cm and 5 mm thick. Spread over half the filling.

Roll another piece of dough out to the same size and place it over the top. Cut into 5 x 2 cm pieces and place on the baking tray. Repeat with remaining dough and filling.

Bake for 15–20 minutes, or until crisp and light golden.

Chocolate Cake

Mrs WM Hammond, Wagga Branch

MAKES ONE 20 CM CAKE
125 g (½ cup) butter,
  softened
220 g (1 cup) caster sugar
3 eggs, separated
300 g (2 cups) plain flour
2 tablespoons cocoa powder
1 teaspoon cream of tartar
125 ml (½ cup) milk
½ teaspoon bicarbonate
  of soda
blanched almonds, to
  decorate

Icing
120 g (1 cup) icing sugar
  mixture
2 tablespoons cocoa powder
2 tablespoons soft butter
1 tablespoon milk

Preheat oven to 180°C. Lightly grease and flour a 20 cm cake tin.

Using an electric beater, beat butter and sugar in a bowl until light and creamy. Add the yolks and beat to combine well. Sift the flour, cocoa and tartar into a bowl, then stir into the creamed mixture with the milk.

Using clean beaters, whisk the egg whites in a bowl until firm peaks form, then stir in the soda. Stir the whites into the batter. Spoon the batter into the tin, smoothing the top even.

Bake for about 40 minutes, or until a skewer inserted in the centre comes out clean. Cool the cake in the tin for 10 minutes, then turn out onto a wire rack to cool completely.

For the icing, sift icing sugar and cocoa into a bowl. Add butter and milk and, using an electric beater, mix on low speed until combined and smooth. Continue to mix at medium speed for a further 2 minutes, until light and fluffy.

Spread the icing over the cooled cake.

Decorate the iced Chocolate Cake with blanched almonds, or other nuts if preferred.

Banana Nut Cake

Mrs Evans, Wagga Branch

MAKES ONE 20 CM CAKE

60 g (¼ cup) butter,
  softened
330 g (1½ cups) caster sugar
2 eggs
1 cup mashed ripe bananas
  (about 3 bananas)
1 teaspoon bicarbonate
  of soda
80 ml (⅓ cup) buttermilk
260 g (1¾ cups) plain flour,
  sifted
60 g (½ cup) chopped
  walnuts

Preheat oven to 180°C. Lightly grease and flour a 20 cm cake tin.

Using an electric beater, beat butter and sugar in a bowl until light and creamy. Add eggs one at a time, beating well between each. Stir in the banana, soda, buttermilk, flour and walnuts, mixing well. Spoon the batter into the tin, smoothing the top even.

Bake for 40 minutes, or until a skewer inserted in the centre comes out clean. Cool the cake in the tin for 10 minutes, then turn out onto a wire rack to cool completely.

Hard Times Cake

MAKES ONE 20 CM CAKE

125 g (½ cup) butter, softened
220 g (1 cup) caster sugar
525 g (3½ cups) plain flour
1 teaspoon allspice
1 teaspoon bicarbonate
  of soda
300 ml milk
320 g (3 cups) currants
40 g (¼ cup) mixed peel,
  chopped

Preheat oven to 180°C. Line a 20 cm cake tin with baking paper.

Using an electric beater, beat the butter and sugar in a bowl until light and creamy. Sift the flour and allspice into a bowl. In a cup, combine the soda and milk. Stir the flour mixture, milk mixture and fruits into the creamed mixture and combine well.

Spoon the batter into the tin, smoothing the top even.

Bake for 1½ hours, or until a skewer inserted in the centre comes out clean. Cool the cake in the tin.

Aberdeen Sausage

Mrs Stuart Williams, Cootamundra Branch

SERVES 4

500 g chuck steak, trimmed
and cut into 5 cm pieces
250 g bacon, rind removed
105 g (1¾ cups, lightly packed)
fresh breadcrumbs
2 tablespoons tomato sauce
1 egg, lightly beaten
1½ teaspoons finely grated
lemon zest

Using a mincer, or mincing attachment for an electric mixer, mince the steak and bacon together. Combine in a bowl with the remaining ingredients and season well with salt and pepper. Using clean hands, mix together well.

Form the mixture into a log about 30 cm long and 4 cm thick. Wrap the log firmly in a floured cloth for boiling. To make one large sausage, tie the ends well with kitchen twine to secure; for smaller sausages, tie at intervals along the log.

Cook in boiling water for 2 hours, or until firm. Unwrap sausage and serve hot.

Sponge Pudding

Mrs Kook, Temora Branch

SERVES 6

1 tablespoon butter, softened
110 g (½ cup) caster sugar
2 eggs
150 g (1 cup) plain flour
1 teaspoon baking powder
milk, as required
warmed golden syrup and
whipped cream, to serve

Bring a large saucepan of water to the boil for steaming, placing a small heatproof plate upside down in the water to keep the pudding basin off the base of the pan. Grease a 1 litre (4 cup) capacity pudding basin.

Using an electric beater, beat the butter and sugar in a bowl until light and creamy. Add the eggs, one at a time, beating well between each. Sift the flour and baking powder into a bowl, then stir into the creamed mixture, adding a few tablespoons of milk as required to make a heavy batter.

Spoon batter into the basin, cover tightly and lower it into the boiling water. Steam for 1 hour or until cooked through, adding more water to the pan as required.

Serve Sponge Pudding hot with golden syrup and whipped cream.

Australian Rice

Miss LM Northcott, Mosman Branch

SERVES 6

2 tablespoons rice bran oil
2 onions, peeled and cut
  into rings
200 g (1 cup) white
  long-grain rice
3 large, ripe tomatoes,
  sliced into rounds
375 ml (1½ cups) water

Heat the oil in a saucepan over medium heat, add the onion and cook, stirring often, for 6–7 minutes, or until browned.

Add the rice and cook for another 3 minutes. Add the tomatoes and water.

Bring to a simmer, cover the pan tightly and cook over low heat for about 15 minutes. Remove from the heat and stand the rice for 5 minutes, or until the liquid is absorbed and the rice is tender.

Season to taste with salt and pepper and serve hot.

Baked Fruit Rolls

Mrs FJ Le Lievre, Coolamon Branch

SERVES 6

225 g (1½ cups) plain flour
½ teaspoon salt
75 g (⅓ cup) caster sugar
1½ teaspoons baking powder
1½ tablespoons butter,
  chopped
80 ml (⅓ cup) milk
165 g (½ cup) raspberry jam
375 ml (1½ cups) boiling
  water

Preheat oven to 170°C. Grease a 1.5 litre (6 cup) capacity baking dish.

Combine the flour, salt, 1 tablespoon of the sugar and the baking powder in a bowl. Using your fingertips, rub in half of the butter, then stir in the milk to form a soft dough.

Turn the dough out onto a lightly floured surface. Roll the dough to about 3 cm thickness and cut into six even-sized pieces (about 14 x 10 cm). Place 1 tablespoon of jam on each piece, roll and pinch the ends to seal, like a dumpling. Place the rolls in the baking dish.

Combine the butter and remaining sugar with the boiling water and pour over the rolls.

Bake for 20 minutes, or until rolls are cooked through and syrup is bubbling.

Banana Fritters

Mrs Douglas Mackellar, Leeton Branch

SERVES 6

50 g butter, softened
2 eggs, well beaten
50 g (¼ cup) caster sugar
50 g (⅓ cup) plain flour,
   sifted
330 ml (1⅓ cups) milk,
   warmed
6 bananas
juice of 1 lemon
vegetable oil, for
   deep-frying
icing sugar, for dusting

For the batter, beat the butter with a wooden spoon until very soft. Add the egg and sugar and combine well. Add the flour and milk and stir until smooth.

Peel the bananas, removing any stringy fibres, and cut in half lengthwise. Place in a dish and gently toss in lemon juice, leaving to stand for 30 minutes.

Heat enough oil for deep-frying in a large saucepan to 180°C, or until a cube of bread browns in 15 seconds.

Dip bananas in the batter in batches, allowing excess to drain off. Deep-fry, in batches, for 3–5 minutes, or until golden. Place on paper towels to drain off excess oil.

Serve fritters hot, dusted with icing sugar.

Baked Apples

Mrs Johnston, Bathurst Branch

SERVES 6

6 granny smith apples, peeled
125 g (½ cup) butter, melted
90 g (1 cup) desiccated
   coconut

Filling
45 g (¼ cup) dried mixed
   fruit
30 g (¼ cup) mixed nuts,
   chopped finely
60 g (¼ cup) butter, melted
60 g (¼ cup, firmly packed)
   brown sugar,

Preheat oven to 180°C. Grease a 1.5 litre (6 cup) capacity baking dish.

Peel the apples and, using an apple corer, remove and discard the cores. Brush each apple with melted butter then roll each in coconut to coat well.

For the filling, combine the fruit, nuts, butter and sugar in a bowl. Stuff the apple cavities with the filling.

Place the apples in the dish and bake for 20–30 minutes, or until the apples are tender. Serve hot.

Chocolate Meringue

Mrs JWC Beveridge, Junee Branch

SERVES 8

80 g (¾ cup) cocoa powder
30 g (¼ cup) cornflour
3 eggs, separated
75 g (⅓ cup) caster sugar
900 ml milk
50 g butter
1 teaspoon vanilla essence

Preheat oven to 180°C. Grease a 20 cm baking dish.

Combine the cocoa and cornflour in a bowl and whisk to combine well. Whisk the egg yolks and sugar in a bowl and set aside. Add enough of the milk to the cocoa mixture to form a paste, whisking until smooth.

Heat the remaining milk in a saucepan until simmering. Stirring constantly, add the cocoa mixture. Cook over medium–low heat, stirring constantly, until the mixture boils and thickens. Stir in the yolk mixture and simmer for 2 minutes, then remove from the heat. Stir in the butter and vanilla.

Spoon the chocolate mixture into the dish. Whisk the egg whites in a bowl until firm peaks form, then spoon the whites over the chocolate mixture.

Bake for 1 hour, or until the meringue is golden.

'Curyo' Loaf

Mrs Fred Simmons, Trundle Branch

SERVES 8

155 g (1 cup) peas, fresh or
    frozen, cooked
60 g (1 cup, lightly packed)
    fresh breadcrumbs
3 large carrots, cooked, mashed
185 g (1 cup) cooked
    medium-grain white rice
250 ml (1 cup) tomato purée
2 eggs, well beaten

Preheat oven to 180°C. Grease a 1.5 litre (6 cup) capacity baking dish.

Combine all the ingredients in a bowl, season well with salt and pepper and mix well. Spoon into dish, smoothing the top even.

Bake for 45 minutes, or until loaf is firm and golden.

Lemon Bread Pudding

Mrs Percy Stacy, Singleton Branch

SERVES 4–6

180 g (3 cups, lightly packed)
   fresh breadcrumbs
3 tablespoons butter, softened
110 g (½ cup) caster sugar
juice and finely grated zest
   of 3 lemons
250 ml (1 cup) boiling water
4 eggs, separated
750 ml (3 cups) milk

Preheat oven to 160°C. Grease a 1.5 litre (6 cup) capacity baking dish.

Combine the crumbs, butter, half of the sugar, lemon juice and zest in a bowl and stir to mix well. Add the boiling water and mix well.

In a bowl, whisk the egg yolks then stir in the milk. Add to the crumb mixture. Spoon into the dish and bake for 30 minutes, or until set.

Using an electric beater, whisk the egg whites in a clean bowl until firm peaks form. Whisking constantly, gradually add the remaining sugar and whisk until it has dissolved and mixture is thick and glossy.

Spoon whites over the pudding. Bake for a further 15 minutes, or until the meringue is golden.

Mysterious Pudding

Mrs Stevenson, Boorowa Branch

SERVES 8

3 firm, ripe bananas, sliced
1 day-old 18 cm sponge
   cake
1 packet fruit jelly, preferred
   flavour
cream or custard, to serve.

Line the inside of a 1.25 litre (5 cup) capacity bowl or mould with some of the banana slices. Cut the cake into 2 cm pieces. Place about one third of the cake pieces in the bowl. Lay more banana over the cake and continue layering until bowl is half full.

Make the jelly according to packet instructions. Pour the hot jelly mixture over the cake and banana. Stand pudding until cooled to room temperature, then refrigerate for 3–4 hours, or until firm.

To serve, turn the pudding out of the mould and serve with cream or custard.

Cowra Savoury Biscuits

Mrs Durrell, Cowra Branch

SERVES 10–12

70 g chopped walnuts
90 g olives, pitted, chopped
1 tablespoon white vinegar
125 ml (½ cup) pouring
   cream, whipped
1 packet water cracker
   biscuits
sliced gherkins, to decorate

Combine walnuts and olives in a bowl and stir in the vinegar. Season with salt and pepper then gently stir into the whipped cream.

Spoon the mixture onto the crackers, decorating each with a slice of gherkin.

Serve immediately.

Coffee Cake No 1

Miss Valerie Weeks, Cremorne

MAKES ONE 20 CM CAKE

125 g (½ cup) butter,
   softened
110 g (½ cup) caster sugar
2 eggs, well beaten
1 tablespoon coffee essence
60 ml (¼ cup) milk
450 g (3 cups) self-raising
   flour, sifted
toasted flaked almonds,
   chopped, to decorate

Coffee Icing
1½ tablespoons butter
120 g (1 cup) icing sugar
coffee essence, to flavour

Preheat oven to 180°C. Lightly grease and flour a 20 cm cake tin.

Using an electric beater, beat the butter and sugar in a bowl until light and creamy. Add the eggs one at a time, beating well between each. Combine the coffee essence and milk in a bowl and add to the creamed mixture with the flour, stirring until smooth.

Spoon batter into the tin, smoothing the top even. Bake for 45 minutes, or until a skewer inserted in the centre comes out clean. Cool the cake in the tin for 10 minutes, then turn out onto a wire rack to cool completely.

For the icing, beat the butter and sugar in a bowl until light and creamy. Flavour with 1–2 teaspoons of coffee essence, adding a little hot water if icing is too thick.

Spread the cake with icing. Sprinkle with flaked almonds to decorate.

Ginger Sandwich

Mrs Frank Turner, Trundle Branch

MAKES ONE 18 CM CAKE
25 g butter
220 g (1 cup) caster sugar
2 eggs
2 tablespoons treacle
125 ml (½ cup) milk
½ teaspoon bicarbonate
   of soda
150 g (1 cup) plain flour,
1 teaspoon ground ginger
raspberry jam, for filling

Caramel Glaze
60 g (¼ cup) butter
100 g (½ cup, firmly packed)
   dark brown sugar
60 ml (¼ cup) thickened
   cream

Preheat oven to 180°C. Lightly grease and flour two 18 cm cake tins.

Using an electric beater, beat the butter and sugar in a bowl until light and creamy. Add the eggs one at a time, beating well between each. Beat in the treacle. Combine milk and soda in a bowl. Sift the flour and ginger into another bowl. Add the milk and flour mixtures to the creamed mixture, then stir to form a smooth batter.

Spoon batter into the tins, smoothing the top even. Bake for 15–20 minutes, or until a skewer inserted in the centre comes out clean. Cool the cakes in the tins for 10 minutes, then turn out onto a wire rack to cool completely.

Spread the raspberry jam over one cake and top with the other cake.

For the caramel glaze, combine all the ingredients in a small saucepan and bring to the boil. Cook over medium heat, stirring, until smooth. Remove from the heat and cool slightly then beat with a wooden spoon until thick and creamy.

Spread caramel over the layered cakes.

Egg and Tomato Luncheon Dish

20 MAR

Mrs AS Wheatley, Condoblin Branch

SERVES 4

4 large tomatoes, thinly
   sliced
50 g butter
4 eggs
a few sprigs of parsley,
   to serve

Preheat oven to 180°C.

Layer the tomatoes in a 1 litre (4 cup) capacity baking dish, seasoning layers with salt and pepper. Dot the top of the tomatoes with butter.

Bake for 15–20 minutes, or until tomatoes have softened and are bubbling. Remove from the oven.

Break the eggs over the tomatoes. Bake a further 8–10 minutes, or until the eggs are set. Garnish with parsley and serve hot.

Passionfruit Sandwich

29 MAR

Mrs Durrell, Cowra Branch

MAKES ONE 18 CM CAKE

250 g (1⅔ cups) plain flour
1 teaspoon cream of tartar
½ teaspoon bicarbonate
   of soda
110 g butter, softened
110 g (½ cup) caster sugar
2 eggs
150 ml milk

Passionfruit Icing
1 teaspoon melted butter
185 g (1½ cup) icing sugar
2 tablespoons milk
pulp of 1 passionfruit

Preheat oven to 180°C. Lightly grease and flour two 18 cm cake tins.

Sift the flour, tartar and soda into a bowl. Using an electric beater, beat the butter and sugar in a bowl until light and creamy. Add the eggs one at a time, beating well between each. Add the flour mixture and the milk, stirring until smooth.

Spoon the batter into the tins, smoothing the tops even. Bake for 15–20 minutes, or until a skewer inserted in the centres comes out clean. Cool cakes in the tins for 10 minutes, then turn out onto wire racks to cool completely.

For the icing, combine all the ingredients in a bowl. Beat with a wooden spoon until smooth.

Spread icing over one cake and top with the other cake.

Apple Soufflé

Mrs WH Kook, Narrandera Branch

SERVES 6

6 medium pink lady apples,
   peeled, cored and chopped
300 ml of water, plus
   1 tablespoon extra
85 g caster sugar
1 tablespoon cornflour
3 eggs, separated

Preheat oven to 180°C. Grease a 1.5 litre (6 cup) capacity soufflé dish. Tie a 3 cm high collar of baking paper around rim of dish.

Combine the apples in a saucepan with 300 ml of water. Bring to a simmer, cover the pan and cook for 20 minutes, or until apples are very soft. Stir in the sugar, then remove from the heat and stand to cool slightly.

Combine the cornflour and egg yolks with 1 tablespoon of water to form a smooth paste. Stir into the apple mixture.

Using an electric beater, whisk the egg whites in a bowl until firm peaks form. Fold the whites into the apple mixture.

Spoon batter into the dish and bake for 20 minutes, or until puffed and golden.

Rhubarb Snow

Mrs J Matthews, Wagga Branch

SERVES 4–6

500 g rhubarb, trimmed
   and chopped
150 g (⅔ cup) caster sugar
2 tablespoons water
1 tablespoon lemon juice
2 egg whites
whipped cream, to serve

Combine the rhubarb, sugar, water and lemon juice in a medium saucepan. Cover and bring to a simmer over low heat. Simmer, stirring occasionally, for 10–12 minutes, or until the rhubarb is very tender. Remove from heat and cool to room temperature.

Using an electric beater, whisk the egg whites in a bowl until firm peaks form. Gently fold the whites into the rhubarb mixture.

Spoon into a serving bowl and refrigerate for 2–3 hours, or until chilled. Serve with whipped cream.

Family recipes

❧ Family recipes ❧

		1	2	3
		Cheese Meringue	Malt Biscuits	Coffee Blancmange
4	5	6	7	8
Orange Shape	Bacon and Scrambled Rice	Eggless Cake	American Salad	Date Spice Cake
9	10	11	12	13
Onion Fritters	Melters	Carrot Soup	Cheese Custard	Doughnuts
14	15	16	17	18
Ginger Pudding	Bananas and Bacon	Apple and Rice Meringue	Honeycomb Pudding	Chocolate Sauce Pudding
19	20	21	22	23
Steamed Lemon Pudding	Apple Roses	Baked Steak	Apple Omelette	Boston Scones
24	25	26	27	28
Carrot Pudding	Anzac Biscuits	Seed Cake	Meringue Sandwich	Almond Fingers
29	30			
Dolly Varden Cake	Passionfruit Velvet Cream with Meringues			

APRIL

Cheese Meringue

Mrs J Kiley, Cootamundra

MAKES ABOUT 12
1 batch of cheese dough
   (see Cheese Straws,
   10 February)
2 egg whites
40 g grated cheddar cheese
pinch cayenne pepper

Preheat oven to 180°C. Line a 40 x 27 cm baking tray with baking paper.

On a lightly floured surface, roll the dough out into a 24 x 24 cm square. Using a 6 cm round pastry cutter, cut rounds from pastry. Re-roll scraps to make more rounds.

Place the biscuits on the tray and bake for 10 minutes, or until crisp and golden. Remove biscuits from the oven and allow to cool slightly.

Using an electric beater, whisk the egg whites in a bowl until firm peaks form. Stir in the grated cheese and cayenne and season with black pepper. Spoon the egg mixture on top of the biscuits.

Bake for 5 minutes, or until the meringue is golden.

Malt Biscuits

MAKES ABOUT 22 BISCUITS
160 g (⅔ cup) butter,
   softened
220 g (1 cup) caster sugar
2 eggs
125 ml (½ cup) treacle
1½ tablespoons malt extract
450 g (3 cups) plain flour
1 teaspoon bicarbonate
   of soda
2 teaspoons cream of tartar
milk, as required

Preheat oven to 180°C. Line a baking tray with baking paper.

Using an electric beater, beat butter and sugar in a bowl until light and creamy. Add the eggs one at a time, beating well between each. Add the treacle and malt extract. Sift the flour, soda and tartar into a bowl. Stir into the butter mixture, adding a few tablespoons of milk, as required, to form a firm dough.

On a lightly floured surface, roll the dough out to 5 mm thickness. Cut rounds using a 6 cm round pastry cutter and place on the tray.

Bake for 10–15 minutes, or until crisp. Transfer to a wire rack to cool.

Coffee Blancmange

Mrs F Hylton Kelly, Crookwell Branch

SERVES 6–8

600 ml milk

75 g (⅓ cup) caster sugar

1 tablespoon coffee essence

3 eggs, separated

12 g (1 tablespoon) powdered
  gelatine

2 tablespoons water

pinch of salt

Warm milk over medium heat in a small saucepan until nearly simmering. Remove from heat, then stir in the sugar, coffee essence and a pinch of salt. Stir to dissolve the sugar.

Beat the egg yolks well in a bowl. Pour 125 ml (½ cup) of the hot milk mixture over the egg yolks. Stir to combine well, then return mixture to the pan. Stirring constantly with a wooden spoon, cook the mixture over medium–low heat for 5 minutes, or until the mixture has thickened a little – do not overheat or the yolks will scramble.

Sprinkle the gelatine over the water in a small heatproof cup and stand for 5 minutes, or until the gelatine softens. Place the cup in a small saucepan of simmering water coming halfway up the side of the cup. Heat for 4–5 minutes, or until the gelatine dissolves. Stir the gelatine into the milk mixture. Stand until the mixture is at room temperature. Refrigerate, stirring occasionally, until it begins to set.

Using an electric beater, whisk the egg whites in a bowl until firm peaks form, then fold into the milk mixture. Spoon the blancmange into five wet 250 ml (1 cup) moulds. Refrigerate overnight, or until firm.

To serve, dip the moulds briefly into hot water, then turn the blancmange out onto a plate.

Orange Shape

Mrs Bromley, Bowral Branch

SERVES 4
60 g caster sugar
600 ml milk
finely grated zest and juice
    of 2 oranges
15 g powdered gelatine
juice of 1 lemon

Combine sugar, half the milk and the orange zest in a saucepan and warm over medium heat until nearly simmering.

Sprinkle the gelatine over the remaining milk in a small heatproof bowl and stand for 5 minutes, or until the gelatine softens. Add to the hot milk mixture and stir until the gelatine dissolves.

Strain the mixture into a bowl and cool to room temperature. Refrigerate until nearly set.

Stir in the orange and lemon juice and return to the refrigerator until set.

Bacon and Scrambled Rice

Mrs SJ Thomas, Mosman Branch

SERVES 4–6
8 bacon rashers
1 tablespoon butter
370 g (2 cups) cold cooked
    rice
2 tablespoons milk
2 eggs, well beaten

Preheat oven grill to medium heat. Place the bacon, in a single layer, in a large frying pan with a heatproof handle. Grill bacon, turning it once, for 5 minutes, or until golden.

Heat the oven to 160°C. Transfer the bacon to another dish, reserving fat in the pan, and keep the bacon warm in the oven.

Melt the butter in the reserved pan. Add the rice and cook, stirring, over medium heat for 5 minutes, or until the rice is hot. Add the milk and eggs and cook, stirring, for 2 minutes, or until eggs are broken up and just cooked through. Season to taste.

Serve the rice hot, with bacon on the side.

Eggless Cake

6 APR

Mrs JJ Fisher, Warren Branch

MAKES ONE 20 CM CAKE
440 g (2 cups) caster sugar
500 ml (2 cups) water
320 g (2 cups) sultanas
2 tablespoons butter,
  chopped
600 g (4 cups) plain flour
1 teaspoon bicarbonate
  of soda
1 teaspoon mixed spice
1 teaspoons cinnamon
1 teaspoon ground nutmeg

Preheat oven to 150°C. Line a 20 cm cake tin with baking paper.

Combine the sugar in a saucepan with the water, sultanas and butter and bring to a simmer. Remove from heat and stand until cool. Transfer to a large bowl.

Sift the flour, soda and spices into a bowl. Add to the sultana mixture and stir to mix well. Spoon the batter into the tin, smoothing the top even.

Bake for 90 minutes, or until a skewer inserted in the centre comes out clean.

Cool the cake in the tin for 10 minutes, then turn out onto a wire rack to cool completely.

American Salad

7 APR

Mrs Vida Spencer, Merriwa Branch

SERVES 6–8
1 pineapple, peeled, cored
  and trimmed
2 bananas, sliced
2 teaspoons sugar
1 iceberg lettuce

Dressing
250 ml (1 cup) pineapple juice
2 tablespoons plain flour
2 teaspoons mustard powder
55 g (¼ cup) caster sugar
2 egg yolks, well beaten
2 tablespoons lemon juice
250 ml (1 cup) whipped cream

Cut the pineapple into bite-sized chunks and combine in a bowl with the banana. Sprinkle with sugar and toss well. Refrigerate for 1 hour.

For the dressing, place pineapple juice in a heatproof bowl. Set the bowl in a saucepan of simmering water. Whisk in the flour, mustard and sugar and cook until mixture thickens, whisking constantly to prevent lumps forming. Add egg yolks and lemon juice and cook, whisking, for a further 3 minutes, or until thick and creamy. Remove from heat and stand until cool, then stir in the whipped cream.

Scatter the fruit mixture over lettuce leaves on a platter. Drizzle over the dressing.

Date Spice Cake

MAKES ONE 20 CM CAKE

285 g (1½ cups, lightly packed)
   brown sugar
2 tablespoons butter, melted
1 egg, beaten
260 g (1¾ cups) self-raising
   flour
1 teaspoon ground cinnamon
¼ teaspoon ground cloves
½ teaspoon ground mace
160 g (1 cup) chopped
   pitted dates
125 ml (½ cup) milk

Preheat oven to 180°C. Grease and flour a 20 cm cake tin.

Combine brown sugar, butter and egg in a bowl and beat well. Sift the flour and spices into a bowl. Add the dates to the sugar mixture. Stir in the flour mixture alternately with the milk. Beat for 5 minutes. Spoon the batter into the tin, smoothing the top even.

Bake for 30 minutes, or until a skewer inserted in the centre comes out clean. Cool the cake in the tin for 30 minutes, then turn out onto a wire rack to cool completely.

Onion Fritters

Mrs DG Munro, Nevertire Branch

SERVES 4–6

vegetable oil, for deep-frying
1 egg, well beaten
125 ml (½ cup) milk,
   or as required
150 g (1 cup) plain flour
1 teaspoon baking powder
4 large onions, peeled and
   cut into 3 mm thick rings

Heat the oil in a large saucepan to 180°C, or until a cube of bread turns golden brown in 15 seconds.

Whisk the egg and milk in a bowl. Add the flour and baking powder and continue whisking until a smooth, thin batter forms, adding a little more milk if required. Season with salt and pepper.

Working in batches, drop onion rings in the batter, coating well and allowing excess to drain. Fry, in batches, for 5 minutes, or until crisp and golden. Drain excess oil on paper towels.

Season fritters to taste with salt and pepper. Serve immediately.

Melters

MAKES ABOUT 22
2 eggs
110 g (½ cup) caster sugar
120 g butter, softened
1 teaspoon vanilla essence
110 g (¾ cup) plain flour
90 g (¾ cup) cornflour
½ teaspoon bicarbonate
  of soda
1 teaspoon cream of tartar

Preheat oven to 180°C. Line a baking tray with baking paper.

Using an electric beater, whisk the eggs and sugar in a bowl until thick and pale. In another bowl, beat the butter until soft and creamy and add to the egg mixture with the vanilla.

Sift the dry ingredients into a bowl. Gently stir into the egg mixture until combined well.

Drop tablespoons of mixture onto the prepared tray. Bake for 10–15 minutes, or until golden.

Carrot Soup

Mrs G Spring, Rylstone Branch

SERVES 6–8
30 g butter
3 large carrots, peeled
  and chopped
1 onion, peeled and chopped
900 ml chicken stock
2 teaspoons lemon juice

Melt the butter in a saucepan over medium heat. Add the carrot and onion and cook, stirring occasionally, for 8 minutes, or until the vegetables start to soften.

Add 300 ml of the stock, bring to a simmer and cook for 30 minutes, or until vegetables are very tender. Transfer to a food processor (or use a stick blender) and purée the mixture until very smooth.

Return purée to the pan with the remaining stock and the lemon juice. Bring to a simmer.

Season to taste with salt and pepper and serve hot.

Cheese Custard

Mrs SJ Thomas, Mosman Branch

12 APR

SERVES 4–6

125 g (¾ cup) grated cheddar
  cheese
2 eggs, well beaten
600 ml milk
buttered toast, to serve
  (optional)

Preheat oven to 180°C. Grease a 1 litre
(4 cup) capacity baking dish.

Place the cheese, eggs and milk in a bowl
and whisk to combine well. Season to taste
with salt and pepper.

Bake for 1 hour, or until set. Serve in the
dish or cut into squares and serve on hot
buttered toast.

Doughnuts

Mrs Hickson, Albury Branch

13 APR

MAKES 15–20

200 g (1⅓ cups) plain flour
½ teaspoon baking powder
60 g caster sugar
60 g (¼ cup) butter,
  chopped
1 egg, well beaten
60 ml (¼ cup) milk
85 g (½ cup) raisins
vegetable oil, for deep-frying
icing sugar, for dusting

Sift the flour and baking powder into a
bowl. Stir in the sugar. Using your fingertips,
rub in the butter until mixture resembles
breadcrumbs. Add the egg and milk, stirring
to form a stiff dough.

Roll the dough out on lightly floured surface
to 1 cm thickness. Using a 6 cm round pastry
cutter, cut rounds out of dough. Sprinkle
some raisins over half the rounds, leaving
a 1 cm border, and brush the edge of the
rounds with water. Place another round on
top, pressing edges to seal.

Place enough oil to deep-fry doughnuts
in a large frying pan and heat to 180°C, or
until a cube of bread turns golden brown
in 15 seconds. Fry doughnuts, in batches,
for 5–10 minutes, or until deep golden and
cooked through. Transfer to paper towels
to drain excess oil.

Dust doughnuts with icing sugar and serve
hot, or at room temperature.

Ginger Pudding

Mrs Lord, Kurrajong Branch

SERVES 8

300 g (2 cups) plain flour
1 tablespoon ground ginger
60 g (¼ cup) butter, chopped
2 tablespoons caster sugar
2 tablespoons treacle
1 teaspoon bicarbonate of soda
200 ml milk
custard, to serve

Bring a large saucepan of water to the boil for steaming, placing a small heatproof plate upside down in the water to keep the pudding basin off the base of the pan. Flour a 1 litre (4 cup) capacity pudding basin.

Sift the flour and ginger into a bowl. Using your fingertips, rub in the butter then stir in sugar. Combine treacle with soda and milk. Stir treacle mixture into the dry ingredients to form a thick batter.

Spoon batter into the basin, cover tightly and lower it into the boiling water. Steam for 3 hours, or until cooked through, adding more water to the pan as required.

Turn the pudding out onto a plate. Cut into wedges and serve with custard.

Bananas and Bacon

Mrs OK Steindl, Glen Innes Branch

SERVES 4

1 tablespoon vegetable oil
8 bacon rashers
4 bananas, sliced lengthways
8 slices of buttered toast, to serve

Heat the oil in a large frying pan over medium heat. Add the bacon and cook, turning once, for 7–8 minutes, or until golden. Remove and keep warm, reserving fat in the pan.

Add the bananas to the pan and cook, turning once, for 3–4 minutes, or until they are light golden.

Divide the bananas and bacon between the buttered toast and serve.

Apple and Rice Meringue

Mrs JH Head, Stroud Branch

SERVES 4–6

2 cloves
110 g (½ cup) caster sugar
4 granny smith apples,
    peeled, cored and coarsely
    chopped
150 ml water
50 g (¼ cup) long-grain rice
125 ml (½ cup) boiling water
80 ml (⅓ cup) milk
1 egg white

Preheat oven to 180°C.

Combine the cloves, 80 g (⅓ cup) of the sugar, the apples and water in a saucepan and bring to a simmer. Cook over medium heat for about 20 minutes, or until apples are soft and mixture resembles a coarse purée.

Rinse the rice well and place in a small saucepan with the boiling water. Cook, covered, for about 12 minutes, or until the water is absorbed. Add 1 tablespoon of the remaining sugar and milk to the mixture and continue cooking until rice is soft.

Place the rice in a 20 cm (6 cup capacity) baking dish. Spoon the apple mixture into the centre of the dish over the rice.

Using an electric beater, whisk the egg white in a bowl until firm peaks form. Add the remaining sugar, whisking constantly until it has dissolved and mixture is thick and glossy.

Spoon whites over the apples and rice. Bake for 15–20 minutes, or until light golden.

Honeycomb Pudding

Mrs D Diggs, Quambone Branch

SERVES 4–6

75 g (½ cup) plain flour
110 g (½ cup) caster sugar
4 eggs, well beaten
125 ml (½ cup) milk
1 tablespoon butter, melted
175 g (½ cup) golden syrup
1 teaspoon bicarbonate
   of soda
custard, to serve

Preheat oven to 180°C. Grease a 1 litre (4 cup) capacity baking dish. Mix flour and sugar in a bowl.

Place eggs, milk, butter, golden syrup in a bowl and whisk to combine well. Stir in the soda until mixture is foamy then add into the flour mixture and stir until smooth. Spoon mixture into the baking dish.

Bake for 20–30 minutes, or until a skewer inserted in the centre comes out clean.

Serve hot, with custard.

Chocolate Sauce Pudding

Mrs Flannery, Stroud Branch

18 APR

SERVES 4

1 tablespoon butter,
   softened
220 g (1 cup) caster sugar
2 tablespoons plain flour
1 tablespoon cocoa powder
2 eggs, separated
250 ml (1 cup) milk
boiling water, for baking
whipped cream, to serve

Preheat oven to 180°C. Grease a 1.5 litre (6 cup) capacity baking dish.

Using an electric beater, beat the butter and sugar until well combined. Sift the flour and cocoa into a bowl, then stir into the butter mixture with the egg yolks and milk.

Using clean electric beaters, whisk the egg whites in a bowl until firm peaks form. Fold into the chocolate mixture.

Spoon batter into the baking dish, then place in a larger baking dish filled with enough boiling water to come half way up the side of the baking dish. Bake for about 45 minutes.

Serve hot, with whipped cream.

Steamed Lemon Pudding

Mrs J McLennan, Temora Branch

SERVES 6–8
finely grated zest and juice
    of 2 lemons
75 g butter, softened
110 g (½ cup) caster sugar

Suet Pastry
360 g plain flour
180 g shredded suet (see note)
1 teaspoon baking powder
¾ teaspoon salt
180 ml (¾ cup) iced water,
    or as required

>

For the pastry, combine the flour, suet and baking powder in a bowl and mix well. Add ½ teaspoon salt and mix in the iced water, adding a little extra water if necessary to make a firm dough. Add suet and mix well together. Add the remaining ¼ teaspoon of salt and baking powder and a little more iced water to make into a fairly stiff dough. Knead lightly to bring it together.

Bring a large saucepan of water to the boil for steaming, placing a small heatproof plate upside down in the water to keep the pudding basin off the base of the pan. Grease a 1 litre (4 cup) capacity pudding basin.

In a bowl, stir together the lemon zest and juice, butter and sugar to combine well.

Gently roll out the pastry on a lightly floured surface to a 40 cm circle. Place inside the basin, leaving excess pastry hanging over the edges.

Spoon the lemon mixture into the basin. Bring the edges of the pastry over the top of the filling to meet in the middle and press together to seal.

Cover the basin with a tight-fitting lid and lower it into the boiling water. Steam for 3 hours, or until cooked through, adding more water to the pan as required.

Note: shredded suet is available as a packet mix at supermarkets, or fresh from your butcher.

Apple Roses

Miss Freda Cameron, Weetangera Branch

20 APR

SERVES 6

300 g (2 cups) plain flour
2 teaspoons baking powder
2 tablespoons butter,
    chopped
125 g caster sugar, plus extra,
    to sprinkle
1 egg, well beaten
500 ml (2 cups) water
2 granny smith apples, peeled,
    cored and thinly sliced

Preheat oven to 180°C. Grease a 24 × 16 cm (6 cup capacity) baking dish.

Combine flour and baking powder in a bowl. Using your fingertips, rub in butter until mixture resembles breadcrumbs, then stir in 2 teaspoons of the sugar. Add the egg with enough cold water to mix to a firm dough.

Turn the dough out onto a floured surface and lightly knead to bring it together. Roll the dough out to about 4 mm thickness and cut into 10 cm squares. Divide apple slices among the squares, sprinkle with sugar and roll to form log shapes.

Combine the remaining sugar with the water in a saucepan and bring to a simmer. Simmer for 5 minutes.

Place the apple rolls in the baking dish, pour over the syrup and bake for 30 minutes, or until cooked through and sauce is bubbling.

Baked Steak

Mrs HE Ashcroft, Baan Baa Branch

21 APR

SERVES 4–6

1 kg shin or gravy beef cut
    into strips about 5 mm thick
2 tablespoons plain flour
1 tablespoon caster sugar
1 teaspoon salt
1 tablespoon balsamic
    vinegar
500 ml (2 cups) tomato
    passata
500 ml (2 cups) beef stock

Preheat oven to 180°C. Place the beef in a 2 litre (8 cup) capacity baking dish.

Combine the flour, sugar, salt and vinegar in a small bowl. Stir to form a smooth paste and pour over the meat. Season with salt and pepper, then pour over the passata and stock.

Cover the dish tightly with foil. Bake for 90 minutes. Uncover and bake for a further 30 minutes, or until the steak is very tender.

Apple Omelette

Mrs LM Armstrong, Hillston Branch

SERVES 10

6 large granny smith apples,
   peeled, cored and
   chopped
50 g butter, chopped
100 g caster sugar
½ teaspoon freshly grated
   nutmeg
3 eggs, separated

Preheat oven to 180°C. Lightly grease
a 24 cm (6 cup capacity) pie dish.

Place the apples in a saucepan with just
enough water to cover. Cook, covered, over
medium heat for 30 minutes, or until very soft.

Add the butter, sugar and nutmeg and beat
the mixture with a wooden spoon to break
up the apples. Cool slightly. Beat the egg yolks
in a bowl, then stir in the apple mixture.

Using an electric beater, whisk the egg
whites in a bowl until firm peaks form.
Carefully fold into the apple mixture.

Spoon batter into the dish and bake for
50 minutes, or until golden. Serve hot.

Boston Scones

MAKES 20–24

600 g (4 cups) plain flour
65 g (⅓ cup) caster sugar
1 tablespoon cream of tartar
2 teaspoons bicarbonate
   of soda
2 teaspoons mixed spice
2 teaspoons ground
   cinnamon
2 tablespoons butter,
   chopped
250 ml (1 cup) milk

Preheat oven to 180°C. Lightly grease and
flour two baking trays.

Sift all the dry ingredients into a large bowl
then, using your fingertips, rub in the butter.
Add a large pinch of salt and the milk and mix
to form a firm dough.

Turn the dough out onto a lightly floured
board and knead briefly if necessary to bring
dough together – take care not to overwork
or scones will be tough. Roll out to 2–3 mm
thickness. Using a knife or square pastry
cutter, cut the dough into 4 cm squares.

Place scones on trays and bake for
10–15 minutes, or until golden and
cooked through.

Carrot Pudding

Mrs Davis, Wagga Branch

SERVES 8

250 g (1 cup) shredded suet
   (see note)
60 g (1 cup, lightly packed)
   fresh breadcrumbs
220 g (1 cup) caster sugar
55 g (1 cup) grated carrots
145 g (1 cup) currants,
   or 170 g (1 cup) sultanas
150 g (1 cup) plain flour
1 teaspoon bicarbonate
   of soda
finely grated zest of 1 lemon
60 ml (¼ cup) milk

Lemon Sauce
165 g (¾ cup) caster sugar
1½ teaspoons cornflour
310 ml (1¼ cups) hot water
1 tablespoon butter
1 tablespoon lemon juice
1½ teaspoons vanilla
   extract

Bring a large saucepan of water to the boil for steaming, placing a small heatproof plate upside down in the water to keep the pudding basin off the base of the pan. Grease and lightly flour the inside of a 6 cup capacity pudding basin.

Place the suet, crumbs, sugar, carrots and sultanas in a bowl and stir to combine well. Stir in the flour. Mix the soda with the lemon zest and milk, then stir into the mixture to form a stiff batter.

Spoon batter into the basin, cover tightly and lower it into the boiling water. Steam for 3 hours, or until cooked through, adding more water to the pan to the pan as required.

For the lemon sauce, mix together the sugar, cornflour and a pinch of salt in a small saucepan. Stir in the hot water, butter, lemon juice and vanilla. Stirring constantly, cook over medium heat until mixture boils and thickens.

To serve, pour hot sauce over the pudding.

Note: shredded suet is available as a packet mix at supermarkets, or fresh from your butcher.

Anzac Biscuits

Aylmerton Branch

MAKES 30

95 g (1 cup) rolled oats
220 g (1 cup) caster sugar
90 g (1 cup) desiccated
  coconut
150 g (1 cup) plain flour
2 tablespoons butter,
  chopped
1 tablespoon golden syrup
1 teaspoon bicarbonate
  of soda
2 tablespoons of boiling
  water

Preheat oven to 180°C. Line a baking tray with baking paper.

Combine the oats, sugar, coconut and flour in a large bowl and stir to combine well. Combine the butter and golden syrup in a small saucepan and heat until smooth. Remove from heat. Combine the soda with the boiling water, add to the butter mixture then stir into the dried ingredients and mix well.

Using your hands, roll teaspoons of the biscuit mixture into balls. Place on the tray, leaving room to spread.

Bake biscuits for 15–20 minutes, or until golden and crisp. Transfer to a wire rack to cool.

Seed Cake

Mrs Lea, Manildra Branch

MAKES ONE 22 CM LOAF

125 g (½ cup) butter,
  softened
220 g (1 cup) caster sugar
4 eggs
2 tablespoons mixed peel,
  chopped
2 tablespoons caraway
  seeds
300 g (2 cups) plain flour
1 teaspoon baking powder
milk, to mix, as required

Preheat oven to 180°C. Line a 22 x 12 cm loaf tin with baking paper.

Using an electric beater, beat butter and sugar until light and creamy. Beat in the eggs, one at a time, beating well between each. Stir in the peel and caraway seeds.

Sift the flour and baking powder into a bowl. Stir into the creamed mixture, adding a little milk, if required, to make a stiff batter.

Spoon the batter into the tin, smoothing the top even.

Bake for 1 hour, or until a skewer inserted in the centre comes out clean.

Meringue Sandwich

Mrs E Giffen, Manildra Branch

MAKES ONE 18 CM CAKE
4 egg whites
160 g caster sugar
300 ml pouring cream,
    whipped
pulp of 6 passionfruit

Preheat oven to 120°C. Grease and flour two 18 cm cake tins.

Using an electric beater, whisk the egg whites in a bowl until firm peaks form. Gradually add the sugar, whisking constantly until it has dissolved and the mixture is firm and glossy.

Spoon into the tins, smoothing the tops even. Bake for 1 hour, or until the meringue feels dry. Carefully turn out onto a wire rack to cool.

When cool, spread one meringue with whipped cream, drizzle with passionfruit pulp and place remaining meringue on the top. Serve immediately.

Almond Fingers

Mrs JE Cameron, Dungog Branch

MAKES 22
175 g plain flour
1 teaspoon baking powder
125 g (½ cup) butter,
    chopped
120 g (1 cup) icing sugar
1 egg
1 teaspoon almond essence
1 teaspoon vanilla essence
milk, to mix, as required
100 g slivered almonds

Preheat oven 180°C. Line a baking tray with baking paper.

Combine the flour and baking powder in a bowl. Rub in the butter until mixture resembles breadcrumbs. Stir in the icing sugar, egg and essences and mix to form a firm dough, adding a little milk if required.

Roll the dough out on a lightly floured surface to a 4 mm thick square. Cut into 6 x 3 cm rectangles and sprinkle the almonds over the top.

Place fingers on the tray. Bake for 8 minutes, or until golden brown. Cool on the tray.

Dolly Varden Cake

Miss Peterson, Manildra Branch

MAKES ONE 20 CM CAKE

250 g (1 cup) butter,
   softened
220 g (1 cup) caster sugar
4 large eggs
250 g (1⅔ cups) plain flour
1 teaspoon baking powder

Butter Icing

250 g (1 cup) butter,
   softened
375 g (3 cups) icing sugar,
   sifted
1–2 tablespoons milk

Filling

85 g (½ cup) sultanas
80 g (½ cup) chopped pitted
   dates
85 g (½ cup) raisins
75 g (½ cup) currants
75 g (½ cup) mixed peel
1 tablespoon sugar
1 tablespoon butter
175 ml brandy
½ teaspoon each of ground
   cinnamon, ginger and
   allspice
glacé cherries and blanched
   almonds, to decorate.

Preheat oven to 180°C. Line the base and side of a 20 cm round cake tin with baking paper.

Using an electric beater, beat the butter and sugar until light and creamy. Add the eggs, one at a time, beating well between each. Sift the flour and baking powder into a bowl, then stir into the creamed mixture. Spoon the batter into the tin, smoothing the top even.

Bake for 1 hour, or until a skewer inserted in the centre comes out clean. Cool the cake in the tin for 15 minutes, then turn out onto a wire rack to cool completely.

Cut a 10 cm-deep hole out of the centre of the cake, leaving a border around the edge. Remove this cut piece from the middle of the cake and reserve for another use.

For the icing, beat butter and sugar until pale and creamy. Add 60 g (½ cup) of icing sugar at a time and mix well. Add enough milk to make a thick, spreadable icing. Ice the edge and side of the cake.

For the filling, combine all the ingredients in a saucepan and bring to a simmer. Cook uncovered, stirring occasionally, for 15 minutes, or until thick. Cool completely to room temperature, then spoon the filling into the cavity in the cake. Decorate and serve.

To serve, decorate the top of the Dolly Varden Cake with cherries and almonds.

Passionfruit Velvet Cream with Meringues

Mrs Ronald Cuttle, Junee Branch

SERVES 4–6
600 ml milk
60 g (¼ cup) butter, chopped
110 g (½ cup) caster sugar
2 tablespoons cornflour
1 tablespoon water
2 eggs, separated
pulp of 6 passionfruit
100 g sifted icing sugar

Preheat oven to 180°C.

Combine milk, butter and sugar in a saucepan and bring to a simmer, stirring occasionally to dissolve the sugar. Combine the cornflour with the water and egg yolks in a small bowl and stir until smooth. Stirring constantly to prevent lumps forming, add to the simmering milk mixture in the pan and cook for 2–3 minutes or until it simmers and thickens. Remove from the heat, then stir in the passionfruit.

Pour mixture into a 1 litre (4 cup) capacity dish and cool to room temperature, then refrigerate to chill. Serve with the meringues.

For the meringues, preheat oven to 100°C. Line a baking tray with baking paper.

Using an electric beater, whisk egg whites until firm peak form then, whisking constantly, gradually add the icing sugar and whisk until firm and glossy. Drop tablespoons of the mixture, or pipe small rounds, onto the tray.

Bake for 40 minutes. Turn oven off and cool the meringues in the oven, with the door slightly ajar.

❧ Family recipes ❧

Family recipes

		1	2	3
		Savoury Steak	Chocolate Rice	Potato Cakes and Bacon
4	5	6	7	8
Prune Delight	Cheese Wafers	Chester Cake	Savoury Sausages	Wholemeal Cake
9	10	11	12	13
Salmon Puffs	Orange Delicious Pudding	Lemon Snow	Brown Fricassee of Rabbit	Vegetable Soup
14	15	16	17	18
Curry Paste	Rainbow Cake No 1	Warren Pudding	Cream Scones	Peach and Raisin Pie
19	20	21	22	23
Apple and Celery Salad	Apricot Sponge	Baked Pumpkin	Tennis Cake	Wallaga Savoury
24	25	26	27	28
Snowden Pudding	Temora Date Pudding	Weethalle Chocolate Pudding	Raspberry Sponge Pudding	Dark Cake No 1
29	30	31		
Apple Batter	Australian Shortcake	Curried Eggs		

MAY

Savoury Steak

Miss Ivy Quinton, Maitland Branch

1 MAY

SERVES 4
1 kg piece rump steak
1 tablespoon malt vinegar
2 tablespoons tomato sauce
1 tablespoon Worcestershire
    sauce

Stuffing
60 g (1 cup, lightly packed)
    fresh breadcrumbs
1 large onion, peeled and
    finely chopped
1 tablespoon finely
    chopped sage leaves
50 g butter, softened

Using a sharp knife, make a horizontal slit in the side of the steak to form a deep pocket, taking care not to cut all the way through. Place the steak in a bowl with the remaining ingredients, turning to coat well. Cover the bowl and stand for 1½ hours.

Preheat oven to 180°C.

For the stuffing, combine all the ingredients in a bowl, season with salt and pepper and stir to mix well.

Drain the steak well and stuff with the crumb mixture. Tie the steak up at 2.5 cm intervals using kitchen string to secure, making a neat shape.

Oil a 2 litre baking dish. Place steak in the dish, season well with salt and pepper and bake for 1 hour, or until the meat is tender.

Chocolate Rice

Mrs Hunter, Albury Branch

2 MAY

SERVES 4
70 g short-grain rice
600 ml milk
110 ml boiling water
60 g dark chocolate, grated
1½ tablespoons caster sugar
2 tablespoons condensed milk
½ teaspoon vanilla essence
chocolate sauce or whipped
    cream, to serve

Combine the rice and milk in a double saucepan over boiling water and add a pinch of salt. Cover and cook over medium heat for 10–15 minutes, or until rice is tender and milk has been absorbed.

Pour the boiling water over the chocolate in a bowl and stir until smooth. Add to the rice with the sugar, condensed milk and vanilla then pour into a bowl. Stand to cool.

Serve with sauce or whipped cream.

Potato Cakes and Bacon

Mrs AV Booth, Yathella Branch

MAKES 10

125 g plain flour
50 g butter, chopped
460 g (2 cups) cold mashed
  potato
pinch cayenne pepper
60 ml (¼ cup) milk, plus extra,
  as required
10 bacon rashers, rind
  removed
vegetable oil, for frying
sprigs of parsley, to serve

Place the flour in a bowl. Using your fingertips, rub in the butter until mixture resembles breadcrumbs. Add the potato, salt to taste and the cayenne. Add the milk to form a firm dough.

Turn the dough out onto a lightly floured surface and briefly knead until smooth. Roll out to 2 cm thickness. Using a 7 cm round pastry cutter, cut rounds from dough, re-rolling any scraps for more rounds.

Preheat oven grill to medium. Heat the oil in a large, heavy based frying pan over medium heat. Add the cakes and cook for 7–8 minutes on each side, or until deep golden.

Cook the bacon under oven grill for 7–8 minutes, or until golden, turning once. Serve with the hot potato cakes.

Serve the Potato Cakes topped with bacon slices and decorated with parsley sprigs.

Prune Delight

Mrs PJ Purcell, Woodstock Branch

4 MAY

SERVES 4–6

250 g (1 cup) pitted prunes,
  chopped
55 g (¼ cup) caster sugar
juice of 2 lemons
600 ml water, plus
  60 ml (¼ cup), extra
1 tablespoon powdered
  gelatine
whipped cream, to serve

Combine the prunes, sugar, lemon juice and water in a saucepan. Bring to a simmer, cover and cook over medium–low heat for 20 minutes, or until the prunes are very tender.

Sprinkle the gelatine over 60 ml of water in a small heatproof cup and stand for 5 minutes, or until the gelatine softens. Place the cup in a small saucepan of simmering water coming halfway up the side of the cup. Heat for 4–5 minutes, or until the gelatine dissolves. Add to the prune mixture, stirring to break up prunes.

Spoon the mixture into a dampened 1 litre (4 cup) capacity mould. Refrigerate for 2–3 hours, or until set.

To serve, dip the mould into hot water then turn out onto a plate.

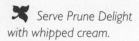

Serve Prune Delight with whipped cream.

Cheese Wafers

Mrs H Bollinger, Parkes Branch

MAKES 16

50 g (½ cup) grated
   cheddar cheese
50 g butter, chopped
pinch cayenne pepper
2 egg yolks
juice of 1 lemon
2 sheets frozen puff
   pastry, thawed

Preheat oven to 180°C. Line a baking tray with baking paper.

Combine the cheddar, butter and cayenne in a small saucepan over low heat. Combine one of the egg yolks and lemon juice in a small bowl, stir to mix well and add to the pan. Cook, stirring constantly, until the cheese melts and the mixture is smooth. Do not let the mixture overheat or it will curdle.

Using a 4 cm round pastry cutter, cut 32 rounds from the pastry. Spread a little cheese mixture over half the rounds, leaving a slight border around each edge. Lightly wet the edges with water, place another round on top and press the edges to seal.

Place wafers on the baking tray. Combine remaining egg yolk with a little water and brush over the wafers. Bake for 12–15 minutes, or until puffed and deep golden.

Chester Cake

Mrs Blessing, Penrith Branch

MAKES ONE 22 CM TART

Filling

160 g (1 cup) chopped
  pitted dates
85 g (½ cup) sultanas
1 teaspoon ground
  cinnamon
1 tablespoon golden
  syrup
2 tablespoons water

225 g (1½ cups) plain flour
1 teaspoon baking powder
2 tablespoons butter
110 g (½ cup) caster sugar
1 egg, well beaten
60 ml (¼ cup) milk

Preheat oven to 180°C. Lightly grease and flour a 22 cm tart tin.

For the filling, combine the dates, sultanas, cinnamon, golden syrup and water in a small saucepan. Bring to a simmer, cover and cook over low heat for 10–15 minutes, or until the dates are soft. Cool to room temperature.

Combine flour and baking powder in a bowl. Using your fingertips, rub in the butter until mixture resemble breadcrumbs. Stir in the sugar. Add the egg and milk and mix to form a firm dough.

Divide the dough in half. Roll one half out to cover base and side of tin. Spread filling over. Roll remaining pastry out to fit over the top. Trim edges and crimp to seal well.

Bake tart for 20–30 minutes, or until pastry is golden.

Savoury Sausages

Mrs Hanstock, Quandialla Branch

SERVES 6

2 eggs, beaten
600 ml milk
250 g (1⅔ cups) plain flour
500 g cooked pork or beef
  sausages, skinned and
  sliced

Preheat oven to 180°C. Grease a 1.5 litre (6 cup) capacity baking dish.

Whisk the eggs and milk together in a bowl. Add the flour, whisking constantly until smooth. Season with salt and pepper.

Pour the batter into the baking dish and place sausages in the batter. Bake for 45 minutes, or until puffy and golden. Serve hot.

Wholemeal Cake

Mrs Borrowdale, Nowra Branch

MAKES ONE 18 CM CAKE
80 g (4 tablespoons) butter,
  softened
220 g (1 cup) caster sugar
2 eggs
2 tablespoons golden syrup
1 teaspoon ground cinnamon
300 g (2 cups) wholemeal
  self-raising flour
1 teaspoon baking powder
160 ml hot water

Icing
125 g (1 cup) icing sugar
1 tablespoon butter
1 teaspoon coffee essence

Preheat oven to 160°C. Lightly grease and flour an 18 cm cake tin.

Using an electric beater, beat butter and sugar in a bowl until light and creamy. Add the eggs, one at a time, beating well between each. Add the golden syrup and mix well. Stir in the cinnamon, flour and baking powder, then add the hot water.

Spoon batter into the tin, smoothing the top even. Bake for 40 minutes, or until a skewer inserted in the centre comes out clean. Cool the cake in the tin for 15 minutes, then turn out onto a wire rack to cool completely.

For the icing, using an electric beater, beat all the ingredients in a bowl until smooth. Spread over the cooled cake.

Salmon Puffs

Miss Helen Sandilands, Uralla Branch

SERVES 4–6
150 g (1 cup) self-raising flour
2 eggs, well beaten
60 ml (¼ cup) milk
pinch cayenne pepper
1 small handful of parsley,
  chopped
415 g tin salmon, drained
  and flaked
vegetable oil, for cooking

Combine flour, eggs, milk and cayenne in a bowl. Stir until smooth and season with salt and pepper. Stir in the parsley and salmon.

Heat the oil in a large, non-stick frying pan over medium heat. Drop heaped tablespoons of the mixture into the pan to form small cakes.

Cook for about 7 minutes on each side, or until golden, puffed and cooked through.

 *Salmon Puffs are best served hot.*

Orange Delicious Pudding

10 MAY

Mrs L Chapman, Braidwood Branch

SERVES 4

1 tablespoon butter,
  softened
165 g (¾ cup) caster sugar
2 tablespoons self-raising
  flour
juice of 2 oranges
finely grated zest of
  1 orange
310 ml (1¼ cups) milk
2 eggs, separated
boiling water, for baking

Preheat oven to 180°C. Grease a 1 litre
(4 cup) capacity baking dish.

Using an electric beater, beat the butter
and sugar in a bowl until well combined.
Stir in the flour, orange juice and zest, milk
and egg yolks.

Using clean beaters, whisk the egg whites
in a bowl until stiff peaks form. Fold into the
creamed mixture, then pour into the dish.

Stand the prepared dish in a larger baking
dish, filled with enough boiling water to come
halfway up the side. Bake for 45 minutes, or
until golden – the top of the pudding will be
fluffy and the base will be creamy. Serve hot.

Lemon Snow

11 MAY

Miss Mabel Romano, Younger Set, Gunnedah Branch

SERVES 4–6

500 ml (2 cups) boiling
  water
grated zest and juice of
  2 lemons
110 g (½ cup) caster sugar
2 tablespoons arrowroot
1½ tablespoons water
2 egg whites
custard, to serve

Combine the boiling water, lemon juice,
zest and sugar in a saucepan and stir over
medium heat for 10–15 minutes, or until
the sugar dissolves.

Combine the arrowroot with the water
in a small bowl to form a smooth paste. Add
to the simmering mixture, stirring constantly,
and cook for 2–3 minutes, or until the mixture
thickens. Remove from the heat, cover, and
cool to room temperature.

Using an electric beater, whisk the egg
whites until firm peaks form. Fold the whites
into the lemon mixture. Pour into a dampened
750 ml (3 cup) capacity mould and refrigerate
for 2–3 hours, or until well chilled.

Serve with custard.

Brown Fricassee of Rabbit

Mrs D A Thompson, Albury Branch

SERVES 4—6
1.5 kg rabbit
plain flour, for dusting
2 tablespoons butter,
   chopped
1 onion, peeled and
   finely chopped
600 ml chicken stock
large pinch ground mace
2 tablespoons red wine

Cut the rabbit into six pieces through the bone. Dust the pieces with flour, shaking off excess.

Heat the butter in a large non-stick frying pan over medium heat. Add the onion and cook, stirring often, for 5 minutes, or until golden. Remove onion to a saucepan large enough to hold the rabbit.

Add a little extra butter to the frying pan if needed. Add the rabbit pieces, in batches if necessary, and cook for 5 minutes or until browned all over, turning often. Season the rabbit to taste.

Transfer rabbit to the saucepan. Add some of the stock to the frying pan and bring to a simmer, stirring to remove any cooked residue. Add both lots of stock to the rabbit mixture, adding a little extra stock or water to just cover rabbit if necessary.

Bring mixture to a simmer. Reduce heat to low, cover the pan and cook for 2 hours, or until the rabbit is very tender. Skim off any fat, add the red wine, and serve hot.

Vegetable Soup

Mrs Chas. J Redman, Quandialla Branch

SERVES 6
1 tablespoon pearl barley
250 ml (1 cup) water
1 carrot, peeled and chopped
1 turnip, peeled and chopped
2 desiree potatoes, peeled
   and chopped
boiling water, as required
1.2 litres (6 cups) chicken
   stock
1 tomato, chopped
¼ teaspoon celery seed
1 tablespoon chopped parsley

Combine the pearl barley and 250 ml (1 cup) water in a saucepan. Bring to a simmer then cook for 30 minutes, or until tender. Drain well.

Combine the carrot, turnip and potatoes in a saucepan with enough boiling water to just cover. Bring to a simmer and cook for 1 hour over low heat, or until very tender.

Combine cooked barley, cooked vegetable mixture, the stock and tomato in a large saucepan. Add the celery seeds and parsley. Season to taste with salt and pepper.

Bring to a simmer and cook for 10 minutes over medium heat. Serve hot.

Curry Paste

Mrs WR Glasson, Molong Branch

MAKES ABOUT 125 ML (½ CUP)
2 hard-boiled eggs, peeled
2 teaspoons curry powder
1 teaspoon butter, softened
1 teaspoon Worcestershire
   sauce
1 teaspoon tomato sauce
1 tablespoon pouring cream
lemon juice and cayenne
   pepper, to taste

Chop the eggs and push them through a sieve.

Combine the eggs in a small bowl with the remaining ingredients, adding lemon juice, cayenne pepper, salt and pepper to taste.

Use Curry Paste as a sandwich spread or on toast, sprinkled with chopped gherkins or capers.

Rainbow Cake No 1

Mrs Bateman, Leeton Branch

MAKES ONE 20 CM CAKE
250 g (1 cup) butter,
  softened
220 g (1 cup) caster sugar
3 eggs
260 g (1¾ cups) plain flour
2 teaspoons baking powder
125 ml (½ cup) milk
1 teaspoon vanilla essence
1 tablespoon cocoa powder
red food colouring

Cream Filling
440 g (2 cups) caster sugar
80 ml (⅓ cup) water
125 g (½ cup) butter,
  softened
½ teaspoon vanilla essence

Preheat oven to 180°C. Lightly grease and flour two 20 cm sandwich tins.

Using an electric beater, beat butter and sugar in a bowl until light and creamy. Add the eggs, one at a time, beating well between each. Sift the flour and baking powder into a bowl, then stir into the creamed mixture. Add the milk and vanilla, stirring to form a smooth batter.

Divide mixture among three bowls. Stir the cocoa into one bowl of mixture. In the second bowl, add enough red food colouring to tint the mixture pink. Leave the third bowl of mixture uncoloured. Drop alternating spoonfuls of the three mixtures into the cake tins. Smooth the tops even.

Bake for 25–30 minutes, or until a skewer inserted in the centres comes out clean. Cool cakes in the tins for 10 minutes, then turn out onto wire racks to cool.

For the cream filling, heat the sugar and water in a small saucepan, over medium–low heat, stirring occasionally until the sugar dissolves. Increase the heat to high and bring to the boil. Immediately remove from heat and allow to cool completely.

Beat butter and vanilla in a bowl until white and creamy then gradually pour in the cold syrup, beating constantly, until the mixture is thick and pale. Refrigerate until ready to use. (If cream should separate in refrigerator, allow it to return to room temperature and beat well until it is smooth.)

Spread filling over one cake, top with the remaining cake and serve.

Warren Pudding

Mrs Percy Russell, Warren Branch

16 MAY

SERVES 4

225 g (1½ cups) plain flour
110 g (½ cup) caster sugar
1 teaspoon ground cinnamon
1 teaspoon ground nutmeg
160 g (1 cup) chopped pitted
  dates
170 g (1 cup) sultanas
40 g (¼ cup) mixed peel
1½ tablespoons butter
1 teaspoon bicarbonate
  of soda
125 ml (½ cup) boiling water
125 ml (½ cup) milk

Bring a large saucepan of water to the boil
for steaming, placing a small heatproof plate
upside down in the water to keep the pudding
basin off the base of the pan. Grease and flour
a 1.5 litre (6 cup) capacity pudding basin.

Combine the flour, sugar and spices in a
bowl and stir to combine well. Add the dates,
sultanas and peel. Place butter and soda in a
small bowl, pour the boiling water over and
add the milk. Stir into the flour mixture until
combined well.

Spoon batter into the basin, cover tightly
and lower it into the boiling water. Steam for
2 hours, or until cooked through, adding more
water to the pan as required.

Cream Scones

Mrs A Latimer, Delungra Branch

17 MAY

MAKES 24

450 g (3 cups) plain flour
4 teaspoons baking powder
½ teaspoon salt
125 ml (½ cup) pouring
  cream
250 ml (1 cup) milk

Preheat oven to 200°C. Line a baking tray
with baking paper.

Sift the flour and baking powder into a large
bowl and make a well in the middle. Add the
salt, cream and half the milk to the well and
mix, adding enough of the remaining milk to
form a soft dough.

Turn the dough out onto a lightly floured
surface. Briefly knead to bring it together –
take care not to overwork or the scones will
be tough. Roll out to 2 cm thickness. Using a
4 cm round pastry cutter, cut out 24 rounds,
re-rolling scraps as necessary.

Place on the baking tray, close together
Bake for 12–15 minutes, or until golden.

Peach and Raisin Pie

Miss Valerie Holcombe, Burren Junction Branch

SERVES 6–8

50 g (⅓ cup) plain flour
90 g self-raising flour
125 g (½ cup) butter, chopped
1 egg, lightly beaten

Filling

215 g (1½ cups) dried peaches, chopped
boiling water, as required
170 g (1 cup) raisins
60 ml (¼ cup) lemon juice
110 g (½ cup) caster sugar
2 teaspoons cornflour

For the pastry, combine the flours in a bowl. Using your fingertips, rub in butter until mixture resembles breadcrumbs. Add enough of the egg to form a coarse dough; you may not need all the egg. Reserve any unused egg.

Knead dough briefly on a lightly floured surface, taking care not to overwork or pastry will be tough. Form into a disc, cover in plastic wrap then refrigerate for 30 minutes.

Soak the dried peaches in just enough boiling water to cover for 1 hour, or until softened. Transfer to a saucepan and bring to a simmer. Cook, covered, for 10 minutes, or until tender. Drain well, reserving 125 ml (½ cup) of the cooking liquid. Cool the liquid.

Combine the peaches, raisins, lemon juice and sugar in a saucepan and bring to a simmer. In a small bowl, combine the cornflour with the reserved peach liquid, stirring until smooth. Add to the peach mixture and cook, stirring constantly, for 1–2 minutes, or until thickened. Stand until cool.

Preheat oven to 190°C.

Divide dough into two pieces, one slightly larger than the other. On a lightly floured surface, roll the larger piece of dough out into a circle 3 mm thick and use to line the base and side of an 18 cm tart tin. Spoon cooled peach mixture over the pastry.

Roll out remaining dough into a circle large enough to cover the filling. Place over the tart then press edges to seal, trimming any excess pastry. Brush any reserved egg over the top of the pie.

Bake for 25–30 minutes, or until pastry is golden and cooked through.

Apple and Celery Salad

Mrs AS Wheatley, Condoblin Branch

SERVES 4

3 pink lady apples
1 celery heart, base trimmed
1 small handful parsley,
   chopped

Dressing
150 ml pouring cream
3 egg yolks
2 tablespoons malt vinegar
mustard powder and
   cayenne pepper, to taste

For the dressing, combine all ingredients in a bowl and whisk to mix well. Season to taste with salt and pepper.

Cut apples in half, remove cores and cut into 1 cm pieces. Cut celery into 5 mm pieces and combine with apples in a bowl.

Pour over the dressing, scatter over the parsley and serve immediately.

Apricot Sponge

Mrs RJ Johnston, Bega Branch

SERVES 6

250 g dried apricots
500 ml (2 cups) boiling water
55 g (¼ cup) caster sugar
18 g (1½ tablespoons)
   powdered gelatine
125 ml (½ cup) water
2 egg whites
custard or whipped cream,
   to serve

Serve Apricot Sponge with custard or whipped cream.

Place apricots in a bowl, pour over the boiling water and stand for 1 hour, or until softened. Transfer mixture to a saucepan with the sugar, bring to a simmer and cook over medium for 15–20 minutes, or until apricots are tender.

Sprinkle the gelatine over the water in a small heatproof cup and stand for 5 minutes, or until the gelatine softens. Place cup in a small saucepan of simmering water coming halfway up the side of the cup. Heat for 4–5 minutes, or until the gelatine dissolves. Add to the apricot mixture and cool to room temperature.

Using an electric beater, whisk the egg whites in a bowl until firm peaks form. Fold whites into the apricot mixture and spoon into a 1 litre (4 cup) capacity bowl.

Refrigerate for 2–3 hours, or until set.

Baked Pumpkin

Mrs Robards, Nevertire Branch

SERVES 10

1 small jap pumpkin
  (about 2.5 kg)
240 g (4 cups, lightly
  packed) fresh
  breadcrumbs
4 small onions, peeled
  and finely chopped
8 sprigs of thyme, leave
  finely chopped
oil, for cooking

Peel the pumpkin and cut a round from the top. Using a spoon, scrape out all the seeds. Sprinkle the inside of the pumpkin with salt then stand pumpkin for 30 minutes, with the hole facing down to drain excess liquid.

Preheat oven to 180°C.

Place breadcrumbs, onion and thyme in a bowl and mix to combine well. Season to taste with salt and pepper. Stuff the pumpkin cavity with the breadcrumb mixture.

Lightly oil the base of a 30 x 20 cm baking dish. Place pumpkin in dish, cut side up. Bake for 2 hours, or until cooked through.

Tennis Cake

Mrs Douglas Mackellar, Leeton Branch

MAKES ONE 23 CM CAKE

375 g (1½ cups) butter,
  softened
375 g caster sugar
500 g (3⅓ cups) plain flour
8 eggs, beaten well
90 g mixed peel
120 g (½ cup) glacé cherries
65 g (½ cup) slivered
  almonds
125 g currants

Lemon Icing

125 g (1 cup) pure icing
  sugar, sifted
1 tablespoon lemon juice
pink food colouring

Preheat oven to 180°C. Line a 23 cm cake tin with baking paper.

Using an electric beater, beat butter and sugar in a bowl until light and creamy. Add the flour and beat for 5 minutes. Add the remaining ingredients, stirring to mix well. Spoon the mixture into the tin, smoothing the top even.

Bake for 1½ hours, or until a skewer inserted in the centre comes out clean. Cool the cake in the tin for 30 minutes, then turn out onto a wire rack to cool completely.

For the lemon icing, combine icing sugar and lemon juice in a bowl. Add 1 drop of food colouring and beat well, adding a little extra lemon juice if required to make a smooth, spreadable icing. Spread cooled cake with icing.

Wallaga Savoury

Mrs JF Sampey, Tilba Tilba Branch

SERVES 4–6

2 slices day-old bread
2 large ripe tomatoes,
   thinly sliced
2 granny smith apples,
   peeled, cored and grated
2 onions, peeled and
   thinly sliced
500 ml (2 cups) milk
2 teaspoons butter

Preheat oven to 190°C. Generously grease a 1 litre (4 cup) capacity baking dish.

Soak the bread briefly in water, then squeeze as much out as possible. Place a layer of sliced tomatoes over the base of the dish and season with salt and pepper. Crumble some of the bread over the tomatoes and scatter over some of the apple and onion, seasoning with salt and pepper.

Repeat layering until ingredients are used, finishing with a layer of crumbled bread. Pour the milk over and dot with butter.

Bake for 1 hour, or until golden and bubbling. Serve warm.

Snowden Pudding

Her Excellency Lady Somers, Patroness
of the Country Women's Assoc. of Victoria

SERVES 4–6

125 g (½ cup) shredded suet
   (see note)
120 g (2 cups, lightly packed)
   fresh breadcrumbs
110 g (½ cup) caster sugar
2 eggs, beaten well
2 tablespoons marmalade
240 g (2 cups) raisins
flour, for coating
custard, to serve

Bring a large saucepan of water to the boil for steaming, placing a small heatproof plate upside down in the water to keep the pudding basin off the base of the pan. Grease a 450 ml (3 cup) capacity pudding basin.

Mix together the suet, crumbs and sugar in a bowl. Add the beaten eggs and marmalade. Scatter a little flour over the raisins to coat, then add to the mixture and stir to combine well. Spoon batter into the basin.

Cover basin tightly and steam for 2 hours. Serve pudding hot, with custard.

Note: shredded suet is available as a packet mix at supermarkets, or fresh from your butcher.

Temora Date Pudding

25 MAY

Miss R Overs, Temora Branch

SERVES 6–8
250 g pitted dates, chopped
250 ml (1 cup) milk
75 g (½ cup) plain flour
1 teaspoon baking powder
125 g (½ cup) butter,
    chopped
125 g caster sugar
125 g fresh breadcrumbs
1 teaspoon ground nutmeg

Bring a large saucepan of water to the boil for steaming, placing a small heatproof plate upside down in the water to keep the pudding basin off the base of the pan. Grease a 1.6 litre (6 cup) capacity pudding basin.

Combine the dates and milk in a small saucepan. Bring to a simmer and cook over medium–low heat for 5 minutes, or until dates are soft. Stand to cool.

Combine flour and baking powder in a bowl. Rub in the butter until mixture resembles breadcrumbs. Add the sugar, crumbs, nutmeg and cooled date mixture, stirring to combine.

Spoon batter into the basin, cover tightly and lower it into the boiling water. Steam for 2 hours, or until cooked through, adding more water to the pan as required.

Weethalle Chocolate Pudding

26 MAY

Mrs AE Hill, Weethalle Branch

SERVES 6
250 g (4¼ cups) fresh
    breadcrumbs
600 ml milk
1 tablespoon cocoa
2 eggs, beaten well
75 g (⅓ cup) caster sugar
custard or whipped cream,
    to serve

Preheat oven to 180°C. Lightly grease a 7 cm deep, 19 cm round baking dish.

Combine crumbs and milk in a saucepan and cook over medium–low heat, stirring often, for 5–10 minutes, or until the mixture forms a thick paste. Remove from the heat and cool slightly. Stir in the remaining ingredients and pour batter into the baking dish.

Bake for 30 minutes, or until firm.

Serve pudding hot or at room temperature, with custard or whipped cream.

Raspberry Sponge Pudding

Miss Joy Jennings, Merriwa Branch

MAKES ONE 20 CM CAKE

60 g (¼ cup) butter,
   softened
220 g (1 cup) caster sugar
1 egg, lightly beaten
300 g (2 cups) plain flour
1 teaspoon baking powder
170 ml (⅔ cup) milk
85 g (⅓ cup) raspberry jam
whipped cream, custard
   or ice cream, to serve

Bring a large saucepan of water to the boil for steaming, placing a small heatproof plate upside down in the water to keep the pudding basin off the base of the pan. Lightly grease a 1 litre (4 cup) capacity pudding basin.

Using an electric beater, beat butter and sugar in a bowl until light and creamy. Add the egg and beat well. Sift the flour and baking powder into a bowl and add to the creamed mixture alternately with milk.

Spoon mixture into the basin and drop spoonfuls of jam on top. Using a knife, cut through the jam and partially mix it into the pudding.

Cover basin tightly and lower it into the boiling water. Steam for 90 minutes, or until cooked through, adding more water to the pan as required.

Remove basin from the water. Stand pudding for 5 minutes, then turn it out onto a serving plate. Serve with cream, custard or ice cream.

Dark Cake No 1

Mrs Douglas Mackellar, Leeton Branch

MAKES ONE 25 CM CAKE
350 g butter, softened
330 g (1½ cups, firmly
   packed) brown sugar
6 eggs
80 ml (⅓ cup) milk
115 g (⅓ cup) treacle
600 g (4 cups) plain flour, sifted
1.1 kg mixed dried fruit
60 g blanched almonds,
   chopped
40 g (¼ cup) mixed peel
½ teaspoon mixed spice
1 teaspoon bicarbonate
   of soda
1 tablespoon water

Preheat oven to 140°C. Line the base and side of a 25 cm cake tin with several layers of baking paper.

Using an electric beater, beat butter and sugar in a large bowl until light and creamy. Add eggs one at a time, beating well between each. Beat in the milk and the treacle. Stir in the flour, fruit, almonds, peel and spice. Combine the soda with the water in a cup, then stir into cake mixture.

Spoon mixture into lined cake tin, smoothing top even. Bake for 3 hours, or until a skewer inserted in the centre comes out clean. Cool the cake in the tin.

Apple Batter

Mrs RJ Bennie, Gunnedah Branch

SERVES 6
150 g (1 cup) plain flour
1 egg, well beaten
250 ml (1 cup) milk
2 tablespoons butter
3 granny smith apples,
   peeled, cored and sliced
brown sugar, to sprinkle

Combine the flour with a pinch of salt in a bowl and make a well in the centre. Add the egg to the well with half the milk and, using a whisk, gradually work the flour into the milk mixture until smooth. Add the remaining milk, stir until smooth, then cover and stand for 30 minutes.

Preheat oven to 180°C. Melt the butter and pour it into a greased 20 cm round pie dish. Lay the apples over the base of the dish and pour over the batter. Bake for 20–30 minutes, or until crisp and brown.

Serve immediately, sprinkled with brown sugar to taste.

Australian Shortcake

Miss Jean Lamont, Kooringal, Harefield

30 MAY

MAKES ABOUT 20 PIECES
115 g butter, softened
60 g caster sugar
250 g rolled oats
½ teaspoon almond essence,
    or to taste

Preheat oven to 180°C. Grease and flour a 30 × 18 cm slice tin.

Using an electric beater, beat butter and sugar in a bowl until light and creamy. Stir in the oats and essence, combining well. Press the mixture into the tin.

Bake for 45 minutes, or until golden. Cool the cake in the tin. Cut into squares or fingers.

Curried Eggs

Mrs TL Purvis, Kickabel Branch

31 MAY

SERVES 4
60 g (¼ cup) butter
2 onions, peeled and very
    finely chopped
3 teaspoons curry powder,
    or to taste
35 g (¼ cup) plain flour
560 ml (2¼ cups) milk,
    heated
8 large hard-boiled eggs,
    peeled and thickly sliced
2 tablespoons finely chopped
    parsley
hot buttered toast, to serve

Heat the butter in a saucepan over medium heat. Add the onion and cook, stirring often, for 5–6 minutes, or until onion has softened. Add the curry powder and cook, stirring, for 1 minute, or until fragrant. Add the flour and stir for 1–2 minutes.

Add the milk a little at a time, stirring constantly, allowing the mixture to simmer between additions. When all the milk is added, cook over low heat, stirring to prevent lumps forming, for 4–5 minutes, then season to taste with salt and pepper.

Add the sliced eggs and parsley, stirring gently to combine. Cook for a few minutes to allow eggs to heat through. Serve on hot buttered toast.

Family recipes

		1 Potato and Cheese Balls	2 Coconut Puddings	3 Welsh Rarebit
4 Scotch Apple Fritters	5 Taunton Hot Pot	6 St Barnabas Pudding	7 Curried Vegetables	8 Raisin Puffs
9 Baked Lemon Pudding	10 Rolled Oat Biscuits	11 Orange Cake	12 Cheese and Rice Croquettes	13 Cornflour and Golden Syrup Pudding
14 Queen Pudding	15 Apple Roll	16 Hermits	17 Rice Flummery	18 Jam Roll
19 Cheeside	20 Artichoke Soup	21 Baked Ginger Pudding	22 Butter and Jam Pudding	23 Children's Delight
24 Scalloped Parsnips	25 Buttermilk Cake	26 Country Women's Raffle Cake	27 Lamingtons	28 Dark Cake No 2
29 Peanut Cookies	30 American Nut Cake			

JUNE

Potato and Cheese Balls

1 JUN

Mrs Beer, Gunnedah Branch

MAKES 10–15

4 pontiac potatoes
125 g (1¼ cups) grated
  cheddar cheese, plus
  extra, to serve
2 egg yolks
flour, for dusting
butter, for frying

Preheat oven to 180°C.

Bake unpeeled potatoes for 45–50 minutes, or until very tender. Leave potatoes to cool, then remove flesh, discarding the skins. Push flesh through a potato ricer.

Combine potato in a bowl with the cheese, egg yolks and salt and pepper to taste. Take heaped teaspoons of mixture and roll into balls. Dust lightly with flour, shaking off excess.

Melt enough butter for shallow frying in a large, heavy-based frying pan over medium heat. Add the balls, in batches if necessary, and cook, turning often, for 8–10 minutes, or until golden and hot through.

Serve hot, scattered with extra grated cheese to taste.

Coconut Puddings

2 JUN

Mrs McKnight, Glen Innes Branch

SERVES 8

625 ml (2½ cups) milk
120 g (2 cups, lightly packed)
  fresh breadcrumbs
165 g (¾ cup) caster sugar
90 g (1 cup) desiccated
  coconut
4 eggs, separated
2 tablespoons icing sugar

Preheat oven to 180°C. Grease a 1.5 litre (6 cup) capacity baking dish.

Pour the milk over the crumbs in a bowl and stand for 5 minutes. Add the sugar, coconut and egg yolks and stir to combine well.

Pour mixture into the baking dish. Bake for 15–20 minutes, or until set.

Using an electric beater, whisk the egg whites in a bowl until firm peaks form. Add the icing sugar and whisk well. Spoon whites over the pudding.

Bake a further 10 minutes, or until meringue is light golden.

Welsh Rarebit

Mrs W Nesbit, Cudal Branch

3 JUN

SERVES 4

1 tablespoon butter
1 teaspoon cornflour
125 ml (½ cup) milk
200 g (2 cups) grated
   cheddar
½ teaspoon mustard
   powder
pinch cayenne pepper
slices of hot toast, to serve

Melt butter in a small saucepan over medium–low heat. Stir the cornflour into the milk in a small bowl. Gradually add milk mixture to the butter, stirring constantly until mixture simmers and thickens slightly.

Add the cheese and stir until melted. Add the mustard, cayenne and salt and pepper to taste.

Serve over slices of toast.

Scotch Apple Fritters

Mrs D Henderson, Urunga Branch

4 JUN

SERVES 4

50 g (⅓ cup) plain flour
1 teaspoon baking powder
1 tablespoon caster sugar
1 egg, well beaten
60 ml (¼ cup) milk
4 granny smith apples,
   peeled, cored and sliced
vegetable oil, for
   deep-frying

Combine the flour, baking powder and sugar in a bowl, making a well in the centre. Add the egg and milk to the well, stirring gradually to form a smooth batter.

Heat enough oil for deep-frying in a saucepan to 170°C, or until a cube of bread turns golden brown in 20 seconds.

Working in batches, dip the apple slices into the batter, allowing excess batter to drain. Fry for 5 minutes, or until batter is crisp and golden. Drain well on paper towels and serve hot.

Taunton Hot Pot

Mrs Jas. Rawsthorne, Forbes Branch

SERVES 6

1 kg lamb neck, trimmed
  of fat
flour, for dusting
1 kg desiree potatoes, peeled
  and cut into 2 cm pieces
3 onions, peeled and
  thinly sliced
750 ml (3 cups) chicken stock

Preheat oven to 160°C.

Remove meat from the bones and cut into 2.5 cm pieces, reserving the bones for another use. Dust the meat with flour, shaking off excess, then season well with salt and pepper.

Place a layer of potatoes in the bottom of a 2 litre (8 cup) capacity casserole dish. Scatter over a layer of onions, then a layer of the meat. Repeat until all the ingredients are used, ending with a layer of potatoes.

Pour over the stock and cover the dish tightly. Bake for 3 hours, adding a little more stock or water if required. Serve hot.

St Barnabas Pudding

Mrs GB Johnson, Broken Hill Branch

SERVES 4–6

125 g (½ cup) shredded suet
  (see note)
125 g (1 cup) chopped
  walnuts
170 g (1 cup) raisins
225 g (1½ cups) self-raising
  flour
2 eggs
165 g (¾ cup) caster sugar

Bring a large saucepan of water to the boil for steaming, placing a small heatproof plate upside down in the water to keep the pudding basin off the base of the pan. Grease and flour a 1.5 litre (6 cup) capacity pudding basin.

Combine the suet, walnuts and raisins in a food processor and chop finely. Combine with the flour in a bowl. Beat eggs and sugar well in another bowl, then add to the flour mixture, stirring well.

Spoon the batter into the basin, cover tightly and lower it into the boiling water. Steam for 2½ hours or until cooked through, adding more water to the pan as required.

Note: shredded suet is available as a packet mix at supermarkets, or fresh from your butcher.

Curried Vegetables

Miss Valerie Holcombe, Burren Junction Branch

SERVES 4

1½ tablespoons (30 g) butter
1 tablespoon (15 g) plain
   flour
1 tablespoon curry powder,
   or to taste
300 ml milk
2–3 cups leftover cooked
   vegetables (e.g., peas,
   cauliflower, broccoli,
   carrots, potatoes, parsnips)
   cut into bite-sized pieces

Melt the butter in a saucepan over medium heat. Add the flour and curry powder and stir until smooth.

Gradually add the milk, stirring constantly to avoid lumps forming and bringing the mixture to a simmer between additions. Cook, stirring, for 1–2 minutes, or until thickened and smooth.

Add the vegetables and season to taste with salt and pepper. Reduce heat to low and cook, stirring occasionally, for 15 minutes. Serve hot.

Raisin Puffs

Mrs H Murray, Bathurst Branch

SERVES 4

boiling water, for soaking
120 g (2 cups, lightly packed)
   fresh breadcrumbs
250 ml (1 cup) boiling water
60 g (¼ cup) caster sugar
2 eggs, beaten well
170 g (1 cup) raisins, chopped

Lemon Sauce
1 egg, beaten
220 g (1 cup) caster sugar
finely grated zest of 1 lemon
juice of 2 lemons
1 tablespoon butter

Pour boiling water over the crumbs in a bowl, then cool to room temperature.

Preheat oven to 170°C. Grease 4 x 185 ml (¾ cup) capacity ramekins.

Stir the remaining ingredients into the crumb mixture, combining well. Spoon into the prepared ramekins. Bake for 30 minutes, or until firm.

For the lemon sauce, combine the egg, sugar, lemon juice and zest in small saucepan. Cook over low heat, stirring constantly, for 10–12 minutes, or until mixture has thickened – do not overheat or the egg will scramble. Add the butter and stir until the mixture is smooth. Remove from the heat.

To serve, turn the puffs out of the ramekins onto serving plates and pour sauce over.

Baked Lemon Pudding

9 JUN

Mrs BF Cox, Mudgee Branch

SERVES 6

500 ml (2 cups) milk
2 tablespoons cornflour
1 tablespoon butter
3 eggs, well beaten
220 g (1 cup) caster sugar
juice and grated zest of
   1 lemon
freshly grated nutmeg,
   for sprinkling

Preheat oven to 180°C. Grease a 1 litre (4 cup) capacity baking dish.

Reserve 2 tablespoons of the milk, then heat the rest in a saucepan until nearly simmering. Combine the reserved milk in a cup with the cornflour to form a smooth paste.

Add paste to the milk in the saucepan, stirring constantly, and cook over medium for 2 minutes, or until mixture simmers and thickens. Remove from the heat and beat in the butter. Set aside to cool and become firm.

Beat the eggs, sugar, juice and zest in a bowl.

Break up the milk mixture into 2 cm pieces and place in the baking dish. Pour egg mixture over and sprinkle with nutmeg.

Bake for 20 minutes, or until set.

Rolled Oat Biscuits

10 JUN

Mrs RK Wood, Adelaide

MAKES ABOUT 24

240 g (2½ cups) rolled oats
165 g (¾ cup) caster sugar
125 g (½ cup) butter,
   softened
1 teaspoon vanilla essence

Preheat oven to 180°C. Lightly grease and flour a 30 x 20 cm slice tin.

Combine the rolled oats and sugar in a bowl. Add the butter and vanilla and stir to mix well. Press mixture into the tin, smoothing the top even.

Bake for 15–20 minutes, or until light golden. Cool in the tin. When cold, cut into 4 x 5 cm pieces.

Orange Cake

Mrs Arthur Colquhoun, Albury Branch

MAKES ONE 18 CM CAKE
125 g (½ cup) butter,
  softened
220 g (1 cup) caster sugar
3 eggs
grated zest of 1 orange
1 teaspoon bicarbonate
  of soda
125 ml (½ cup) milk
2 teaspoons cream of tartar
150 g (1 cup) plain flour
60 g (½ cup) cornflour

Orange Butter Icing
60 ml (¼ cup) orange juice
1 teaspoon butter
60 g (½ cup) sifted icing
  sugar, or as required

Preheat oven to 180°C. Lightly grease and flour two 18 cm cake tins.

Using an electric beater, beat butter and sugar in a bowl until light and creamy. Add eggs, one at a time, beating well between each. Combine the orange zest, soda and milk in a cup. Sift the tartar, flour and cornflour into a bowl and add to creamed mixture alternately with the milk mixture, stirring until smooth.

Spoon batter into tins, smoothing the top even. Bake for 30–40 minutes, or until a skewer inserted in the centre comes out clean. Cool the cakes in the tins for 10 minutes, then turn out onto a wire rack to cool completely.

For the icing, combine juice and butter in saucepan and heat gently until butter has melted. Remove from the heat and beat in icing sugar, a little at a time, adding enough to form a light, spreadable icing.

When cakes are cold, spread one cake with icing and layer with the second cake.

Cheese and Rice Croquettes

12 JUN

Mrs P Styles, Yass Branch

SERVES 6–8
60 g (¼ cup) butter
50 g (⅓ cup) plain flour
250 ml (1 cup) milk
100 g (1 cup) grated
cheddar cheese
370 g (2 cups) cold cooked
white long-grain rice
220 g (2 cups) dried bread
crumbs
2 eggs, well beaten
oil, for deep-frying

Melt butter in a small saucepan over medium heat. Add the flour, stirring until the mixture is smooth. Slowly add the milk, stirring constantly to prevent lumps forming, until the mixture boils and thickens. Add cheese and stir until melted. Remove from the heat and cool.

Stir the rice into the cheese mixture and season to taste with salt and pepper. Using wet hands, form the mixture into golf ball-sized balls, then roll each in breadcrumbs to coat well. Dip each ball into the beaten egg, draining off excess. Dip in crumbs again to coat well.

Heat enough oil in a saucepan for deep-frying to 170°C, or until a cube of bread turns brown in 20 seconds.

Fry croquettes, in batches, for 4 minutes, or until golden brown. Drain well on paper towels. Serve hot.

Cornflour and Golden Syrup Pudding

13 JUN

Mrs AS Wheatley, Condoblin Branch

SERVES 6–8
1 tablespoon cornflour
600 ml milk
1 tablespoon caster sugar
1 tablespoon golden syrup
1 egg, beaten

Preheat oven to 180°C. Lightly grease a 1 litre (4 cup) capacity baking dish.

Combine the cornflour in a cup with enough of the milk to make a smooth paste. Place the sugar, syrup and egg in a bowl, add the paste and stir to mix well. Bring the remaining milk just to the boil then add to the egg mixture, stirring to mix well.

Pour mixture into the baking dish. Bake for 30 minutes, or until set and golden.

Queen Pudding

Mrs F Hylton Kelly, Crookwell Branch

SERVES 4

600 ml milk
120 g (2 cups, lightly packed) fresh breadcrumbs
15 g butter, melted
75 g (⅓ cup) caster sugar
4 eggs, separated
2 tablespoons raspberry jam

Preheat oven to 180°C. Grease a 1 litre (4 cup) capacity baking dish.

Heat milk in a small saucepan until nearly simmering and pour over the crumbs in a bowl. Cool slightly. Add butter, half the sugar and the egg yolks and stir to combine well.

Spread crumb mixture over the base of the baking dish. Bake for 30 minutes, or until set.

Using an electric beater, whisk egg whites in a bowl until firm peaks form. Gradually add remaining sugar and whisk until thick and glossy.

Spread the jam over the pudding, then spoon the whites over jam. Bake a further 10–15 minutes, or until meringue is light golden.

Apple Roll

Mrs WJ Keast, Junee Branch

SERVES 8

225 g (1½ cups) self-raising flour
60 g (¼ cup) butter, chopped
220 g (1 cup) caster sugar
125 ml (½ cup) milk
2 granny smith apples, peeled, cored and finely chopped
250 ml (1 cup) boiling water
custard or whipped cream, to serve

Serve Apple Roll hot, with custard or whipped cream.

Preheat oven to 180°C. Grease a 1 litre (4 cup) capacity baking dish.

Place flour in a bowl. Using your fingertips, rub in the butter until mixture resembles breadcrumbs. Stir in half the sugar, add the milk and mix to form a coarse dough.

Turn the dough out onto a lightly floured surface and knead briefly to bring together – do not overwork or the dough will be tough. Roll out to a rectangle about 20 × 30 cm. Scatter apples over the dough. Roll up to form a log. Cut log into slices about 2 cm thick.

Scatter remaining sugar over the base of baking dish and pour over the boiling water. Place slices on top, cut side down. Bake for 30–40 minutes, or until golden and bubbling.

Hermits

MAKES 30

245 g (1½ cups, lightly
    packed) brown sugar
250 g (1 cup) butter, softened
3 eggs
125 g (1 cup) walnut
    pieces, chopped
500 g dates, pitted and
    chopped
2 teaspoons ground cinnamon
375 g (2½ cups) plain
    flour, sifted
1 teaspoon bicarbonate
    of soda
80 ml (⅓ cup) hot water

Preheat oven to 180°C. Line two baking trays
with baking paper.

Using an electric beater, beat sugar and
butter in a bowl until light and creamy. Add
eggs, one at a time, beating well between
each. Stir in the walnuts and dates.

Sift the flour and cinnamon into a bowl.
Combine the soda with the hot water in
a cup. Stir soda mixture into the creamed
mixture, add the sifted flour and mix well.

Drop heaped teaspoons of the mixture
onto baking trays, leaving room for spreading.

Bake for 10–15 minutes, or until golden and
cooked through. Transfer to a wire rack to cool.

Rice Flummery

Mrs J Wilesmith, Yathella

SERVES 4–6

110 g (½ cup) short-grain rice
875 ml (3½ cups) milk
110 g (½ cup) caster sugar
60 g (¼ cup) butter
grated zest of 1 small lemon
4 eggs, separated
30 g (¼ cup) icing sugar

Preheat oven to 160°C.

Combine rice and milk in a saucepan and
bring to a simmer. Cook over medium–low
heat, stirring often, for 12–15 minutes, or until
rice is tender and mixture is thick. Remove
from the heat and cool slightly.

Add the sugar, butter, lemon zest and egg
yolks to the rice. Pour into a 1.5 litre (6 cup)
capacity baking dish.

Using an electric beater, whisk the egg
whites in a bowl until firm peaks form. Add
the icing sugar and whisk until thick and glossy.
Spoon whites over the rice mixture.

Bake flummery for 20 minutes, or until rice
is set and meringue is deep golden.

Jam Roll

Mrs Cameron, Dungog Branch

SERVES 12

3 eggs
120 g caster sugar
60 ml (¼ cup) water
1 teaspoon baking powder
150 g (1 cup) plain flour
85 g (¼ cup) raspberry jam

Preheat oven to 180°C. Grease and flour the sides of a 23 x 33 cm swiss roll tin and line the base with baking paper.

Using an electric beater, whisk the eggs and sugar until thick and pale and the mixture leaves a trail when beaters are lifted. Whisk in 60 ml (¼ cup) water. Sift the baking powder and flour into a bowl, then carefully fold into the egg mixture.

Pour the batter into the tin. Bake for 10–15 minutes, or until the surface springs back when pressed.

Heat the jam in a small saucepan over low heat for about 3 minutes. Working quickly, turn out cake while hot onto a piece of baking paper and spread with the hot jam. Working with a long side facing you, roll up the cake using the paper as a guide. Leave to cool in the paper. Remove paper to serve.

Cheeside

Mrs WB Studdy, North Sydney Branch

MAKES 185 ML (¾ CUP)

125 g (1¼ cups) grated
   cheddar cheese
1 tablespoon malt vinegar
1 tablespoon Worcestershire
   sauce
1 teaspoon butter, softened
1 teaspoon vegetable oil
1 teaspoon mustard powder
pinch cayenne pepper

Combine all ingredients in a bowl. Season to taste with salt and pepper and stir to combine well. Transfer to small jar, seal and store in refrigerator.

Serve spread on crackers or in sandwiches.

Artichoke Soup

Mrs F Oliver, Running Stream Branch

20 JUN

SERVES 4–6

1 kg jerusalem artichokes,
scrubbed well and sliced
1.25 litres (5 cups) chicken
stock, or as required
30 g butter
2 tablespoons (30 g) plain
flour
600 ml milk

Combine artichokes and stock in a saucepan and bring to a simmer. Cook, covered, for 30 minutes over medium heat, or until the artichokes are very tender. Place mixture in a food processor or blender and purée until very smooth. Push mixture through a sieve, discarding solids.

Melt the butter in a saucepan over medium, add the flour and stir to form a smooth paste. Gradually add the milk, stirring constantly to prevent lumps forming, until mixture boils and thickens. Add the artichoke mixture, stirring to mix well, and season to taste with salt and pepper. Add a little extra stock if soup is too thick. Serve hot.

Baked Ginger Pudding

Mrs EJ Keating, Broken Hill Branch

21 JUN

SERVES 4

1 tablespoon butter, softened
55 g (¼ cup) caster sugar
1 tablespoon treacle
1 egg, well beaten
150 g (1 cup) plain flour
1 teaspoon ground ginger
1 teaspoon bicarbonate
of soda
125 ml (½ cup) milk

Preheat oven to 180°C. Lightly grease a 1 litre (6 cup) capacity baking dish.

Using an electric beater, beat butter and sugar in a bowl until light and creamy. Stir in the treacle. Sift the flour and ginger into a bowl. Mix the soda and milk in a cup. Add flour and milk mixtures alternately to the treacle mixture to form a smooth batter.

Spoon batter into the dish, smoothing the top even. Bake for 90 minutes, or until a skewer inserted in the centre comes out clean. Serve warm.

Butter and Jam Pudding

22 JUN

Mrs Valerie Weekes, Cremorne

SERVES 6
50 g (⅓ cup) plain flour
2 eggs, separated
600 ml milk
1 tablespoon melted butter
85 g (¼ cup) raspberry jam

Preheat oven to 200°C. Lightly grease a 1 litre (4 cup) capacity baking dish.

Whisk together the flour, egg yolks and milk until smooth, then stir in the melted butter.

Using an electric beater, whisk the egg whites in a bowl until soft peaks form, then fold into the batter. Spoon batter into the dish, then place spoonfuls of jam on top.

Bake for 45 minutes, or until firm and the surface is golden and bubbling.

Children's Delight

23 JUN

Mrs WH McEachern, Wagga Branch

SERVES 8
100 g (½ cup) tapioca
500 ml milk
4 eggs, separated
220 g (1 cup) caster sugar
25 g (¼ cup) desiccated coconut, plus extra, for sprinkling

Soak the tapioca overnight in water to cover, then drain well.

Preheat oven to 160°C. Grease a 24 x 16 x 6 cm deep baking dish.

Combine the tapioca and milk in a saucepan and bring to a simmer. Cook over low heat, stirring occasionally, for 10–15 minutes, or until tapioca is translucent and mixture is thick.

Combine the yolks, 165 g (¾ cup) of the sugar and the coconut in a bowl. Stir into the tapioca mixture. Cook briefly over low heat, stirring constantly, until sugar dissolves. Pour into the baking dish.

Using an electric beater, whisk the egg whites in a bowl until firm peaks form. Gradually whisk in the remaining sugar until the mixture is thick and glossy. Spoon whites over the tapioca mixture and sprinkle with coconut.

Bake for 15–20 minutes, or until meringue is golden.

Children's Delight is best served cold.

Scalloped Parsnips

Mrs JM Trezise, Kentucky Branch

24 JUN

SERVES 4
500 g parsnips, peeled and
    cut into 2 cm pieces
500 ml (2 cups) water
40 g butter, plus extra,
    for baking
2 tablespoons plain flour
375 ml (1½ cups) milk,
    heated
100 g (1 cup) grated
    cheddar cheese
60 g (1 cup, lightly packed)
    fresh breadcrumbs

Place the parsnips in a large saucepan with the water. Cover, bring to the boil, and cook for 12–15 minutes, or until the parsnips are very tender. Drain well.

Preheat oven to 180°C. Grease a 1.5 litre (6 cup) capacity baking dish.

Melt the butter in a small saucepan over medium heat, then add the flour and stir until smooth. Add the milk a little at a time, stirring constantly, and allowing the mixture to simmer between additions. Cook over low heat, stirring to prevent lumps forming, for 4–5 minutes. Season to taste with salt and pepper.

Spread the parsnips evenly over the base of the dish and pour over the sauce. Scatter over the cheese, then the crumbs, in even layers. Dot the top with butter.

Bake for 30–35 minutes, or until golden and bubbling.

Buttermilk Cake

25 JUN

MAKES ONE 23 CM CAKE
250 g (1 cup) butter,
    softened
440 g (2 cups) caster sugar
1½ teaspoons bicarbonate
    of soda
500 ml (2 cups) buttermilk
600 g (4 cups) plain flour
500 g mixed dried fruit

Preheat oven to 160°C. Line the base and side of a 23 cm cake tin with baking paper.

Using an electric beater, beat butter and sugar in a bowl until light and creamy. Combine the soda and buttermilk in a cup, then stir into the creamed mixture alternately with the flour. Stir in the dried fruit.

Spoon batter into the tin, smoothing the top even. Bake for 1½–2 hours, or until a skewer inserted in the centre comes out clean. Cool the cake in the tin.

Country Women's Raffle Cake

Mrs WM Hammond, Wagga Branch

MAKES TWO 25 CM CAKES

625 g (2½ cups) butter,
  softened
500 g caster sugar
12 eggs
2 tablespoons plum jam
1 tablespoon sweet
  orange marmalade
500 g raisins
500 g sultanas
500 g currants
250 g dates, pitted,
  chopped
625 g plain flour
2 tablespoons ground
  mixed spice
1 nutmeg, freshly grated
125 g (1 cup) slivered
  almonds
250 ml (1 cup) brandy
1½ teaspoons vanilla
  essence
1½ teaspoons lemon
  essence

Preheat oven to 150°C. Line two 25 cm cake tins with several layers of baking paper.

Using an electric beater, beat butter and sugar in a bowl until light and creamy. Add the eggs, one at a time, beating well between each. Add the jam and marmalade.

Combine all the dried fruits in a large bowl with enough of the flour to lightly coat the fruit, tossing to combine well.

Sift the remaining flour with the spices into a bowl. Combine the flour mixture with the creamed mixture in a very large bowl, stirring to mix well. Stir in the fruits, almonds, brandy and essences.

Spoon batter into tins, smoothing the top even. Bake for 4½–5 hours, or until a skewer inserted in the centres comes out clean.

Cool the cakes in the tins.

Lamingtons

MAKES 20
125 g (½ cup) butter,
 softened
220 g (1 cup) caster sugar
2 eggs
1 egg yolk
½ teaspoon bicarbonate
 of soda
125 ml (½ cup) milk
225 g (1½ cup) plain flour
1 teaspoon cream of tartar
450 g (5 cups) desiccated
 coconut, or as required

Icing
85 g butter, softened
215 g (1¾ cups) icing sugar
1 tablespoon cocoa powder
1 teaspoon vanilla essence
1 tablespoon hot water

Preheat oven to 180°C. Lightly grease and flour a 30 x 21 cm cake tin.

Using an electric beater, beat butter and sugar in a bowl until light and creamy. Add the eggs, one at a time and beating well between each, then beat in the egg yolk.

Dissolve the soda in the milk in a cup. Sift the flour and tartar into a bowl. Add the milk mixture and the flour to the creamed mixture, stirring to combine well. Spoon the batter into the tin, smoothing the top even.

Bake for 30 minutes, or until a skewer inserted in the centre comes out clean. Cool the cake in the tin for 10 minutes, then turn out onto a wire rack to cool completely. Cut the cake into 6 cm square pieces. If possible, leave the cake uncovered for one day, to dry out a little.

For the icing, using an electric beater, beat the butter and icing sugar in a bowl until smooth. Sift in the icing sugar and cocoa. Add the vanilla and hot water and stir until smooth.

Place the coconut on a plate. Roll each piece of cake in the icing to coat, allowing any excess to drip off, then dip into the coconut to cover well.

Dark Cake No 2

Mrs C Horgan, Nowra Branch

MAKES TWO 23 CM CAKES

250 g (1 cup) butter, softened
220 g (1 cup, firmly packed) brown sugar
4 eggs
250 ml (1 cup) treacle
250 ml (1 cup) milk
450 g (3 cups) plain flour
½ teaspoon ground nutmeg
½ teaspoon cream of tartar
1 teaspoon bicarbonate of soda
850 g (5 cups) raisins
1½ teaspoons finely grated lemon zest

Preheat oven to 150°C. Line the base and sides of two 23 x 13 x 7 cm loaf tins with baking paper.

Using an electric beater, beat butter and sugar in a bowl until light and creamy. Add eggs, beating well between each. Beat in the treacle and milk. Sift the dry ingredients into a bowl, then stir into the creamed mixture with the raisins and lemon zest.

Spoon the batter into the tins, smoothing the tops even. Bake for about 1¼ hours, or until a skewer inserted in the centre comes out clean. Cool the cakes in the tins.

Peanut Cookies

Mrs Dowling, Manildra Branch

MAKES 30

2 tablespoons butter, softened
165 g (¾ cup) caster sugar
1 egg
150 g (1 cup) self-raising flour
125 g blanched peanuts, coarsely chopped
milk, as required

Preheat oven to 180°C and line a baking tray with baking paper.

Using an electric beater, beat the butter and sugar in a bowl until light and creamy. Add the egg and beat to combine well. Stir in the flour and peanuts to form a stiff dough, adding a little milk if required.

Drop heaped teaspoons of the dough on the tray, leaving room for cookies to spread.

Bake for 10–12 minutes, or until golden. Cool cookies on the tray for 5 minutes, then transfer to a wire rack to cool.

American Nut Cake

Mrs Clarence, Boggabri Branch

MAKES ONE 20 CM CAKE

125 g (½ cup) butter,
    softened
220 g (1 cup) caster sugar
2 eggs, separated
½ teaspoon bicarbonate
    of soda
125 ml (½ cup) milk
300 g (2 cups) plain flour
1 teaspoon cream of tartar
125 g (1 cup) chopped
    walnuts
170 g (1 cup) raisins

Lemon Icing

2 tablespoons milk, or as
    required
2 teaspoons lemon juice
2 teaspoons butter,
    softened
200 g (1⅓ cups) sifted icing
    sugar, or as required
1 teaspoon finely grated
    lemon zest

Preheat oven to 180°C. Lightly grease and flour a 20 cm cake tin.

Using an electric beater, beat butter in a bowl until very light and creamy. Beat in the sugar and egg yolks. Mix the soda and milk in a cup, then stir into the creamed mixture. Sift the flour and tartar into a bowl, then stir into the creamed mixture with the walnuts and raisins.

Whisk the egg whites until firm peaks form and fold into the mixture. Spoon batter into the tin, smoothing the top even.

Bake for 30–40 minutes, or until a skewer inserted in the centre comes out clean Cool the cake in the tin for 30 minutes, then turn out onto a wire rack to cool completely.

For the icing, using an electric beater, combine the milk, lemon juice, butter and icing sugar in a bowl and beat well. Stir in the lemon zest. Add a little more icing sugar if the mixture is too thin, or more milk if it is too thick: it should have a smooth, spreadable consistency. Spread icing on the cooled cake.

Family recipes

	1	2	3
	Cheese Crescents	Delicious Pudding (hot)	Savoury Rabbit
4	5	6	7	8
Windsor Pudding	Scrambled Bacon and Corn	Baked Roly Poly	Date Cookies	Coffee Cake No 2
9	10	11	12	13
Steak and Kidney Pudding	Shortbread No 1	Oyster Toast	Golden Pudding	Apricot Batter
14	15	16	17	18
Potato Soup	Pound Cake	Fruit Cake (eggless)	Cup Pudding	Raspberry Bun
19	20	21	22	23
Scotch Broth	Sponge Sandwich No 1	Bowral Tart	Prune Pudding	Vanity Puffs
24	25	26	27	28
Eggs Baked in Potato Cases	Currant Pudding	Treacle Sauce	Muffins	Cheese Pyramids
29	30	31		
Date Drops	Spaghetti Savoury	Rose Cake		

JULY

Cheese Crescents

Mrs RH Oakes, Maitland Branch

MAKES 36

90 g (1 cup) grated cheddar
  cheese
70 g (¼ cup) chutney
1 tablespoon dried
  breadcrumbs
1 egg, lightly beaten
4 sheets frozen puff pastry,
  thawed

Preheat oven to 180°C. Line a baking tray with baking paper.

Combine the cheese, chutney, breadcrumbs and egg in a bowl and stir to mix well. Using a 7 cm round pastry cutter, cut rounds from the pastry and place on the trays.

Spoon small amounts of the filling onto half of each round, leaving a small border. Fold the pastry over to form a semicircle and press the edges to seal.

Bake for 10–15 minutes, or until puffed and deep golden. Serve hot or at room temperature.

Delicious Pudding (hot)

Mrs Edwards, Emerald Hill Branch

SERVES 4–6

60 g (¼ cup) butter,
  softened
220 g (1 cup) caster sugar
2 tablespoons plain flour
juice and grated zest of
  1 lemon
2 eggs, separated
250 ml (1 cup) milk
boiling water, for baking

Preheat oven to 170°C.

Using an electric beater, beat the butter and sugar well in a bowl. Mix in the flour, lemon juice and zest, egg yolks and milk.

Using clean beaters, whisk the egg whites in a bowl until firm peaks form. Fold the whites into the lemon mixture.

Pour the batter into a 1 litre (4 cup) capacity baking dish. Place the dish in a larger baking dish filled with enough boiling water to come halfway up the side.

Bake for 45 minutes, or until the top is light golden and the base is creamy. Serve hot.

Savoury Rabbit

Mrs Tate, Yass Branch

3 JUL

SERVES 4–6

1.5 kg rabbit
¼ cup plain flour
3 bacon rashers
1 onion, peeled and finely
    chopped
2 large carrots, trimmed
    and sliced
1 small handful of parsley,
    chopped
2–3 teaspoons finely grated
    lemon zest
600 ml chicken stock, or
    as required

Preheat oven to 170°C. Liberally grease a 1.5 litre (6 cup) capacity baking dish with butter.

Cut the rabbit into 6–8 pieces through the bone. Season the flour with salt and pepper in a bowl. Dust the rabbit with the flour, shaking off any excess.

Place the rabbit in the dish and cover with the bacon, onion, carrot, parsley and zest. Pour over the stock, adding a little extra stock or water if required to just cover the rabbit.

Bake for 1 hour, or until the rabbit is tender.

Windsor Pudding

Mrs Taylor, Moulamein Branch

4 JUL

SERVES 8

6 granny smith apples,
    peeled, cored and
    chopped
2 tablespoons lemon
    juice
2 strips lemon peel
50 g butter, softened
75 g (⅓ cup) caster sugar
125 ml (½ cup) water
1 egg, well beaten
35 g (¼ cup) plain flour
1 teaspoon baking
    powder
icing sugar, for dusting

Combine the apples, lemon juice and peel, 2 teaspoons of the butter, half the sugar and the water in a saucepan. Bring to a simmer, cover and cook over medium–low heat for 15 minutes, or until the apples are very tender.

Preheat oven to 180°C.

Using an electric beater, beat the remaining butter and sugar in a bowl until light and creamy. Add the egg and beat well. Sift the flour and baking powder into a bowl, then stir into the butter mixture to combine well.

Place the apples in a 1.5 litre (6 cup) capacity baking dish and spoon pudding mixture over.

Bake for 30 minutes, or until the top is deep golden. Dust with icing sugar and serve hot.

Scrambled Bacon and Corn

Mrs F Williams, Walgett Branch

SERVES 4

250 g bacon rashers,
  chopped
420 g tin of sweet corn
  kernels, drained
4 eggs, lightly beaten
125 ml (½ cup) milk
hot buttered toast and
  chopped parsley, to serve

Heat a large, non-stick frying pan over medium heat. Add the bacon and cook, stirring, for 5 minutes, or until golden. Add the corn and cook, stirring for a further 3 minutes, or until the corn is heated though.

Add the eggs and stir to combine, then add the milk and salt and pepper to taste. Cook, stirring occasionally, for a further 5 minutes, or until the eggs have set lightly.

Serve on toast, sprinkled with parsley.

Baked Roly Poly

Mrs Westerdale, Tallimba Branch

SERVES 8

150 g (1 cup) self-raising
  flour
125 g (½ cup) butter,
  chopped, plus
  1 tablespoon extra
85 g (¼ cup) raspberry jam
55 g (¼ cup) caster sugar
250 ml (1 cup) boiling
  water

Preheat oven to 180°C.

Place the flour in a bowl. Using your fingertips, rub in the butter until the mixture resembles breadcrumbs. Gradually add enough cold water to make a soft dough.

Turn the dough onto a floured surface and roll out to a rectangle about 24 x 20 cm. Spread with the jam, leaving a 1.5 cm border around the edge. Starting from a long side, roll up the dough to form a log.

Place the roll, seam side down, in a 1.5 litre (6 cup) capacity baking dish. Combine the sugar, remaining butter and boiling water in a bowl and pour it over.

Bake for 30 minutes, or until the roly poly is deep golden and the sauce is bubbling.

Date Cookies

MAKES 18
75 g butter, softened
110 g (½ cup) caster sugar
1 egg
1 teaspoon vanilla essence
185 g (1¼ cup) self-raising flour
½ teaspoon ground nutmeg
1 teaspoon ground cinnamon
35 g (⅓ cup) rolled oats
160 g (1 cup) chopped pitted
   dates
60 ml (¼ cup) milk

Preheat oven to 175°C. Line two baking trays with baking paper.

Using an electric beater, beat the butter and sugar in a bowl until light and creamy. Add the egg and vanilla and beat to combine well. Sift the flour and spices into a bowl, then add to the butter mixture with the oats, dates and milk and stir to combine well.

Drop slightly heaped tablespoons of the mixture onto the trays. Bake for about 12 minutes, or until golden. Transfer to a wire rack to cool.

Coffee Cake No 2

Mrs Lamrock, Penrith Branch

MAKES ONE 20 CM CAKE
125 g (½ cup) butter,
   softened
80 g caster sugar
2 eggs
2 tablespoons milk
1 tablespoon coffee essence
150 g (1 cup) plain flour
1 teaspoon baking powder

Icing
150 g (1¼ cup) icing sugar
55 g butter, softened
1 tablespoon coffee essence
boiling water, as required

Preheat oven to 180°C. Lightly grease and flour a 20 cm cake tin.

Using an electric beater, beat the butter and sugar in a bowl until light and creamy. Add the eggs, one at a time, beating well between each. Stir in the milk and coffee essence.

Sift the flour and baking powder into a bowl. Stir into the creamed mixture to combine well, then spoon the batter into the tin, smoothing the top even.

Bake for 40–50 minutes, or until a skewer inserted in the centre comes out clean. Cool the cake in the tin for 10 minutes, then turn out onto a wire rack to cool completely.

For the icing, combine all the ingredients in a bowl and add a few teaspoons of boiling water, or enough to form a smooth, thick icing. Spread over the cooled cake.

Steak and Kidney Pudding

9 JUL

Mrs Hadlow, Collector Branch

SERVES 4–6

1 batch Suet Pastry
  (see April 19)
750 g beef chuck steak,
  trimmed and cut into
  2.5 cm pieces
125 g beef kidney,
  trimmed and cut into
  1 cm pieces
1 large onion, peeled and
  finely chopped
1 teaspoon dried mixed
  herbs
35 g (¼ cup) plain flour

Bring a large saucepan of water to the boil for steaming, placing a small heatproof plate upside down in the water to keep the pudding basin off the base of the pan. Lightly grease and flour a 1 litre (4 cup) capacity pudding basin.

Cut a third off the pastry and set aside. On a lightly floured surface, roll the larger piece of pastry out into a circle large enough to line the basin.

Mix together the steak, kidney, chopped onion and herbs in a bowl. Sprinkle over the flour and mix well. Spoon the mixture into the pastry-lined basin and add enough cold water to come halfway up the filling.

Roll out the remaining pastry into a round large enough to cover the basin. Place over the top of the pudding, pressing the pastry together at the edges to seal well.

Cover the basin with pleated baking paper, to allow the pastry to expand, then cover that with pleated foil. Secure tightly with string.

Lower the basin into the boiling water. Simmer for 2–2½ hours, or until cooked through, adding more water to the pan as required.

Shortbread No 1

Mrs RK Wood, Adelaide

MAKES 16
250 g (1⅔ cups) plain flour
80 g (½ cup) rice flour
170 g butter, chopped
85 g caster sugar

Preheat oven to 150°C. Lightly grease and flour the sides of two 20 cm cake tins and line the bases with baking paper.

Combine the flours in a bowl. Using your fingertips, rub in the butter until the mixture resembles breadcrumbs. Add the sugar.

Knead with your hands until a firm dough forms, then divide in half. Press each piece of dough into a tin, using a palette knife to smooth the top even. Mark the edges with the tines of a fork.

Bake for 40 minutes, or until firm. Cool shortbread in the tin, cutting into wedges from the centre while still a little warm.

Oyster Toast

Mrs CV Robertson, Yass Branch

MAKES 12
12 freshly shucked oysters
25 g butter, plus extra,
    for spreading
30 g (½ cup, lightly packed)
    fresh breadcrumbs
100 ml milk
2½ tablespoons thickened
    cream
1½ tablespoons finely chopped
    parsley
6 thin slices white bread, toasted
    and crusts trimmed
a few sprigs of parsley, to serve

Preheat oven to 170°C. Cut each oyster into quarters and set aside.

Melt the butter in a small saucepan over medium heat, add the breadcrumbs and stir to combine well. Add the milk, bring the mixture to a simmer, then cook, stirring, for 5 minutes, or until it thickens. Stir in the cream and bring to a boil. Stir through the oysters and chopped parsley and season to taste with salt and pepper, then remove from the heat.

Butter the toast and place on a baking tray. Spread each piece with oyster mixture then bake for 5–6 minutes, or until heated through.

Remove the toast from the oven, cut each piece in half on the diagonal and serve immediately, garnished with parsley sprigs.

Golden Pudding

Mrs S Wood, Stroud Branch

SERVES 6

2 tablespoons butter,
  softened
2 tablespoons caster sugar
1 egg
½ teaspoon bicarbonate
  of soda
125 ml (½ cup) milk
2 tablespoons golden syrup
150 g (1 cup) plain flour

Bring a large saucepan of water to the boil for steaming, placing a small heatproof plate upside down in the water to keep the pudding basin off the base of the pan. Lightly grease and flour a 1.5 litre (6 cup) capacity pudding basin.

Using an electric beater, beat the butter and sugar in a bowl until light and creamy. Add the egg and beat well. Dissolve the soda in a little of the milk in a cup. Add the syrup, remaining milk, flour and dissolved soda to the butter mixture, stirring to mix well.

Spoon the batter into the basin, cover tightly and lower it into the boiling water. Steam for 1½ hours, or until cooked through, adding more water to the pan as required.

Apricot Batter

Mrs WN Alley, Braidwood Branch

SERVES 4

120 g (⅓ cup) dried apricots
boiling water, for soaking
60 g caster sugar
1 egg, beaten
1 tablespoon melted butter
80 ml (⅓ cup) boiling water
150 g (1 cup) plain flour
1 teaspoon baking powder
cream or custard, to serve

Place the apricots in a bowl and pour the boiling water over. Leave to stand for 1 hour, or until the apricots have softened.

Heat the apricot mixture in a saucepan over medium heat and bring to a simmer. Cover and cook for 20 minutes, or until the apricots are soft. Stir in the sugar.

Preheat oven to 190°C.

Whisk together the egg, melted butter and boiling water in a bowl. Sift the flour and baking powder in a bowl and stir it into the mixture to form a smooth batter.

Spoon the hot apricots into a 20 cm pie dish and pour the batter over. Bake for 30 minutes, or until golden.

Serve Apricot Batter hot with cream or custard.

Potato Soup

Mrs H Marr, Cootamundra Branch

14 JUL

SERVES 4–6

60 g (¼ cup) butter, plus
   extra, for frying
1 onion, peeled and chopped
500 g desiree potatoes, peeled
   and chopped
1 stalk of celery, chopped
600 ml chicken stock
250 ml (1 cup) pouring cream
2–3 slices of day old bread,
   crusts removed and cut
   into small cubes

✖ *Serve the Potato
Soup hot, with the fried
bread scattered over.*

Heat the butter in a large saucepan. Add the onion, potatoes and celery and cook, stirring, over medium heat for 10 minutes, or until vegetables have started to soften.

Add the stock, bring to a simmer and cook for a further 20–30 minutes, or until the vegetables are very tender.

Transfer the vegetables and stock to a food mill (mouli) and pass the mixture through to form a smooth purée. Discard any solids. Return the purée to the pan, add the cream and season with salt and pepper.

Heat enough butter to coat the base of a large frying pan over medium heat. Add the cubes of bread and cook, tossing in the pan often, for 5–6 minutes, or until light golden.

Pound Cake

Mrs Stan Wild, Wagga Branch

15 JUL

MAKES ONE 28 CM ROUND CAKE
OR ONE 25 CM SQUARE CAKE

500 g (2 cups) butter,
   softened
500 g caster sugar
8 eggs
750 g (5 cups) plain flour
1 teaspoon baking powder
420 g (3 cups) currants
510 g (3 cups) sultanas
240 g (1½ cups) chopped
   pitted dates
225 g (1½ cups) mixed peel

Preheat oven to 150°C. Line a 28 cm round (or 25 cm square) cake tin with baking paper.

Using an electric beater, beat the butter and sugar in a bowl until light and creamy. Add the eggs, one at a time, beating well after each.

Sift the flour and baking powder into a bowl, then stir into the creamed mixture. Add the dried fruit and peel and stir to combine well. Spoon the batter into the tin, smoothing the top even.

Bake for 3½–4 hours, or until a skewer inserted in the centre comes out clean. Cool the cake in the tin.

Fruit Cake (eggless)

MAKES ONE 23 CM CAKE

250 g (1 cup) butter,
   softened
220 g (1 cup, firmly packed)
   brown sugar
215 g (1½ cups) currants
255 g (1½ cups) sultanas
255 g (1½ cups) raisins
25 g chopped almonds
25 g chopped walnuts
450 ml water
1 teaspoon mixed spice
1 teaspoon ground nutmeg
525 g (3⅓ cups) plain flour
1 teaspoon bicarbonate
   of soda
2 teaspoons water

Preheat oven to 160°C. Line a 23 cm cake tin with baking paper.

Combine the butter, sugar, fruits, nuts and water in a saucepan and slowly bring to a simmer. Cook over medium–low heat for 5 minutes, stirring constantly. Remove from the heat and cool to room temperature.

Sift the spices and flour into a bowl, then stir into the cooled fruit mixture. Dissolve the soda in the water in a cup, then stir into the mix. Spoon the batter into the tin.

Bake for 2½ hours, or until a skewer inserted in the centre comes out clean. Cool the cake in the tin.

Cup Pudding

Mrs Westerdale, Tallimba Branch

SERVES 8

150 g (1 cup) plain flour
185 g (1 cup) mixed dried
   fruit
250 ml (1 cup) milk
1 tablespoon melted butter
1 teaspoon bicarbonate
   of soda

Bring a large saucepan of water to the boil for steaming, placing a small heatproof plate upside down in the water to keep the pudding basin off the base of the pan. Grease and flour a 1.5 litre (6 cup) capacity pudding basin.

Stir the flour and dried fruit in a bowl. Add half the milk and the butter. Dissolve the soda in the remaining milk in a cup, then stir it into the batter to combine well.

Spoon the batter into the basin, cover tightly and lower it into the boiling water. Steam for 3 hours, or until cooked through, adding more water to the pan as required.

Raspberry Bun

Miss Elsie Segaert, Manly Branch

SERVES 6–8
125 g (½ cup) butter, softened
220 g (1 cup) caster sugar
2 eggs
225 g (1½ cups) self-raising
    flour, sifted
165 g (½ cup) raspberry jam
90 g (1 cup) desiccated
    coconut

Preheat oven to 180°C. Lightly grease and flour a 1.5 litre (6 cup) capacity baking dish.

Using an electric beater, beat the butter and half the sugar in a bowl until light and creamy. Add one of the eggs and beat well. Stir in the flour.

Spread the mixture over the base of the dish then spread over the jam. Mix together the remaining sugar, egg and coconut in a bowl. Spread the coconut mixture over the jam.

Bake for 50–60 minutes, or until golden and cooked through.

Scotch Broth

Mrs Reid, Binalong Branch

SERVES 6–8
155 g (⅔ cup) green split peas
boiling water, for soaking
2.75 litres (5½ cups) water
200 g (1 cup) pearl barley
750 g lamb neck chops, fat
    trimmed and cut into
    2 cm pieces
1 teaspoon salt
2 carrots
1 turnip, peeled and finely
    chopped
4 spring onions, trimmed
    and chopped
1 tablespoon finely chopped
    parsley
3 teaspoons sugar

Place the peas in a bowl and cover with boiling water. Stand for 30 minutes, then drain well.

Bring 2.75 litres (5½ cups) of water to a simmer in a large saucepan. Add the peas, barley, meat and salt. Return to a simmer, skimming off any scum that rises to the surface.

Finely chop 1 carrot and grate the other. Add the chopped carrot, turnip and onions to the pan. Cover and cook over medium–low heat for 30 minutes. Add the grated carrot, parsley, sugar and salt and pepper to taste.

Simmer for a further 2½–3 hours, or until meat is very tender.

Sponge Sandwich No 1

Mrs Percy Stacy, Singleton Branch

MAKES ONE 18 CM CAKE
4 eggs
220 g (1 cup, firmly packed)
   brown sugar
150 g (1 cup) plain flour
1 teaspoon baking powder
60 ml (¼ cup) milk
2 teaspoons melted butter
icing sugar, for sprinkling

Filling
25 g butter, softened
60 g (½ cup) icing sugar
1 teaspoon vanilla essence
2 tablespoons jam of choice
   (optional)

Preheat oven to 180°C. Lightly grease and flour two 18 cm cake tins.

Combine the eggs and sugar in a bowl. Using an electric beater, whisk until very thick and pale and the mixture leaves a trail when beaters are lifted.

Sift the flour and baking powder into a bowl and gently fold into the egg mixture. Add the milk and butter, then stir to combine well.

Spoon the batter into the tins and bake for 15–20 minutes, or until the surface springs back when gently pressed. Cool the cakes in the tins for 15 minutes, then turn out onto wire racks to cool.

For the filling, using an electric beater, beat all the ingredients in a bowl until light and creamy. Spread the mixture over one of the cooled cakes. (Option: spread a layer of jam over the base of the second cake before joining them together.) Layer the other cake on top.

To serve, sprinkle cake with icing sugar.

Bowral Tart

Bowral Branch

21 JUL

SERVES 8
1 tablespoon butter
110 g (½ cup) caster sugar
1 egg
150 g (1 cup) plain flour
1 teaspoon baking powder
2 teaspoons jam

Preheat oven to 180°C. Grease and flour a 20 cm cake tin.

Using an electric beater, beat the butter and sugar until well combined. Add the egg and beat well. Sift the flour and baking powder into a bowl, then stir it into the mixture.

Spoon the batter into the tin, smoothing the top even. Make a hole in the centre of the batter and spoon in the jam.

Bake for 20 minutes, or until cooked through. Cool slightly in the tin, then turn out onto a serving plate.

Prune Pudding

Mrs CA Lamont, Wagga Branch

22 JUL

SERVES 8
60 g (¼ cup) butter, melted
1 egg, beaten well
90 g (¼ cup) golden syrup
½ teaspoon almond essence
95 g (1 cup) rolled oats
75 g (½ cup) plain flour
1 teaspoon bicarbonate
of soda
250 ml (1 cup) buttermilk
or milk
375 g (1½ cups) pitted prunes,
coarsely chopped
custard, to serve

Bring a large saucepan of water to the boil for steaming, placing a small heatproof plate upside down in the water to keep the pudding basin off the base of the pan. Grease and flour a 1 litre (4 cup) capacity pudding basin.

Combine the butter, egg, syrup and essence in a bowl. Combine the oats and flour in another bowl, making a well in the centre. Dissolve the soda in the buttermilk in a cup and pour it into the well. Pour in the egg mixture and stir until smooth. Add the prunes, stirring to combine.

Spoon the batter into the basin, cover tightly and lower it into the boiling water. Steam for 2½ hours or until cooked through, adding more water to the pan as required. Serve hot with custard, if desired.

Vanity Puffs

P Marina, Young Branch

23 JUL

MAKES ABOUT 24

250 ml (1 cup) milk
75 g (½ cup) plain flour
3 eggs
1 tablespoon melted butter
vegetable oil, for deep-frying
55 g (¼ cup) caster sugar
1 teaspoon ground
  cinnamon

Bring the milk to a simmer in a saucepan. Working quickly, add the flour and stir with a wooden spoon until a smooth, thick paste forms. Remove from the heat and cool slightly.

Add the eggs, one at a time, stirring well between each until smooth. Stir in the butter.

Heat the oil in a large saucepan to 170°C, or until a cube of bread turns golden brown in 20 seconds.

Mix together the sugar and cinnamon in a bowl and set aside.

Drop tablespoons of the mixture into the hot oil and cook for about 5 minutes, or until puffed and golden. Transfer puffs to paper towels to drain the excess oil.

Toss the puffs in the sugar mixture to coat. Serve hot.

Eggs Baked in Potato Cases

Mrs A Webb, Orange Branch

24 JUL

SERVES 4

4 large desiree potatoes,
  washed
2 tablespoons butter, cut
  into 8 pieces
8 eggs
chopped parsley

Preheat oven to 180°C.

Bake the potatoes for 20–30 minutes, or until tender. Set aside until cool enough to handle.

Cut the potatoes in half lengthwise. Scoop out some of the cooked flesh, leaving a 5 mm wall. Reserve the remainder of the flesh for another use.

Place a piece of butter in each potato half. Carefully break an egg into each and sprinkle with parsley and salt and pepper.

Bake for 10–15 minutes, or until the eggs are just set. Serve hot.

Currant Pudding

Mrs AF Leeson, Dunedoo Branch

SERVES 8

300 g (2 cups) plain flour
1 teaspoon baking powder
250 g (1 cup) shredded suet
(see note)
½ teaspoon salt
60 ml (¼ cup) iced water,
or as required
140 g (1 cup) currants
55 g (¼ cup) caster sugar
2 teaspoons mixed spice

Bring a large saucepan of water to the boil for cooking the pudding.

Sift the flour and baking powder into a bowl. Stir in the suet and salt. Add enough iced water to form a soft dough.

Roll the dough out onto a lightly floured surface to about 20 × 18 cm. Scatter over the currants, sugar, spice and a few tablespoons of water to dampen. Working from a long edge, roll up the dough to form a log. Place the log in a heavily floured pudding cloth and roll the cloth around the log, leaving a little room for expansion. Tie the ends tightly with string.

Place the log into the boiling water. Boil for 1½ hours, or until pudding is cooked through, adding more water to the pan as required.

Note: shredded suet is available as a packet mix at supermarkets, or fresh from your butcher.

Treacle Sauce

Mrs Westerdale, Tallimba Branch

MAKES ABOUT 1½ CUPS

175 g (½ cup) treacle
1½ tablespoons lemon juice,
or to taste
250 ml (1 cup) water, plus
1 tablespoon, extra
2 teaspoons cornflour

Combine the treacle, juice and water in a small saucepan and bring to a simmer, stirring until smooth.

Combine the cornflour with the tablespoon of water in a small bowl, stirring until smooth. Stirring constantly to prevent lumps forming, add to the treacle mixture and cook for 1–2 minutes, or until thickened slightly.

Remove from the heat and cool slightly, adding a little extra lemon juice to taste if required. Serve warm on puddings or desserts.

Muffins

Mrs F G McFaul

MAKES 12
1 egg, beaten
250 ml (1 cup) milk
225 g (1½ cups) plain flour
1 tablespoon caster sugar
2 teaspoons baking powder

Preheat oven to 180°C. Grease and butter a 12-hole 60 ml (⅓ cup) capacity muffin tin.

Place the egg and milk in a bowl and whisk to combine well. Sift the flour, sugar and baking powder into a bowl, then stir into the milk mixture.

Pour the batter into the tin and bake for 25–30 minutes, or until a skewer inserted in the centres comes out clean. Turn out onto a wire rack to cool.

Cheese Pyramids

Mrs Stuart Williams, Cootamundra

MAKES ABOUT 60
110 g (¾ cup) plain flour
115 g grated cheddar cheese
60 g chilled butter, chopped
2 eggs yolks
large pinch cayenne pepper
lemon juice, as required

Topping
250 ml (1 cup) pouring
   cream, whipped
100 g (1 cup) grated
   cheddar cheese
large pinch of cayenne
   pepper

Preheat oven to 180°C. Line two baking trays with baking paper.

Combine the flour, cheese and butter in a bowl and, using your fingertips, rub in the butter until mixture resembles breadcrumbs. Add the egg yolks, cayenne and enough lemon juice to form a firm dough.

Knead the dough lightly until smooth, then roll out on a floured surface to 5 mm thickness. Using a round 3 cm pastry cutter, cut rounds from the dough, re-rolling scraps for more rounds. Place on the trays.

Bake for 15 minutes, or until light golden. Transfer to a wire rack to cool.

For the topping, combine the ingredients in a bowl, season to taste with salt and pepper and gently stir to combine. Spoon the topping onto the cooled biscuits and serve.

Date Drops

MAKES 30
250 g (1 cup) butter,
  softened
110 g (½ cup) caster sugar
1 egg
1 teaspoon ground
  cinnamon
225 g (1½ cups) plain flour
½ teaspoon bicarbonate
  of soda
1 tablespoon boiling water
120 g (¾ cup) chopped dates
90 g (¾ cup) chopped
  walnuts

Preheat oven to 180°C. Line two baking trays with baking paper.

Using an electric beater, beat the butter and sugar until light and creamy. Add the egg and beat well.

Sift the cinnamon and flour into a bowl, then stir into the creamed mixture with the dates and walnuts. Stir the soda into the boiling water in a cup, add to the flour mixture and stir to combine well.

Drop heaped tablespoons of the mixture onto the trays, leaving room for spreading. Bake for 10–15 minutes, or until light golden and cooked through. Transfer to a wire rack to cool.

Spaghetti Savoury

Miss Ivy Quinton, Maitland Branch

SERVES 2
750 ml (3 cups) chicken
  stock
150 g dried spaghetti
25 g butter
2 large ripe tomatoes,
  chopped
30 g (⅓ cup) grated
  cheddar cheese
vinegar, for poaching
4 eggs

Bring the stock to a simmer in a saucepan. Add the spaghetti and cook, stirring with tongs to separate the spaghetti strands, for 8 minutes, or until the stock is absorbed and the spaghetti is cooked – add a little extra stock or water if required. Stir in the butter, tomatoes and cheese and season well with salt and pepper. Cover and keep hot.

Bring a pan of water to the simmer and add a dash of vinegar. Carefully break the eggs into the water and cook for about 3 minutes, or until the whites are firm. Gently remove the eggs using a slotted spoon and drain well.

Place the spaghetti in serving bowls, top with the eggs and serve immediately.

Rose Cake

Mrs Fraser, Dungog Branch

MAKES ONE 18 CM CAKE
115 g butter, softened
220 g (1 cup) caster sugar
125 ml (½ cup) milk
3 egg whites
225 g (1½ cups) plain flour
1½ teaspoons baking
    powder
1 tablespoon rosewater
red food colouring
unsprayed rose petals,
    to decorate

Snow Glaze
115 g (1¼ cups) icing
    sugar, sifted
1 teaspoon butter,
    softened
¼ teaspoon vanilla
    essence
2–4 teaspoons milk,
    or as required

Preheat oven to 180°C. Line an 18 cm cake tin with baking paper.

Using an electric beater, beat the butter and sugar until light and creamy. Stir in the milk.

Using clean beaters, whisk the egg whites until firm peaks form. Sift the flour and baking powder into a bowl and fold into the creamed mixture with the egg whites and rosewater. Spoon half the mixture into the tin.

Add enough colouring to the remaining mixture in the bowl to tint it pink. Spoon this on top of the mixture in the tin and stir lightly to mix the colours a little.

Bake for 25–30 minutes, or until a skewer inserted in the centre comes out clean. Cool the cake in the tin for 15 minutes, then turn out onto a wire rack to cool completely.

For the snow glaze, combine the icing sugar, butter and vanilla in small bowl and beat well. Gradually add enough milk to make a smooth, thick mixture.

Cover the cake with the icing. Scatter with the rose petals just before serving.

Family recipes

		1	2	3
		Fricassee of Chicken	Banana Shortcake	Spiced Sausage en Casserole
4	5	6	7	8
Haricot Beans and Bacon	Esmeralda Rolls	Velvet Pudding	Oxtail Soup	Nut Loaf
9	10	11	12	13
Cauliflower Savoury	Rock Cakes	Gingernuts	Chocolate Cakes	Salmon Pie
14	15	16	17	18
Gunnedah Pudding	Cinnamon Slice	Oatmeal Apple Pudding	Jam Sauce	Apple Puffs
19	20	21	22	23
Stuffed Shoulder of Lamb	Treacle Pudding	Bobotee or Baked Curry	Apple and Celery Sandwiches	Baked Apple Pudding
24	25	26	27	28
Cup Cake	Pearl Cake	Steamed Sago Plum Pudding	John Bull Biscuits	Mysteries
29	30	31		
Chocolate Sponge	Shortbread Creams	Nutties		

AUGUST

Fricassee of Chicken

Mrs Mitchell McKenzie, Yathella Branch

SERVES 6

1 x 1.8 kg chicken (or 1.8 kg
   chicken pieces)
boiling water, as required
6 black peppercorns
6 sprigs of thyme, tied in
   a bundle
1 small onion, peeled and
   quartered
60 g (¼ cup) butter
35 g (¼ cup) plain flour
1 tablespoon pouring cream
2 egg yolks

Using a large sharp knife, cut the chicken through the bone into eight pieces. Place the chicken in a bowl, pour over the boiling water to cover and stand for 5 minutes. Drain well.

Place the chicken in a saucepan with the peppercorns, thyme and onion and add enough water to cover. Bring to a simmer and cook over medium–low heat for 20 minutes, or until the chicken is cooked through. Strain the liquid and reserve, discarding the herbs, onion and peppercorns. Place the chicken on a warm serving platter, cover and keep warm.

Melt the butter in a saucepan, add the flour, then stir with a wooden spoon over medium–low heat until a smooth paste forms. Gradually add 400 ml of the reserved liquid, stirring well between additions and bringing the mixture to a simmer before adding more liquid. Cook, stirring to prevent lumps forming, for 5 minutes. Add the cream, then remove from the heat.

Add a little of the hot mixture to the egg yolks in a small bowl and stir to combine well. Stir into the mixture in the pan. Cook for 2 minutes over low heat, stirring constantly – do not let it boil or the sauce will curdle. Season to taste with salt and pepper.

Pour the sauce over the chicken and serve immediately.

Banana Shortcake

Mrs Arthur Martin, Wagga

MAKES ONE 18 CM CAKE
125 g (½ cup) butter,
  softened
220 g (1 cup) caster sugar
2 eggs
1 teaspoon vanilla essence
300 g (2 cups) plain flour
1 teaspoons baking powder
125 ml (½ cup) milk
2 large firm, ripe bananas,
  sliced
2 tablespoons lemon juice
250 ml (1 cup) thickened
  cream, whipped

Preheat oven to 180°C. Grease and flour the sides of two 18 cm cake tins and line the bases with baking paper.

Using an electric beater, beat the butter and sugar in a bowl until light and creamy. Add the eggs, one at a time, beating well between each. Beat in the vanilla. Sift the flour and baking powder into a bowl, then stir into the creamed mixture with the milk.

Spoon the batter into the tins, smoothing the tops even.

Bake for 30–35 minutes, or until a skewer inserted in the centre comes out clean. Cool the cakes in the tins for 10 minutes, then turn out onto a wire rack to cool completely.

Gently toss the banana slices in a bowl with the lemon juice to coat. Drain well.

Spoon a layer of whipped cream over one of the cakes and arrange half the bananas over the cream. Place the other cake on top. Spread a layer of cream over the cake and arrange the remaining bananas on top.

Spiced Sausage en Casserole

Mrs AM Munro, Gulargambone Branch

SERVES 4

1½ tablespoons brown sugar
2 tablespoons plain flour
1 tablespoon Worcestershire
  sauce
2 tablespoons malt vinegar
375 ml (1½ cups) boiling water
1 onion, peeled and finely
  chopped
1 carrot, peeled and finely
  chopped
6 pork sausages

Preheat oven to 180°C.

Combine the sugar, flour, Worcestershire sauce, vinegar and boiling water in a casserole dish and stir to mix well. Add the onion and carrot. Prick the sausages, add to the dish and season well with salt and pepper.

Cover the casserole tightly and bake for 2 hours, or until the vegetables are soft and the sausages are cooked through.

Haricot Beans and Bacon

4 AUG

Mrs WS Forsyth, Armidale Branch

SERVES 4

475 g (2⅓ cups) dried
  haricot beans
250 g bacon rashers
chopped parsley,
  for sprinkling

Soak the beans overnight in cold water to cover. Drain well.

Place the beans in a saucepan, add enough water to cover and cook for 40–50 minutes, or until beans are very tender. Drain well, reserving the cooking liquid.

Transfer the beans to a food processor and, using the pulse button, purée coarsely, adding a little reserved liquid as required. Return to the saucepan, season with salt and pepper, cover and keep hot.

Cook the bacon, in batches if necessary, in a large, heavy-based frying pan over medium heat for 5–6 minutes, turning once. Pour any rendered fat over the beans and stir to combine.

Spoon the beans into a warmed serving dish, sprinkle with parsley, top with bacon and serve.

Esmeralda Rolls

Mrs Hartley, Mendooran Branch

MAKES 8–10

300 g (2 cups) plain flour
2 teaspoons baking powder
2 tablespoons butter,
    chopped
125 ml (½ cup) milk,
    or as required
260 g (¾ cup) golden
    syrup
2 tablespoons desiccated
    coconut
500 ml (2 cups) boiling
    water

Preheat oven to 190°C. Generously grease a 30 × 20 cm baking dish.

Sift the flour, baking powder and a large pinch of salt into a bowl. Using your fingertips, rub in the butter until the mixture resembles breadcrumbs. Add enough milk to make a soft dough.

Turn the dough out onto a lightly floured surface and knead briefly to bring it together. Roll the dough out into a 30 × 12 cm rectangle and spread 75 g (½ cup) of the golden syrup over. Roll up dough to form a log and cut it into 12 even-sized pieces. Arrange the pieces in a single layer in the dish, overlapping slightly if necessary.

Combine the remaining golden syrup, coconut and the boiling water in a saucepan and bring to a simmer. Pour over the rolls in the dish.

Bake for 1 hour, or until the rolls are golden and cooked through and the sauce is thick and syrupy.

Esmeralda Rolls are best served hot.

Velvet Pudding

Mrs J Connell, Yass Branch

SERVES 8

3 eggs, separated
110 g (½ cup) caster sugar
2 tablespoons cornflour
900 ml milk
1 teaspoon vanilla essence
3 teaspoons lemon juice
glacé cherries, to decorate

Preheat oven to 180°C. Lightly grease a 20 cm pie dish.

Whisk the egg yolks and half the sugar in a bowl. Place the cornflour in a cup and stir in a little of the milk to make a smooth, thin paste. Stir the paste into the yolk mixture.

Place the remaining milk in a saucepan and bring to a simmer. Stirring constantly, add the yolk mixture to the hot milk and bring back to a simmer. Stir over medium heat for several minutes, or until the mixture boils and thickens, then add the vanilla essence. Pour the mixture into the dish.

Using an electric beater, whisk the egg whites until firm peaks form. Whisking constantly, slowly add the remaining sugar and whisk until it has dissolved and the mixture is glossy. Whisk in the lemon juice. Spoon the whites over the mixture in the dish.

Bake for 15–20 minutes, or until the meringue is light golden.

🦋 *Decorate Velvet Pudding with glacé cherries and serve warm or cold.*

Oxtail Soup

Mrs F Connell, Yass Branch

SERVES 12

1.75 kg pieces of oxtail
plain flour, for dusting
30 g butter
2 bacon rashers, rind
  removed, chopped
1 turnip, peeled and
  finely chopped
2 onions, peeled and
  finely chopped
2 carrots, peeled and
  finely chopped
1 heart of celery,
  trimmed and finely
  chopped
2 teaspoons black
  peppercorns
1 tablespoon caster sugar
2 tablespoons tomato
  sauce
125 ml (½ cup) port

Dust the oxtail lightly with flour in a bowl, shaking off any excess.

Heat the butter in a large, heavy-based saucepan over medium heat and cook the oxtail, turning often, for 10 minutes, or until browned all over. Add enough water to cover then bring to a simmer, skimming off any scum that rises to the surface. Cook over low heat for 4 hours, or until the meat is very tender, adding a little extra water as required to keep the oxtail covered.

Strain the oxtail well, reserving the cooking liquid. Cool the meat to room temperature. Remove the meat and discard fat from the bones. Refrigerate the meat and cooking liquid overnight. The next day, remove any fat from the cooking liquid.

Place the oxtail, reserved cooking liquid, bacon, vegetables, peppercorns and sugar in a pan, adding enough water to cover. Bring to a simmer. Cook for 1 hour, or until the vegetables are tender.

Stir in the tomato sauce and port, then serve hot.

Nut Loaf

Mrs Baird, Gunning Branch

MAKES ONE 28 CM LOAF
125 g (1 cup) chopped
  walnuts
250 ml (1 cup) milk
110 g (½ cup) caster sugar
1 egg
300 g (2 cups) self-raising
  flour

Combine the walnuts and milk in a bowl and soak for 1 hour.

Preheat oven to 180°C. Grease and flour a 28 x 18 x 4 cm loaf tin.

Whisk together the sugar and egg in a bowl. Add the nut mixture and the flour and stir to combine well. Spoon the batter into the tin.

Bake for 40–50 minutes, or until a skewer inserted in the centre comes out clean. Cool loaf in the tin.

Cauliflower Savoury

Mrs BA Tyson, Kuring-gai Branch

SERVES 4–6
1 cauliflower, trimmed
  and cut into florets
1 tablespoon butter
1 tablespoon plain flour
250 ml (1 cup) milk
50 g (½ cup) grated
  cheddar cheese

Preheat oven to 180°C. Grease a 1.5 litre (6 cup) capacity baking dish.

Cook the cauliflower in boiling salted water for 3–4 minutes, or until softened. Drain well and place in the baking dish.

Melt the butter in a small saucepan, add the flour and stir until smooth. Stirring constantly, gradually add the milk, stirring well between each addition to prevent lumps forming. Stir in the cheese and season with salt and pepper. Pour the mixture over the cauliflower.

Bake for 10–15 minutes, or until golden and bubbly.

Rock Cakes

Mrs Percy Stacy, Singleton Branch

MAKES 20

500 g (3⅓ cups) plain flour
2 teaspoons baking powder
120 g butter, chopped
250 g caster sugar
125 g currants
grated zest of 1 lemon
½ teaspoon freshly grated
  nutmeg
3 eggs, well beaten
milk, to mix, as required

Preheat oven to 180°C. Line two baking trays with baking paper.

Sift the flour and baking powder into a bowl. Using your fingertips, rub in the butter until the mixture resembles breadcrumbs. Add the sugar, currants, lemon zest and nutmeg. Add the eggs, stirring until a firm dough forms, adding a little milk if it is too stiff – it should drop heavily from a spoon.

Drop heaped tablespoons of the mixture onto the trays.

Bake for 18–20 minutes, or until light golden and firm. Transfer to a wire rack to cool.

Gingernuts

Yass Branch

MAKES 60

250 g (1 cup) butter,
  softened
220 g (1 cup) caster sugar
350 g (1 cup) treacle
750 g (5 cups) plain flour
1½ tablespoons ground
  ginger
1 teaspoon bicarbonate
  of soda
125 ml (½ cup) milk

Preheat oven to 180°C. Line two baking trays with baking paper.

Using an electric beater, beat the butter and sugar in a bowl until light and creamy. Add the treacle and beat to mix well. Sift the flour and ginger into a bowl. Dissolve the soda in the milk in a cup. Stir the flour and milk mixtures into the butter mixture, then stir to form a dough.

Turn the dough out onto a lightly floured surface and roll out to 5 mm thickness. Using a 4 cm round pastry cutter, cut rounds from the dough and place on the trays. Re-roll scraps and cut out more rounds.

Bake for 10–12 minutes, or until crisp. Transfer to a wire rack to cool.

Chocolate Cakes

MAKES 12
80 g butter, softened
65 g (⅓ cup) caster sugar
2 eggs
225 g (1½ cup) self-raising
   flour
1 tablespoon cocoa
   powder

Preheat oven to 180°C. Grease and flour a 12-hole 60 ml (⅓ cup) capacity muffin tin.

Using an electric beater, beat the butter and sugar in a bowl until light and creamy. Add the eggs, one at a time, beating well between each.

Sift the flour and cocoa into a bowl, then stir into the creamed mixture. Spoon the batter into the tin, smoothing the top even.

Bake for 12–15 minutes, or until a skewer inserted in the centre comes out clean. Turn out onto a covered rack to cool.

Salmon Pie

Mrs FW Parker, Lockhart Branch

SERVES 4
1 x 410 g tin pink or
   red salmon, well
   drained
2 large ripe tomatoes,
   thinly sliced
150 g (2½ cups, lightly
   packed) fresh
   breadcrumbs
3 eggs, well beaten
500 ml (2 cups) milk

Preheat oven to 180°C. Grease a 1.5 litre (6 cup) capacity baking dish.

Flake the salmon in a bowl using a fork and scatter half of it over the base of the dish. Place half the tomato slices over the salmon in an even layer, then scatter over half the crumbs.

Whisk the eggs and milk in a bowl and pour over the mixture in the dish.

Bake for 45 minutes, or until just set. Serve hot.

Gunnedah Pudding

Mrs RJ Bennie, Gunnedah Branch

SERVES 8

250 g (about 8 slices) stale
   bread, chopped
1 tablespoon caster sugar
90 g (¼ cup) golden syrup
175 g shredded suet
   (see note)
1 teaspoon baking powder
2 eggs, well beaten
1 teaspoon vanilla essence

Syrup Sauce
525 g (1½ cups) golden
   syrup
60 g (¼ cup) butter
125 ml (½ cup) water

Bring a large saucepan of water to the boil for steaming, placing a small heatproof plate upside down in the water to keep the pudding basin off the base of the pan. Grease a 1.5 litre (6 cup) pudding basin.

Place the bread in a bowl and cover with cold water. Drain the bread well, squeezing out as much water as possible.

Combine the bread in a bowl with the sugar and syrup. Combine the suet and baking powder in a bowl, then stir into the bread mixture, adding the eggs and vanilla.

Spoon the batter into the basin, cover tightly and lower it into the boiling water. Steam for 3 hours, or until cooked through, adding more water to the pan as required.

For the sauce, combine the syrup and butter with the water in a saucepan and bring to the boil. Cook, stirring, over medium heat for 2–3 minutes, or until smooth. Reduce the heat and simmer until ready to serve.

Note: shredded suet is available as a packet mix at supermarkets, or fresh from your butcher.

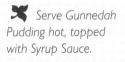 *Serve Gunnedah Pudding hot, topped with Syrup Sauce.*

Cinnamon Slice

Mrs JE Cameron, Dungog Branch

MAKES ABOUT 24

250 g (1 cup) butter,
   softened
440 g (2 cups) caster sugar
4 eggs
300 g (2 cups) plain flour
2 teaspoons baking powder
1 tablespoon ground cloves
1 tablespoon ground
   cinnamon
250 ml (1 cup) milk

Lemon Icing
185 g (1½ cups) icing sugar,
   sifted
60 ml (¼ cup) lemon juice,
   or as required

Preheat oven to 180°C. Grease and flour a 30 x 21 cm slice tin

Using an electric beater, beat the butter and sugar in a bowl until light and creamy. Add the eggs one at a time, beating well between each. Sift the flour, baking powder and spices into a bowl, then stir into the creamed mixture with the milk.

Spoon the batter into the tin, smoothing the top even. Bake for 12–15 minutes, or until a skewer inserted in the centre comes out clean. Cool slice in the tin.

For the icing, combine the icing sugar and lemon juice in a bowl, stirring well until smooth. Add a little extra lemon juice if required to make a spreadable consistency.

Spread the icing over the cooled cake and let stand until the icing has set. Cut the cake into 5 cm squares.

Oatmeal Apple Pudding

Mrs EG Hooke, Dungog Branch

SERVES 6

2 large granny smith apples, peeled, cored and thinly sliced

75 g (⅓ cup) caster sugar

½ teaspoon ground cinnamon

125 g (½ cup) butter, softened

110 g (½ cup, firmly packed) brown sugar

1 egg

1 teaspoon vanilla essence

75 g (½ cup) plain flour

2 teaspoons baking powder

50 g (½ cup) rolled oats

125 ml (½ cup) milk

Preheat oven to 180°C.

Scatter the apples, caster sugar and cinnamon over the base of a 1.5 litre (6 cup) capacity baking dish.

Using an electric beater, beat the butter and brown sugar in a bowl until light and creamy. Add the egg and vanilla and beat well. Sift the flour and baking powder into a bowl, then stir in the oats. Add to the creamed mixture with the milk, stirring until smooth.

Spread the mixture carefully over the apples.

Bake for 45 minutes, or until golden, cooked in the middle and the apples are bubbling.

Jam Sauce

MAKES ABOUT 1½ CUPS

165 g (½ cup) raspberry jam

1 tablespoon lemon juice, or to taste

250 ml (1 cup) water, plus 1 tablespoon extra

2 teaspoons arrowroot

Combine the jam, lemon juice and water in a saucepan. Bring to a simmer, stirring to dissolve the jam.

Combine the arrowroot with the tablespoon of water in small bowl. Add the arrowroot mixture to the pan, stirring constantly. Cook, stirring to prevent lumps forming, for 1–2 minutes, or until the sauce thickens slightly.

Cool slightly, adding a little more lemon juice to taste, if required.

Serve warm with steamed puddings or other desserts.

Apple Puffs

Mrs Arthur Dubois, Rowena Branch

SERVES 6

150 g (1 cup) self-raising
   flour
50 g butter, chopped
1 egg, well beaten
1 tablespoon water, plus
   250 ml (1 cup) extra
3 large granny smith apples
220 g (1 cup) caster sugar
custard or cream, to serve

Preheat oven to 180°C. Grease a 1.5 litre (6 cup) capacity baking dish.

Place the flour in a bowl. Using your fingertips, rub in half the butter until the mixture resembles breadcrumbs. Add the egg and the tablespoon of water and mix to form a firm dough.

Roll the dough out on a lightly floured surface into a 30 cm square. Cut into six even-sized pieces.

Peel the apples, cut each in half and remove the core. Sprinkle 2 teaspoons of sugar into the core cavity of each apple, then place each apple half cut side up on a piece of pastry. Carefully wrap pastry up and around each apple half to enclose, then place in the dish, flat side up.

Combine the remaining sugar and butter in a saucepan with the water and bring to the boil. Pour into the dish, taking care not to splash the hot syrup over the pastry.

Bake for 30–40 minutes, or until the pastry is golden and the apples are tender.

Serve with custard or cream.

Stuffed Shoulder of Lamb

Mrs H Constable, Yarrabandai Branch

SERVES 8–10

2 lamb kidneys, membrane
  and core removed,
  finely chopped
1 bacon rasher, rind
  removed, chopped
1 tablespoon chopped parsley
1 tablespoon butter
1 egg
60 g (1 cup, lightly packed)
  fresh breadcrumbs
250 ml (1 cup) chicken stock
1 x 2 kg boned and
  butterflied shoulder
  of lamb (see note)

Preheat oven to 190°C.

Combine the kidneys, bacon, parsley, butter, egg, crumbs and stock in a bowl. Season with salt and pepper and mix well.

Press the stuffing evenly over the inside of the lamb shoulder. Roll the lamb up to enclose the stuffing, using kitchen string to tie firmly at 2.5 cm intervals. Place the lamb in a roasting dish and season well with salt and pepper.

Roast the lamb for about 1 hour, or until the juices still run a little pink when pierced with a fine skewer.

Note: Ask your butcher to bone and butterfly the lamb shoulder for you.

Treacle Pudding

Miss Elsie M Purvis, Bonshaw Branch

SERVES 8

150 g (1 cup) plain flour
1 teaspoon bicarbonate
  of soda
1 teaspoon salt
2 tablespoons butter
60 g (⅓ cup) caster sugar
90 g (¼ cup) treacle,
  warmed
250 ml (1 cup) milk
custard, to serve

Serve Treacle Pudding hot with custard.

Bring a large saucepan of water to the boil for steaming, placing a small heatproof plate upside down in the water to keep the pudding basin off the base of the pan. Grease and flour a 1.5 litre (6 cup) capacity pudding basin.

Combine the flour, soda and salt in a bowl. Using your fingertips, rub in the butter until the mixture resembles breadcrumbs. Add the sugar, treacle and milk and stir to mix well.

Spoon the batter into the basin, cover tightly and lower it into the boiling water. Steam for 2 hours, or until cooked through, adding more water to the pan as required.

Bobotee or Baked Curry

Mrs Armstrong, Harbourside Branch

SERVES 4

2 slices day-old bread
75 g butter
2 large onions, peeled and
   finely chopped
2 tablespoon curry powder
4 eggs, well beaten
16 blanched almonds,
   very finely chopped
250 ml (1 cup) milk
500 g minced pork or beef
steamed rice, to serve

Serve the Bobotee hot with steamed rice.

Preheat oven to 180°C. Grease a 1.5 litre (6 cup) capacity baking dish.

Soak the bread in water in a bowl. Drain the bread well, squeezing out as much water as possible.

Heat the butter in a frying pan over medium heat. Add the onion and cook, stirring often, for 5–6 minutes, or until softened. Add the curry powder and cook for another 1–2 minutes. Stand to cool a little.

Crumble the bread into a large bowl. Add the onion mixture with the eggs, almonds, milk and minced meat and mix well. Spoon the mixture into the dish.

Bake for 50–60 minutes, or until the juices run clear when the Bobotee is pierced in the middle.

Apple and Celery Sandwiches

Mrs Waddell, Merriwa Branch

SERVES 4

2 pink lady or granny smith
   apples, peeled, cored
   and finely chopped
2 stalks of celery, trimmed
   and finely chopped
2 tablespoons mayonnaise
8 brown bread slices,
   buttered

Combine the apples, celery and mayonnaise in a bowl and season with salt and pepper. Stir to mix well.

Spoon the mixture onto half of the bread slices, spreading to cover evenly. Top with the remaining bread slices and remove the crusts.

Cut the sandwiches into fingers and serve.

Baked Apple Pudding

Mrs TL Badgery, Bowral Branch

SERVES 6–8

225 g (1½ cup) plain flour
1½ teaspoons baking
    powder
2 tablespoons butter
80 ml (⅓ cup) milk
2 granny smith apples,
    peeled, cored and finely
    chopped
45 g (¼ cup) sultanas
1 tablespoon brown sugar
large pinch of ground
    cloves
1 teaspoon finely grated
    lemon zest
180 g caster sugar
250 ml (1 cup) boiling
    water

Preheat oven to 170°C.

Combine the flour and baking powder in a bowl. Using your fingertips, rub in half the butter. Add the milk and stir to form a coarse dough.

Turn the dough out onto a lightly floured surface and knead briefly until it comes together – take care not to overwork it or the dough will be tough. Roll out into a 24 x 18 cm rectangle.

Combine the apples, sultanas, brown sugar, cloves and lemon zest in a bowl and mix well. Spread the apple mixture over the dough and roll up to form a log. Place the log seam side down in a 1.5 litre (6 cup) capacity baking dish.

Combine the caster sugar, the remaining butter and the boiling water in a saucepan and bring to the boil. Pour the syrup over the pudding.

Bake for 1 hour, or until the pudding is golden and the syrup is bubbling.

Cup Cake

Mrs T Beasley, Dubbo Branch

MAKES ONE 20 CM CAKE
125 g (½ cup) butter,
  softened
220 g (1 cup) caster sugar
4 eggs
1½ teaspoons vanilla essence
½ teaspoon ground nutmeg
375 g (2½ cup) plain flour
2 teaspoons baking powder
140 g (1 cup) currants
170 g (1 cup) sultanas
250 ml (1 cup) milk

Preheat oven to 180°C. Line a 20 cm round cake tin with baking paper.

Using an electric beater, beat the butter and sugar in a large bowl until light and creamy. Add the eggs, one at a time, beating well between each. Stir in the vanilla.

Sift the nutmeg, flour and baking powder into a bowl. Stir into the butter mixture with the dried fruit and milk to combine well. Spoon the batter into the tin, smoothing the top even.

Bake for 1½ hours, or until a skewer inserted in the centre comes out clean. Cool the cake in the tin for 30 minutes, then turn out onto a wire rack to cool.

Pearl Cake

Mrs GS Hill, Wingham Branch

MAKES ONE 20 CM CAKE
125 g (½ cup) butter,
  softened
220 g (1 cup) caster sugar
1 teaspoon vanilla essence
125 ml (½ cup) milk
150 g (1 cup) plain flour
125 g (1 cup) cornflour
2 teaspoons baking powder
3 egg whites

Preheat oven to 180°C. Lightly grease and flour a 20 cm cake tin.

Using an electric beater, beat the butter and sugar in a bowl until light and creamy. Stir in the vanilla and the milk. Sift the flour, cornflour and baking powder into a bowl, then stir into the creamed mixture.

Using clean beaters, whisk the egg whites in a bowl until firm peaks form and fold gently into the creamed mixture. Spoon the batter into the tin, smoothing the top even.

Bake for 30 minutes, or until a skewer inserted in the centre comes out clean.

Cool in the tin for 10 minutes, then turn out onto a covered rack to cool completely.

Steamed Sago Plum Pudding

Mrs F Pabst, Holbrook Branch

SERVES 6

65 g (⅓ cup) sago
275 ml milk
1 tablespoon melted butter
2 eggs, well beaten
120 g (2 cups, lightly packed)
    fresh breadcrumbs
170 g (1 cup) sultanas
110 g (½ cup) caster sugar
1 teaspoon bicarbonate
    of soda
custard, ice cream or
    whipped cream, to serve

Place sago in a large bowl, pour over 250 ml (1 cup) of the milk then cover the bowl and refrigerate overnight.

Bring a large saucepan of water for steaming to the boil, placing a small heatproof plate upside down in the water in the pan to keep the pudding basin off the base. Lightly grease and flour a 1.5 litre (6 cup) capacity pudding basin.

Stir the melted butter, eggs, crumbs, sultanas and sugar into the sago mixture in the bowl. Stir the soda into the remaining milk then add to the mixture and stir well. Spoon into the basin then cover tightly. Steam for 3 hours, adding more water as required.

Serve hot, with custard, ice cream or whipped cream.

John Bull Biscuits

Mrs CL Griffith, Albury Branch

MAKES 30

220 g (1 cup) caster sugar
180 g butter, softened
2 eggs
1 teaspoon vanilla essence
225 g (2⅓ cups) rolled oats
2½ teaspoons baking
    powder

Preheat oven to 180°C. Line a baking tray with baking paper.

Using an electric beater, beat the butter and sugar in a bowl until light and creamy. Add the eggs, one at a time, beating well between each. Add the vanilla, oats and baking powder, stirring to combine well.

Roll tablespoons of the mixture into balls and place on the tray, leaving room between each for spreading.

Bake the biscuits for 10–12 minutes, or until golden. Transfer to a wire rack to cool.

Mysteries

Mrs CE Archer, Canowindra Branch

MAKES ABOUT 24
1 egg, well beaten
110 g (½ cup) caster sugar
1 teaspoon vanilla essence
145 g (1½ cup) rolled oats
1 tablespoon melted butter

Preheat oven to 180°C. Line a baking tray with baking paper.

Combine the egg, sugar, vanilla and pinch of salt in a bowl and beat to mix well. Add the oats and melted butter and stir to combine.

Drop heaped teaspoons of the mixture onto the tray, leaving room between each for spreading.

Bake for 12–15 minutes, or until light golden. Transfer to a wire rack to cool.

Chocolate Sponge

Mrs GS Hill, Wingham Branch

MAKES ONE 17 CM CAKE
1 tablespoon butter,
  softened
220 g (1 cup) caster sugar
2 eggs
1 tablespoon cocoa powder
125 ml (½ cup) milk
185 g (1¼ cups) plain flour
1 teaspoon baking powder

Filling
120 g (1 cup) icing sugar
1 teaspoon cocoa powder
1 tablespoon butter,
  softened
1 tablespoon milk
boiling water, as required

Preheat oven to 170°C. Grease and flour two 17 cm cake tins.

Using an electric beater, beat the butter and sugar in a bowl until well combined Add the eggs one at a time, beating well between each. Dissolve the cocoa with the milk in a cup.

Sift the flour and baking powder into a bowl. Add the cocoa and sifted flour to the egg mixture, then stir to combine well. Spoon the batter into the tins, smoothing the tops even.

Bake for 18–20 minutes, or until a skewer inserted in the centre comes out clean. Cool the cakes in the tins for 10 minutes, then turn out onto wire racks to cool.

For the filling, sift the icing sugar and cocoa into a bowl. Add the butter and milk, stirring to combine well. Add enough boiling water to form a thick, smooth icing.

Spread the icing over one cake, top with the other cake and serve.

Shortbread Creams

Mrs McAlister, Finley Branch

MAKES 48
155 g butter, softened
165 g (¾ cup) caster sugar
2 eggs
450 g (3 cups) plain flour
1 teaspoon baking powder
2 teaspoons cream of
  tartar

Icing
125 g (1 cup) icing sugar
1 tablespoon cocoa powder
1 tablespoon butter,
  softened
1 tablespoon milk
1 teaspoon vanilla essence

Preheat oven to 180°C. Line two baking trays with baking paper.

Using an electric beater, beat the butter and sugar until light and creamy. Add the eggs one at a time, beating well between each. Sift the flour, baking powder and tartar into a bowl, then stir into the creamed mixture to form a coarse dough.

Roll the dough out on a floured surface to 4 mm thickness. Using a 5 cm round pastry cutter, cut rounds from the dough, re-rolling scraps for more rounds. Place on the trays.

Bake for 12–15 minutes, or until light golden. Transfer to a wire rack to cool.

For the icing, sift the icing sugar and cocoa into a bowl. Using an electric beater, beat the butter and the sifted mixture until light and creamy. Add the milk and vanilla and beat well.

Spread half the biscuits with icing. Top with the remaining biscuits, pressing together to join.

Nutties

Mrs CA Lamont, Wagga Branch

MAKES ABOUT 35
190 g (2 cups) rolled oats
110 g (¾ cup) plain flour
90 g (¾ cup) chopped walnuts
110 g (½ cup) caster sugar
125 g (½ cup) butter, melted
1 teaspoon honey
½ teaspoon bicarbonate
  of soda
2 tablespoons boiling water

Preheat oven to 180°C. Line a baking tray with baking paper.

Combine the oats, flour, walnuts and sugar in a bowl and stir to mix well. Stir in the butter and honey. Dissolve the soda in the boiling water in a cup and add to the mixture. Drop heaped teaspoons of the mixture on the tray, leaving room for spreading.

Bake for 12–15 minutes, or until firm and light golden. Transfer to a wire rack to cool.

Family recipes

Family recipes

		1 Egg Custard	2 Mint Jelly	3 Cheese Fondue
4 Chicken en Casserole	5 Alpine Pudding	6 Coconut Buns	7 Sausage Muffins	8 Cheese and Celery Pie
9 Gingerbread No 1	10 Prize Scones	11 Almond Cheese Cakes	12 Rolled Oats Shortbread	13 Signora Cake
14 Bran Muffins	15 Velvet Cake	16 Narua Cake	17 Banbury Tart	18 Mungindi Roly Poly
19 Lemon Tart	20 Chocolate Pudding	21 Thatched Pudding	22 Dandy Pudding	23 Pumpkin Cake
24 Savoury Supreme	25 Raspberry Slice	26 Sultana Cake	27 Coconut Biscuits	28 Rich Pound Cake
29 Date Loaf	30 Plum Cake			

SEPTEMBER

Egg Custard

MAKES ABOUT 4 CUPS
600 ml milk
4 eggs, beaten well
1 teaspoon vanilla essence
55 g (¼ cup) caster sugar

Heat the milk over boiling water in a double boiler.

Stir in the remaining ingredients then, stirring constantly to avoid curdling, cook for about 8–10 minutes, or until the mixture thickens enough to coat the back of a spoon. Strain into a serving bowl.

Serve the custard hot, poured over steamed puddings and other desserts, or with stewed fruit.

Mint Jelly

Mrs WB Studdy, Nth Sydney Branch

MAKES ABOUT 3 CUPS
220 g (1 cup) caster sugar
300 ml white vinegar
60 g (5 tablespoons)
   powdered gelatine
125 ml (½ cup) water
170 g (3⅓ cups) chopped
   mint

Combine the sugar and vinegar in a small saucepan and bring to a simmer, stirring to dissolve the sugar.

Sprinkle the gelatine over the water in a small cup and stand for 5 minutes, or until the gelatine softens. Add to the hot vinegar mixture then stir over low heat, until the gelatine dissolves.

Remove from the heat, stir in the chopped mint and cool to room temperature.

Pour the jelly into a bowl and refrigerate for 3–4 hours, or until set.

Mint Jelly is the ideal condiment to serve with roasted or grilled lamb.

Cheese Fondue

3 SEP

Mrs Hollingsworth, Rylstone Branch

SERVES 6

300 ml milk

60 g (1 cup, lightly packed) fresh breadcrumbs

100 g (1 cup) grated cheddar cheese

60 g (¼ cup) butter, chopped

2 eggs, separated

large pinch of cayenne pepper

Preheat oven to 180°C. Grease a 1.5 litre (6 cup) capacity baking dish.

Place the milk in a small saucepan and bring just to a simmer. Pour the milk over the breadcrumbs in a bowl. Add the cheese, butter and egg yolks.

Using an electric beater, whisk the egg whites in a bowl until firm peaks form. Fold the whites into the crumb mixture, season with salt and pepper and add the cayenne. Spoon the mixture into the dish.

Bake for 30 minutes, or until golden and set.

Chicken en Casserole

4 SEP

Mrs EM Widdison, Yathella Branch

SERVES 4–6

1.5 kg chicken pieces

flour, for dusting

2 tablespoons butter

1 onion, thinly sliced

2 carrots, peeled and thinly sliced

2 parsnips, peeled and thinly sliced

2 potatoes, peeled and thinly sliced

Preheat oven to 180°C.

Dust the chicken lightly with flour in a bowl, shaking off any excess.

Melt the butter in a casserole dish and add the chicken. Season well with salt and pepper. Layer each vegetable over the chicken, finishing with the potatoes.

Baked, covered, for 1½ hours. Remove the lid and bake for a further 10 minutes, or until the potatoes are golden.

Alpine Pudding

Mrs TR McCracken, Harefield

SERVES 8

240 g (4 cups, lightly packed) fresh breadcrumbs

500 ml (2 cups) milk

2 eggs, separated

55 g (¼ cup) caster sugar, plus extra, for sprinkling

1 teaspoon vanilla essence

85 g (¼ cup) raspberry or other jam

Preheat oven to 180°C. Grease a 1 litre (4 cup) capacity baking dish.

Place the crumbs in the dish. Bring the milk nearly to a simmer in a saucepan. Combine the hot milk in a bowl with the yolks, half the sugar and the vanilla. Pour over the crumb mixture.

Bake for 30 minutes, or until set. Remove from the oven and, while hot, spread the jam over.

Using an electric beater, whisk the egg whites in a bowl until firm peaks form. Gradually add the remaining sugar and a pinch of salt and whisk until the sugar has dissolved and the mixture is thick and glossy. Spoon the whites over the pudding and sprinkle with a little extra sugar.

Bake for 20 minutes, or until the meringue is light golden.

Coconut Buns

MAKES 18

450 g (3 cups) plain flour

1 teaspoon bicarbonate of soda

2 teaspoons cream of tartar

1 tablespoon caster sugar

90 g (1 cup) desiccated coconut

60 ml (¼ cup) milk, or as required

Preheat oven to 180°C. Line a baking tray with baking paper.

Sift the flour, soda and tartar into a bowl. Stir in the sugar, coconut and the milk and stir to form a dough with a heavy dropping consistency, adding a little more milk if required.

Drop tablespoons of the mixture onto the tray, allowing room for spreading.

Bake for 15–20 minutes, or until golden. Transfer to a wire rack to cool.

Sausage Muffins

Mrs CA Lamont, Wagga Branch

MAKES ABOUT 24

375 g (2½ cups) plain flour
½ teaspoon salt
2 teaspoons baking powder
80 g butter, chopped
60 ml (¼ cup) milk, or as
  required
500 g sausage meat
melted butter, for brushing

Preheat oven to 180°C. Line a baking tray with baking paper.

Sift the flour, salt and the baking powder into a bowl. Using your fingertips, rub in the butter until the mixture resembles breadcrumbs. Add the milk and stir to form a soft dough, adding a little more milk if required.

Roll the dough out on a floured surface to 1 cm thickness. Using a 7 cm round pastry cutter, cut rounds out of the dough. Place 1 tablespoon of the meat mixture in the middle of half the rounds and brush the edges lightly with water. Top with another round and press the edges to seal. Repeat until done. Place on the tray and brush the tops with melted butter.

Bake for 30 minutes, or until golden and cooked through. Serve hot.

Cheese and Celery Pie

Mrs Messiter, Bowral Branch

SERVES 4

80 g (1⅓ cup, lightly packed)
  fresh breadcrumbs
130 g (1⅓ cup) grated
  cheddar cheese
125 ml (½ cup) milk
150 g (1 cup) cooked
  chopped celery
1 onion, finely chopped
1 egg, beaten well

Preheat oven to 180°C. Grease a 22 cm pie dish.

Place 1 cup of the crumbs, 1 cup of the cheese and the remaining ingredients in a bowl. Stir to combine well.

Spoon the mixture into the dish, smoothing the top even. Scatter over the remaining crumbs and cheese.

Bake for 25–30 minutes, or until golden and set. Serve hot or cold.

Gingerbread No 1

Mrs Kennedy, Wagga Branch

MAKES ONE 20 CM CAKE

250 g (1 cup) milk

350 g (1 cup) treacle

250 g (1 cup) butter,
   softened

220 g (1 cup) caster sugar

3 eggs

450 g (3 cups) plain flour

1 teaspoon bicarbonate
   of soda

1 teaspoon mixed spice

2 tablespoons ground
   ginger

Preheat oven to 180°C. Line a 20 cm square cake tin with baking paper.

Place the milk and treacle in a saucepan and stir over low heat until combined well. Remove from the heat and cool slightly.

Using an electric beater, beat the butter and sugar until light and creamy. Add the eggs, one at a time, beating well between each. Sift the dry ingredients into a bowl, then stir into the butter mixture. Add the milk mixture, stirring until smooth. Spoon the batter into the tin.

Bake for 1 hour, or until a skewer inserted in the centre comes out clean. Cool the gingerbread in the tin.

Prize Scones

Mrs HC Smith, Kentucky Branch

10 SEP

MAKES ABOUT 15

300 g (2 cups) plain flour

2 teaspoons baking powder

250 ml (1 cup) pouring
   cream

125 ml (½ cup) milk, or as
   required, plus extra,
   for brushing

Preheat oven to 200°C. Grease and flour a baking tray.

Sift the flour and baking powder into a bowl. Using a flat-bladed knife, mix in a pinch of salt, the cream and enough milk to make a soft dough, adding a little more milk if required.

Turn the dough out onto a lightly floured surface and roll out to about 4 cm thickness. Using a 6 cm round pastry cutter, cut rounds from the dough. Place the rounds on the tray, leaving room for spreading. Brush the tops with a little milk.

Bake for 12–15 minutes, or until risen and golden. Transfer to a wire rack. Serve warm.

Gingerbread No 1 — Mrs Kennedy, Wagga Branch — 9 SEP

Prize Scones — Mrs HC Smith, Kentucky Branch — 10 SEP

186

Almond Cheese Cakes

Mrs Arthur Martin, Wagga Branch

MAKES 24

2 egg whites, beaten well
100 g (1 cup) almond meal
165 g (¾ cup) caster sugar
½ teaspoon almond essence
165 g (½ cup) raspberry jam

Pastry
250 g (1⅔ cup) plain flour
½ teaspoons cream of
  tartar
¼ teaspoon bicarbonate
  of soda
250 g (1 cup) chilled butter,
  chopped
110 g (½ cup) caster sugar
2 egg yolks

Preheat oven to 180°C. Grease two 12-hole round-bottomed patty tins.

For the pastry, sift the flour, tartar and soda into a bowl. Using your fingertips, rub in the butter until the mixture resembles breadcrumbs. Stir in the sugar and egg yolks.

Turn the dough out onto a floured surface and knead briefly until it comes together. Wrap the pastry in plastic wrap and chill for 30 minutes.

Roll out to 5 mm thickness. Using a round 6 cm pastry cutter, cut rounds out of the pastry and use to line the patty holes. Prick the pastry bases and bake for 5–10 minutes.

Combine the egg whites, almond meal, sugar and almond essence in a bowl and stir well. Place 1 teaspoon of jam in each pastry case and spoon filling on top.

Return cakes to oven and bake a further 5 minutes, or until filling is set.

Rolled Oats Shortbread

Miss B Wilson, Neutral Bay

MAKES 30

225 g (2⅓ cups) rolled
  oats
55 g (¼ cup) caster sugar
125 ml (½ cup) boiling
  water

Preheat oven to 180°C. Lightly grease a 28 × 18 cm slice tin.

Combine the oats and sugar in a bowl, pour over the boiling water and stir to combine well. Using your hands, press the mixture into the tin.

Bake for 30 minutes, or until light golden. Cool a little and, while still warm, cut shortbread into fingers. Leave to cool completely in the tin before removing.

Signora Cake

MAKES ONE 18 CM CAKE
115 g butter, softened
220 g (1 cup) caster sugar
2 eggs, separated
260 g (1¾ cups) self-raising
  flour
1 teaspoon ground
  cinnamon
125 ml (½ cup) milk
½ teaspoon vanilla
  essence

Vanilla Butter Cream Icing
200 g butter, softened
250 g (2 cups) sifted icing
  sugar
2½ tablespoons milk,
  or as required
1 teaspoon vanilla
  essence

Preheat oven to 180°C. Lightly grease and flour two 18 cm cake tins.

Using an electric beater, beat the butter and sugar in a bowl until light and creamy. Beat in the egg yolks. Sift the flour and cinnamon into a bowl, then stir into the creamed mixture in batches, alternating with the milk. Stir in the vanilla.

Using clean beaters, whisk the egg whites in a bowl until firm peaks form. Gently fold into the mixture. Spoon the batter into the tins, smoothing the tops even.

Bake for 15–20 minutes, or until a skewer inserted in the centre comes out clean. Cool the cakes in the tins for 10 minutes, then turn out onto a wire rack to cool completely.

For the butter cream, place all the ingredients in a bowl and, using an electric beater or a wooden spoon, beat for 5 minutes, or until smooth and fluffy.

Spread butter cream over one cake – you will not need it all. Top with the other cake and spread any remaining cream over the top.

Bran Muffins

Mrs DG Munro, Nevertire Branch

MAKES 6
1 tablespoon butter, melted
1½ tablespoons honey
1 egg
75 g (½ cup) plain flour
½ teaspoon bicarbonate
  of soda
1 teaspoon baking powder
35 g (½ cup) bran
2 tablespoons milk, or as
  required

Preheat oven to 180°C. Grease a 6-hole 60 ml (⅓ cup) capacity muffin tin.

Mix the butter, honey and egg in a bowl to combine well. Sift the flour, a pinch of salt, the soda and baking powder into a bowl and add it to the butter mixture. Add the bran and enough milk to form a thick batter. Spoon the batter into the tin.

Bake for 25–30 minutes, or until a skewer inserted in the centres comes out clean. Turn out onto a covered rack to cool.

Velvet Cake

15 SEP

Mrs Douglas Mackellar, Leeton

MAKES ONE 20 CM CAKE
250 g (1 cup) butter,
  softened
220 g (1 cup) caster sugar
4 eggs
½ teaspoon bicarbonate
  of soda
60 ml (¼ cup) water
1 teaspoons cream of tartar
500 g (3⅓ cups) plain flour

Preheat oven to 180°C. Lightly grease and flour a 20 cm cake tin.

Using an electric beater, beat the butter and sugar in a bowl until light and creamy. Add the eggs, one at a time, beating well between each. Dissolve the soda in the water in a cup and add to the creamed mixture.

Sift the tartar and flour into a bowl, then stir into the mixture. Beat for a further 3 minutes. Spoon the batter into the tin, smoothing the top even.

Bake for 30–40 minutes, or until a skewer inserted in the centre comes out clean. Turn out onto a covered rack to cool.

Narua Cake

Mrs A Seccombe, Wagga Branch

MAKES ONE 20 CM CAKE
250 g (1 cup) butter,
    softened
220 g (1 cup) caster sugar
3 eggs
300 g (2 cups) self-raising
    flour
2 tablespoons cocoa
1 teaspoon mixed spice
125 ml (½ cup) milk
250 g (2 cups) chopped
    walnuts, plus extra, for
    decorating

Chocolate Honey Icing
250 g (2 cups) icing sugar
1 tablespoon cocoa powder
1 tablespoon butter, softened
2 tablespoons honey
boiling water, as required

Preheat oven to 180°C. Grease and flour
a 20 cm cake tin.

Using an electric beater, beat the butter
and sugar in a bowl until light and creamy.
Add the eggs, one at a time, beating well
between each. Sift the flour, cocoa and
spice into a bowl, then stir into the creamed
mixture with the milk and the walnuts.
Spoon the batter into the tin, smoothing
the top even.

Bake for 30–40 minutes, or until a skewer
inserted in the centre comes out clean. Cool
the cake in the tin for 15 minutes, then turn
out onto a wire rack to cool completely.

For the icing, sift the icing sugar and cocoa
into a bowl. Add the butter, honey and
enough boiling water to mix into a thick,
smooth icing.

When the cake is cool, cover it with
chocolate icing and decorate with the
extra walnut pieces.

Banbury Tart

Miss Valerie Holcombe, Burren Junction Branch

MAKES ONE 20 CM TART

170 g (1 cup) chopped raisins
220 g (1 cup) caster sugar
30 g (¼ cup) plain buttercake
   or sponge cake crumbs
1 egg, beaten
1 tablespoon melted butter
juice and grated zest of
   1 lemon

Shortcrust Pastry
300 g (2 cups) plain flour
1 teaspoon baking powder
140 g chilled butter, grated
iced water, as required

For the pastry, sift the flour and baking powder into a bowl. Divide the butter into thirds. Rub one third of the butter into the dry ingredients, then add enough iced water to form a firm dough.

Turn the dough out onto a lightly floured surface. Roll it into a 20 × 18 cm rectangle. Using another third of the butter, dot pieces of butter over two-thirds of the dough. Fold the third with no butter over to the middle of the rectangle, then fold the other end over the top of that. Roll the pastry out again to the same sized rectangle as before and repeat the process with the remaining butter, folding the pastry in the same way. Wrap in plastic wrap and chill for 30 minutes.

Preheat oven to 190°C.

Divide the dough in two, making one piece slightly larger than the other. Roll the larger piece out to cover the base and side of a 20 cm tart tin.

Place the raisins, sugar, cake crumbs, egg, melted butter, lemon juice and grated zest in a bowl and stir to combine. Spoon the filling into the pastry case.

Roll out the remaining pastry to fit over the tart. Trim the edges, crimping with a fork to seal.

Bake for 30 minutes, or until the pastry is golden.

Mungindi Roly Poly

Miss Nan Bellamey, Mungundi Branch

SERVES 6–8

450 g (3 cups) plain flour
1 teaspoon bicarbonate
  of soda
2 teaspoons cream of tartar
2 tablespoons butter, chopped
2 granny smith apples,
  peeled, cored and thinly
  sliced

Sauce
330 g (1½ cups) caster sugar
115 g butter, chopped
500 ml (2 cups) boiling water

Preheat oven to 180°C. Lightly grease
a 24 × 18 cm baking dish.

Sift the flour, soda and tartar into a bowl.
Using your fingertips, rub in the butter until
the mixture resembles breadcrumbs. Add
enough water to make a soft dough.

Turn the dough out onto a lightly floured
surface and roll out to a 38 × 30 cm rectangle.
Scatter the apples over the dough. Starting
from a long edge, roll up to form a log. Place
the log in the dish, seam side down.

For the sauce, combine the sugar and
butter in a bowl, pour over the boiling water
and stir until the sugar has dissolved and the
butter has melted. Pour over the roly poly.

Bake for 1 hour, or until the pudding is
cooked and the sauce is thick and bubbling.

Lemon Tart

Mrs Jean Lamont, Younger Set, Wagga Branch

19 SEP

SERVES 6

60 g (¼ cup) butter, chopped
1 tablespoon caster sugar, plus extra, for sprinkling
1 egg, separated
125 ml (½ cup) water
1 teaspoon cornflour
juice and grated zest of 1 lemon

Pastry
300 g (2 cups) plain flour
½ teaspoon baking powder
125 g (½ cup) chilled butter, chopped
iced water, as required

For the pastry, combine the flour and baking powder in a bowl. Add the butter and rub in until the mixture resembles breadcrumbs. Add enough iced water to form a firm dough.

Knead briefly until the dough comes together. Form into a disc, wrap in plastic wrap and refrigerate for 30 minutes, or until firm.

Preheat oven to 180°C.

Roll out the pastry on a floured surface to fit the base and side of a 22 cm pie dish. Line the dish with the pastry, trimming the edges even. Prick the pastry all over with a fork and bake for 20 minutes.

Combine the butter, caster sugar, egg yolk and water in a saucepan. Combine the cornflour with the lemon juice in a cup and stir until smooth. Add to the pan with the grated zest. Stirring constantly, cook over medium heat until the mixture boils and thickens. Pour into the pastry case.

Using an electric beater, whisk the egg whites until firm peaks form. Spoon the whites over the lemon filling. Sprinkle with a little caster sugar.

Bake for 18–20 minutes, or until the meringue is lightly browned.

193

Chocolate Pudding

Mrs Heyde, Eastwood-Epping Branch

20 SEP

SERVES 6

125 g dark chocolate, chopped
150 ml milk
125 g caster sugar
125 g (½ cup) butter, softened
2 eggs, separated
180 g (3 cups, lightly packed) fresh breadcrumbs

Bring a large saucepan of water to the boil for steaming, placing a small heatproof plate upside down in the water to keep the pudding basin off the base of the pan. Lightly grease a 1.5 litre (6 cup) capacity pudding basin.

Combine the chocolate and milk in a small saucepan and heat, stirring often, over medium–low heat, until the chocolate has melted and the mixture is smooth. Remove from the heat and cool slightly.

Using an electric beater, beat the sugar and butter in a bowl until light and creamy. Stir in the yolks, breadcrumbs and chocolate mixture.

Using clean beaters, whisk the egg whites in a bowl until firm peaks form. Fold into the pudding batter.

Spoon the batter into the basin, cover tightly and lower it into the boiling water. Steam for 1 hour, or until cooked through, adding more water to the pan as required.

Thatched Pudding

21 SEP

Miss Ursula Barton, Wellington Branch

SERVES 6

125 g (½ cup) butter
2 tablespoons plain flour
300 ml milk
2 tablespoons sugar
finely grated zest of 1 lemon
4 eggs, separated

Preheat oven to 180°C. Grease a 1.5 litre (6 cup) capacity baking dish.

Melt the butter in a saucepan over medium heat. Add the flour and a little of the milk and stir to form a smooth paste. Gradually add the remaining milk, stirring constantly, until the mixture boils and thickens. Remove from the heat, then add the sugar and lemon zest. Cool slightly.

Beat the egg yolks in a bowl and add a little of the hot milk mixture. Stir to combine well, then add to the mixture in the pan.

Using an electric beater, whisk the egg whites until firm peaks form. Gently fold into the milk mixture, then pour into the baking dish.

Bake for 20 minutes, or until golden. Serve immediately.

Dandy Pudding

22 SEP

Mrs RJ Boyle, Wee Waa Branch

SERVES 4–6

600 ml milk
1½ teaspoons finely grated
   orange zest
1½ teaspoons finely grated
   lemon zest
1 tablespoon butter, softened
75 g (⅓ cup) caster sugar
2 eggs
1½ tablespoons plain flour
1½ teaspoons vanilla essence

Preheat oven to 180°C. Grease a 1.5 litre (6 cup) capacity baking dish.

Place milk in a saucepan and bring to the boil. Add the orange and lemon zest and stir to combine. Set aside.

Using an electric beater, beat the butter and sugar in a bowl until well combined. Add the eggs, flour and vanilla and beat until smooth. Add the milk mixture and stir to combine well. Pour the mixture into the baking dish.

Bake for 15–20 minutes, or until just set. Serve hot or cold.

Pumpkin Cake

Mrs WH Keating, Quambone Branch

MAKES TWO 23 CM CAKES
500 g (2 cups) butter, softened
660 g (3 cups) caster sugar
625 g (2½ cups) warm
  mashed pumpkin
4 eggs, beaten
600 g (4 cups) plain flour,
  or as required
3 teaspoons bicarbonate
  of soda
250 ml (1 cup) milk
1 tablespoon mixed spice
1 tablespoon treacle
3 teaspoons vanilla essence
385 g (2¼ cups) sultanas
385 g (2¼ cups) raisins
280 g (2 cups) currants
500 g pitted dates, chopped
120 g (¾ cup) mixed peel

Preheat oven to 150°C. Line two 23 cm cake tins with several layers of baking paper.

Using an electric beater, beat the butter and sugar in a bowl until light and creamy. Add the mashed pumpkin and stir in the eggs.

Sift the flour into a bowl then add 150 g (1 cup) of flour to the creamed mixture. Dissolve the soda in the milk in a cup, then stir into the mixture with the spice, treacle and vanilla. Add the fruit with the remaining flour, adding a little extra flour if the mixture seems thin – it should have a heavy dropping consistency. Spoon the batter into the tins, smoothing the tops even.

Bake for 1½–2 hours, or until a skewer inserted in the centre comes out clean. Cool the cakes in the tins for 30 minutes, then turn out onto a wire rack to cool completely.

Savoury Supreme

MAKES 24
200 g ham, finely chopped
2 tablespoons chopped
  walnuts
90 g (⅓ cup) mango chutney
50 g purchased honey-
  mustard sauce, or to taste
50 g butter, softened
6 slices of bread, toasted
60 g cheddar cheese, sliced

Preheat oven to 180°C.

Combine the ham, walnuts, chutney, honey-mustard sauce and butter in a bowl. Season to taste with salt and pepper and stir to combine well.

Spoon the mixture onto toast slices and spread evenly to cover. Top with the cheese and cut each slice into quarters.

Place on an oven tray and bake for 15 minutes, or until the cheese is bubbling. Serve immediately.

Raspberry Slice

25 SEP

Mrs E McDowall, Braidwood Branch

MAKES ABOUT 28

125 g (½ cup) butter, softened
385 g (1¾ cups) caster sugar
2 eggs
300 g (2 cups) self-raising flour
165 g (½ cup) raspberry jam
90 g (1 cup) desiccated coconut

Preheat oven to 180°C. Grease and flour a 28 × 18 cm slice tin.

Using an electric beater, beat the butter and 180 g (¾ cup) of the sugar in a bowl until light and creamy. Add one egg and beat to combine well. Stir in the flour.

Press the mixture evenly over the base of the tin. Spread the jam over. Combine the coconut with the remaining sugar and egg in a bowl and sprinkle the mixture over the jam.

Bake for 20 minutes, or until the base is cooked through and the top is golden. Cool slice in the tin. Using a sharp knife, cut into squares or rectangles.

Sultana Cake

26 SEP

Mrs Hugh A Jones, Warren Branch

MAKES ONE 20 CM CAKE

250 g (1 cup) butter, softened
250 g caster sugar
3 eggs
350 g (2⅓ cup) plain flour, plus extra, as required
1 teaspoon baking powder
125 ml (½ cup) milk
255 g (1½ cups) sultanas
60 g blanched almonds, chopped
55 g (⅓ cup) mixed peel

Preheat oven to 180°C. Line a 20 cm cake tin with baking paper.

Using an electric beater, beat the butter and sugar in a bowl until light and creamy. Add the eggs, one at a time, beating well between each.

Sift the flour and baking powder into a bowl. Stir into the creamed mixture with the milk. Coat the sultanas in a little extra flour – this will stop them sinking to the bottom of the cake – then stir them into the mixture with the almonds and peel. Spoon the batter into the tin, smoothing the top even.

Bake for 1¼ hours, or until a skewer inserted in the centre comes out clean. Cool the cake in the tin for 20 minutes, then turn out onto a wire rack to cool completely.

Coconut Biscuits

MAKES ABOUT 40
500 g (2 cups) butter, softened
440 g (2 cups) caster sugar
1 egg
500 g (3⅓ cup) plain flour
1 teaspoon bicarbonate
   of soda
2 teaspoons cream of tartar
85 g (1 cup) desiccated
   coconut
1½ teaspoons vanilla
   essence

Preheat oven to 180°C. Line two baking trays with baking paper.

Using an electric beater, beat the butter and sugar in a bowl until light and creamy. Add the egg and beat to combine well. Sift the flour, soda and tartar into a bowl then stir into the creamed mixture with the coconut and vanilla.

Using lightly floured hands, roll tablespoons of the mixture into balls and place on the trays, leaving room for spreading.

Bake for 10–15 minutes, or until golden. Transfer to wire racks to cool.

Rich Pound Cake

Miss Murray, Manildra Branch

MAKES TWO 23 CM CAKES
600 g butter, softened
500 g caster sugar
12 eggs
750 g plain flour
3 teaspoons mixed spice
250 g almond meal
1 teaspoon salt
250 g mixed peel
750 g raisins
750 g currants
125 ml (½ cup) brandy

Preheat oven to 140°C. Line two deep 28 cm cake tins with several layers of baking paper.

Using an electric beater, beat the butter and sugar in a bowl until light and creamy. Add the eggs, one at a time, beating well between each.

Sift the flour and mixed spice into a bowl. Stir the flour mixture and the almond meal into the creamed mixture. Add the salt, dried fruits and brandy and stir well. Spoon the batter into the tins, smoothing the top even.

Bake for 5 hours, or until a skewer inserted in the centres comes out clean – cover the tops with baking paper if the cakes brown too much. Cool the cakes in the tins.

Date Loaf

Mrs J Mackellar, Braidwood Branch

MAKES I LOAF

450 g (3 cups) plain flour
I tablespoon butter
3 teaspoons baking powder
165 g (¾ cup) caster sugar
120 g (¾ cup) pitted dates,
  chopped
I egg
250 ml (I cup) milk

Preheat oven to 170°C. Grease and flour a 24 × 13 × 6 cm loaf tin.

Place the flour in a bowl then, using your fingertips, rub in the butter. Stir in the baking powder and sugar. Add the dates, egg and milk and stir to mix well. Spoon the batter into the tin, smoothing the top even.

Bake for 35–40 minutes, or until a skewer inserted in the centre comes out clean. Cool the loaf in the tin, then turn out onto a covered rack to cool completely.

Plum Cake

Mrs McLeish, Quambone Branch

MAKES TWO 25 CM CAKES

500 g (2 cups) butter, softened
440 g (2 cups) caster sugar
8 eggs
125 g golden syrup
I nutmeg, freshly grated
I teaspoon ground ginger
I teaspoon mixed spice
I kg (6⅔ cups) plain flour
½ teaspoon bicarbonate
  of soda
1.5 kg sultanas
125 g (¾ cup) mixed peel
90 g blanched almonds,
  chopped
125 ml (½ cup) brandy
3 teaspoons vanilla essence

Preheat oven to 150°C. Line two 25 cm cake tins with several layers of baking paper.

Using an electric beater, beat the butter and sugar in a bowl until light and creamy. Add the eggs, one at a time, beating well between each. Beat in the golden syrup.

Sift the spices, flour and soda into a bowl. Stir the sifted mixture gradually into the butter mixture, alternating with the fruit. Stir in the almonds, brandy and essence. Spoon the batter into the tins, smoothing the tops even.

Bake for 3–4 hours, or until a skewer inserted in the centres comes out clean. Cool the cakes in the tins.

Family recipes

Family recipes

| | | 1 | 2 | 3 |
| | | Egg Pie | Savoury Pancakes | Macaroni Cheese |

| 4 | 5 | 6 | 7 | 8 |
| Corn Custard | Celery Soup | Pickled Eggs | Brown Fig Cake | Spiced Cake |

| 9 | 10 | 11 | 12 | 13 |
| One Two Three Four Cake | Brown Sugar Cookies | Gingerbread No 2 | Nut Waffles | West End Cake |

| 14 | 15 | 16 | 17 | 18 |
| Gerrard Steak | Meringues | Chocolate Roll | Date Sponge | Apple Sauce Cake |

| 19 | 20 | 21 | 22 | 23 |
| Fish Scallops | Auntie's Cakes | Calala Pudding | Marmalade Pudding | Sponge Custard |

| 24 | 25 | 26 | 27 | 28 |
| Cinnamon Biscuits | Merriwa Caramel Custard | Coconut Shortbread | Raspberry Buns | Walnut Cake |

| 29 | 30 | 31 | | |
| Cheese Cakes | Stone Cream Pudding | Crisp Biscuits | | |

OCTOBER

Egg Pie

Mrs Helen Sandilands, Uralla Branch

SERVES 6

10 eggs

12 bacon rashers, rind
removed

Pastry

300 g (2 cups) self-raising
flour

185 g chilled butter,
chopped

125 ml (½ cup) iced water,
or as required

For the pastry, combine the flour and
butter in a bowl. Using your fingertips, rub
in the butter until the mixture resembles
breadcrumbs. Add enough of the iced water
to form a firm dough.

Turn the dough out onto a lightly floured
surface and knead briefly to bring it together.
Form the dough into a disc, wrap it in plastic
wrap and chill for 30 minutes.

Preheat oven to 180°C.

Cut the dough into two equal pieces. On
a lightly floured surface, roll out one half until
large enough to line the base and side of a
25 x 4 cm deep pie dish.

Break the eggs into the pastry-lined dish
and season well with salt and pepper. Place
the bacon over the top of the eggs. Roll the
remaining piece of pastry out into a circle
large enough to fit over the pie. Place the
pastry over, trimming the edges even. Prick
the pastry top several times with the tip of
a small, sharp knife.

Bake for about 45 minutes, or until the
pastry is golden and the eggs are firm.

Egg Pie can be
served hot or cold –
it's an ideal picnic dish.

Savoury Pancakes

Mrs Frank Jones, Grenfell Branch

MAKES 10–12
150 g (1 cup) self-raising
  flour
1 egg, well beaten
300 ml milk
butter, for cooking

Filling
2 tablespoons vegetable oil
½ onion, very finely
  chopped
125 g minced pork or beef
2 tablespoons flour
2 tablespoons chicken stock
1 tablespoon tomato sauce

Preheat oven to 150°C.

For the filling, heat the oil in a frying pan over medium heat. Add the onion and mince and cook, stirring often, for 8–10 minutes, or until the onion is soft and the meat is cooked through.

Add the flour and cook, stirring, for 5 minutes, then add the stock. Stirring constantly, bring the mixture to a simmer and cook for 2–3 minutes, or until thickened. Stir in the tomato sauce and season well with salt and pepper. Keep warm.

Place the flour in a bowl and make a well in the centre. Add the egg and the milk to the well and combine, using a whisk.

Working in batches, heat a little butter in the base of a non-stick frying pan over medium heat. Add 80 ml (⅓ cup) of the batter for each pancake, to form 10 cm pancakes. Cook for 2–3 minutes, or until brown, then turn over and cook for a further 2–3 minutes, or until cooked through.

Place the cooked pancakes in the oven in a heatproof dish to keep hot. Repeat with the remaining batter.

Spoon some of the meat mixture over each hot pancake, roll up and serve immediately.

Macaroni Cheese

3 OCT

Mrs F Sheridan, Mount Hope Branch

SERVES 4

180 g (2 cups) dried
  macaroni
600 ml milk
1 tablespoon plain flour
1½ tablespoons water
100 g (1 cup) grated
  cheddar cheese
½ teaspoon mustard
  powder
large pinch of cayenne
  pepper
1 tablespoon fresh
  breadcrumbs
15 g butter

Preheat oven to 200°C. Grease a 1.5 litre (6 cup) capacity baking dish.

Cook the macaroni in a large saucepan of boiling, salted water for 10 minutes, or until *al dente*. Drain the macaroni well and return it to the pan with the milk. Bring to a simmer and cook for a further 10 minutes, or until the macaroni is very tender.

Combine the flour in a cup with the water to make a smooth paste, then stir into the macaroni mixture. Bring to a simmer and cook, stirring, for 3 minutes, or until the mixture thickens. Stir in half the cheese, the mustard powder and the cayenne and season to taste with salt and pepper.

Pour the macaroni mixture into the dish, sprinkle over the remaining cheese and the crumbs. Dot the top with the butter.

Bake for 20 minutes, or until golden. Serve hot.

Corn Custard

4 OCT

Mrs George Cory, Braeside, Dalveen, Queensland

SERVES 4

2 x 415 g tins corn kernels,
  well drained
300 ml milk
2 eggs, beaten
2 tablespoons melted
  butter

Preheat oven to 180°C. Grease a 1.5 litre (6 cup) capacity baking dish.

Combine the corn, milk and eggs in a bowl and whisk to mix well. Season to taste with salt and pepper, then stir in half the butter.

Pour the corn mixture into the dish and drizzle the remaining butter over the top.

Bake for 20–30 minutes, or until set.

Celery Soup

5 OCT

Mrs J Heckendorf, Lockhart Branch

SERVES 6

1 head of celery, trimmed,
 cut into 2 cm pieces
2 litres (8 cups) chicken
 stock
60 g (¼ cup) butter
40 g plain flour
300 ml milk
300 ml pouring cream
croutons, to serve

Combine the celery in a large saucepan with the stock and bring to a simmer. Cook for 35–40 minutes, or until very tender.

Transfer the celery mixture to a food processor and purée until smooth. For a very smooth soup, pass the purée through a sieve and discard the solids.

Melt the butter in a large saucepan. Add the flour and stir to form a smooth paste. Slowly add the milk and cream, stirring constantly to prevent lumps forming, bringing the mixture to a simmer between additions. Add the puréed celery and stir to combine well. Season to taste with salt and pepper.

Serve hot, sprinkled with croutons.

Pickled Eggs

6 OCT

Mrs Armstrong, Harbourside Branch

MAKES TWO 1 LITRE JARS

1 litre (4 cups) malt vinegar
1 teaspoon whole black
 peppercorns
1 teaspoon whole white
 peppercorns
1 teaspoon ground ginger
1 teaspoon yellow mustard
 seeds, optional
16 eggs, hard-boiled and
 peeled

Combine the vinegar, peppercorns, ginger and mustard seeds, if using, in a saucepan and bring to the boil.

Place the eggs in two sterilised 1 litre (4 cup) capacity jars and pour the hot vinegar mixture over.

Allow the liquid to cool, then seal the jars.

Store eggs in a cool, dark place for a month before using.

Pickled Eggs are delicious served with cold meats.

Brown Fig Cake

Mrs Lamrock, Penrith

MAKES ONE 24 CM CAKE

250 g (1 cup) butter, softened

250 g caster sugar

2 tablespoons honey

2 teaspoons vanilla essence

3 eggs

500 g (3⅓ cups) self-raising flour

1½ teaspoons mixed spice

80 ml (⅓ cup) milk, or as required

250 g raisins

350 g dried figs, trimmed and chopped

100 g (⅔ cup) blanched almonds, chopped

Preheat oven to 170°C. Lightly grease and flour the side of a 24 cm cake tin and line the base with baking paper.

Using an electric beater, beat the butter, sugar, honey and vanilla in a bowl until light and creamy. Add the eggs, one at a time and beating well between each.

Sift the flour and spice into a bowl and stir into the creamed mixture with the milk, adding a little more milk if necessary – the mixture will be very thick. Add the raisins, figs and almonds and stir to mix well. Spoon the mixture into the tin, smoothing the surface even.

Bake for about 1½ hours, or until a skewer inserted in the centre comes out clean – cover the cake with foil if it browns too quickly.

Cool the cake in the tin for 30 minutes, then turn it out onto a wire rack to cool completely.

Spiced Cake

Mrs Colless, Come-by-Chance Branch

MAKES ONE 20 CM LOAF

50 g butter, softened
110 g (½ cup) caster sugar
2 eggs
175 g (½ cup) golden syrup
½ teaspoon bicarbonate
  of soda
60 ml (¼ cup) milk
225 g (1½ cups) plain flour
1 teaspoon baking powder
3 teaspoons ground ginger
1 teaspoon freshly grated
  nutmeg

Icing
370 g (2 cups, lightly
  packed) brown sugar
1 tablespoon butter
100 ml milk

Preheat oven to 170°C. Grease and flour the sides of a 20 cm loaf tin and line the base with baking paper.

Using an electric beater, beat the butter and sugar in a bowl until light and creamy. Add the eggs, one at a time, beating well between each. Stir in the syrup.

Dissolve the soda in the milk in a cup. Sift the flour, baking powder and spices into a bowl. Add the milk and flour mixtures to the creamed mixture, stirring to combine well. Spoon the batter into the tin, smoothing the top even.

Bake for 55–60 minutes, or until a skewer inserted in the centre comes out clean. Cool the cake in the tin for 10 minutes, then turn out onto a wire rack to cool completely.

For the icing, combine all the ingredients in a small saucepan and slowly bring to the boil. Cook over medium heat for about 5 minutes, stirring often to prevent the mixture catching. Remove from the heat and cool slightly.

Transfer to a bowl. Using an electric beater, beat until the mixture is cool and thick.

Spread the icing over the cake and leave to stand until the icing is set.

One Two Three Four Cake

Miss D Carter, Quambone Branch

MAKES ONE 20 CM CAKE

250 g (1 cup) butter,
softened
440 g (2 cups) caster sugar
4 eggs
450 g (3 cups) plain flour
2 teaspoons baking
powder
125 ml (½ cup) milk

9 OCT

Preheat oven to 180°C. Lightly grease and flour a 20 cm cake tin.

Using an electric beater, beat the butter and sugar in a bowl until light and creamy. Add the eggs, one at a time, beating well between each.

Sift the flour and baking powder into a bowl, then stir it into the creamed mixture with the milk. Spoon the batter into the tin, smoothing the top even.

Bake for 30–40 minutes, or until a skewer inserted in the centre comes out clean. Cool the cake in the tin for 10 minutes, then turn it out onto a wire rack to cool completely.

Brown Sugar Cookies

10 OCT

MAKES ABOUT 30

330 g (1½ cups, firmly
packed) brown sugar
375 g (2½ cups) plain flour
1¼ teaspoons bicarbonate
of soda
125 g (½ cup) butter,
softened
125 ml (½ cup) boiling
water
1 tablespoon orange juice
2 teaspoons finely grated
orange zest
white sugar, for sprinkling

Preheat oven to 180°C. Line a baking tray with baking paper.

Stir the brown sugar, flour and soda into a bowl. Place the butter in a bowl, add the boiling water and stand until cooled slightly and butter has melted. Add to the sugar mixture with the orange juice and zest, stirring to combine well.

Drop teaspoons of the mixture onto the tray, leaving room for spreading. Sprinkle each lightly with white sugar.

Bake for 15–20 minutes or until cookies are firm. Transfer to a wire rack to cool.

Gingerbread No 2

Mrs Cameron, Dungog Branch

MAKES ONE 20 CM CAKE

250 g (1 cup) butter,
  softened
440 g (2 cups) caster sugar
2 eggs
125 ml (½ cup) treacle
300 g (2 cups) plain flour
1 tablespoon ground
  cinnamon
1 tablespoon ground ginger
2 teaspoons bicarbonate
  of soda
60 ml (¼ cup) boiling
  water

Orange Icing

2 tablespoons milk, at room
  temperature, plus extra,
  as required
2 teaspoons orange juice
2 teaspoons butter,
  softened
200 g icing sugar, sifted,
  plus extra, as required
1 teaspoon grated orange
  zest

Preheat oven to 180°C. Grease and flour a 20 cm cake tin.

Using an electric beater, beat the butter and sugar in a bowl until light and creamy. Add the eggs, one at a time, beating well between each. Stir in the treacle.

Sift the flour, cinnamon and ginger into a bowl and add to the creamed mixture. Dissolve the soda in the boiling water in a cup, then stir into the mixture. Continue stirring until the batter is very smooth. Spoon the batter into the tin.

Bake for 40–50 minutes, or until a skewer inserted in the centre comes out clean. Cool the cake in the tin for 15 minutes, then turn it out onto a wire rack to cool completely.

For the icing, combine the milk, orange juice, butter and icing sugar in a bowl and beat well. Add the orange zest. Add more icing sugar or milk as required, to thicken or thin the icing to a spreadable consistency. Spread the icing over the cooled cake.

Nut Waffles

Mrs Evans, Wagga Branch

MAKES 6–8
300 g (2 cups) plain flour
1 tablespoon baking powder
2 tablespoons caster sugar
2 eggs, separated
80 g butter, melted
250 ml (1 cup) milk
120 g (1 cup) very finely
    chopped walnuts

Combine the flour, baking powder and sugar in a large bowl. Beat the egg yolks, butter and milk in a small bowl and add to the flour mixture, whisking until smooth.

Using an electric beater, whisk the egg whites in a bowl until firm peaks form. Fold the whites and the walnuts into the batter.

Heat an electric waffle iron. Following the manufacturer's instructions, cook the mixture, in batches, until waffles are golden and cooked through. Serve hot.

West End Cake

MAKES ONE 20 CM CAKE
250 g (1 cup) butter,
    softened
220 g (1 cup) caster sugar
2 eggs, beaten well
300 g (2 cups) self-raising
    flour, plus extra, for
    dusting fruit
60 ml (¼ cup) milk
115 g (¾ cup) currants
130 g (¾ cup) sultanas
65 g (½ cup) slivered
    almonds
1 teaspoon ground
    cinnamon

Preheat oven to 180°C. Line a 20 cm cake tin with baking paper.

Using an electric beater, beat the butter and sugar in a bowl until light and creamy. Add the eggs and beat to combine well. Add the flour and milk, stirring until the mixture is smooth.

Combine the currants, sultanas, almonds and cinnamon in a baking dish with enough flour to lightly coat the fruit. Heat in the oven for 5 minutes to warm through. Add to the cake mixture then stir to mix well. Spoon the batter into the tin, smoothing the top even.

Bake for 40–50 minutes, or until a skewer inserted in the centre comes out clean. Cool the cake in the tin for 15 minutes, then turn it out onto a wire rack to cool completely.

Gerrard Steak

Mrs G Hadlow, Collector Branch

SERVES 6

1 kg boneless shin, chuck or other braising beef, trimmed
2 tablespoons plain flour
2–3 tablespoons vegetable oil, or as required
300 ml beef stock
2 tablespoons caster sugar
2½ tablespoons HP Sauce
1 tablespoon Worcestershire sauce
2 tablespoons red wine vinegar

Preheat oven to 165°C.

Cut the steak into 3–3.5 cm pieces and place in a bowl with the flour. Toss to coat well, shaking off and reserving any excess flour.

Heat 2 tablespoons of the oil in a large frying pan over medium–high heat. Add the meat in batches and cook, turning often, for 3–4 minutes, or until browned all over, adding more oil if required. Place the cooked meat in a small roasting dish, reserving the pan.

Pour excess oil from the pan and scatter in the reserved flour. Add the stock to the pan and cook, whisking constantly to dislodge any cooking residue from the base, for 2–3 minutes, or until the stock simmers.

Add the sugar, sauces and vinegar, season well and pour the mixture over the meat in the dish. Cover the dish tightly with foil.

Bake for 2 hours, or until the meat is very tender.

Meringues

Mrs Stubbard, Narrandera Branch

MAKES ABOUT 26
4 egg whites
275 g (1¼ cups) caster
 sugar

Preheat oven to 100°C. Line two baking trays with baking paper.

Using an electric beater, whisk the egg whites in a large bowl until firm peaks form. Whisking constantly, gradually add the sugar and whisk for 10–12 minutes, or until the sugar has dissolved and the mixture is very thick and glossy.

Drop tablespoons of the mixture onto the trays, or use a piping bag fitted with a large, star nozzle to pipe 5 cm rounds.

Bake for 1–2 hours, or until the meringues are firm and dry.

Chocolate Roll

Miss V Haigh, Goulburn Branch

MAKES ONE 23 CM CAKE
110 g (½ cup) caster sugar
2 eggs
150 g (1 cup) self-raising
 flour
95 g (⅓ cup) cocoa powder
1 teaspoon boiling water

Filling
60 g (¼ cup) butter,
 softened
40 g (⅓ cup) icing sugar
¼ teaspoon vanilla essence

Preheat oven to 170°C. Lightly grease and flour a 23 × 13 cm swiss roll tin.

Using an electric beater, whisk the sugar and eggs in a bowl until thick and pale. Sift the flour and cocoa into a bowl and gently fold into the egg mixture with the boiling water. Spoon the batter into the tin, smoothing the top even.

Bake for 15 minutes, or until cooked through. Turn the hot cake out onto a tea towel and carefully roll it up using the towel as a guide. Leave to cool.

For the filling, beat the butter, icing sugar and vanilla in a bowl until very pale and creamy.

Carefully unroll the cake and spread with the filling. Re-roll the cake and serve.

Date Sponge

Miss A Travis, Gilgandra Branch

SERVES 6

160 g (1 cup) pitted dates
125 ml (½ cup) boiling water
2 tablespoons butter
75 g (⅓ cup) caster sugar
1 egg
185 ml (¾ cup) milk
150 g (1 cup) plain flour
1 teaspoon baking powder
custard, to serve

Preheat oven to 180°C.

Place the dates in the base of a 1.5 litre (6 cup) capacity baking dish and pour over the boiling water. Place in the oven while you make the pudding.

Using an electric beater, beat the butter and sugar in a bowl. Add the egg and beat well. Stir in the milk, flour and baking powder and mix well. Pour the batter over the dates.

Bake for 30–40 minutes, or until the sponge is cooked through.

Serve Date Sponge hot or cold – it's delicious hot with custard.

Apple Sauce Cake

Mrs Blessing, Penrith Branch

MAKES ONE 22 CM CAKE

220 g (1 cup) caster sugar
180 g butter, softened
375 ml (1½ cups)
    unsweetened apple
    sauce or apple purée
2 teaspoons bicarbonate
    of soda
2 tablespoons boiling water
1 teaspoon salt
1 teaspoon ground cinnamon
1 teaspoon ground cloves
375 g (2½ cups) plain flour,
    sifted
170 g (1 cup) raisins, chopped

Preheat oven to 180°C. Grease and flour a 22 x 12 x 6.5 cm loaf tin.

Using an electric beater, beat sugar and butter in a bowl until light and creamy. Stir in the apple sauce.

Dissolve the soda in the boiling water in a cup, then stir into the mixture with the salt, spices, flour and raisins, stirring to combine well. Spoon the batter into the tin, smoothing the top even.

Bake for 30–40 minutes, or until a skewer inserted in the centre comes out clean. Cool the cake slightly in the tin, then turn it out onto a wire rack to cool completely.

Fish Scallops

Mrs Hoskings, Binnaway Beach

19 OCT

SERVES 4

1 x 415 g tin salmon, well drained
60 g (¼ cup) butter
35 g (¼ cup) plain flour
300 ml milk
2 tablespoons pouring cream
1 teaspoon finely chopped anchovies
60 g (1 cup, lightly packed) fresh breadcrumbs

Preheat oven to 180°C.

Place the salmon in a bowl and flake coarsely with a fork, removing any bones if necessary. Set aside.

Combine half the butter with the flour in a small saucepan and stir over medium heat until the butter melts and a paste forms. Stirring constantly to prevent lumps forming, gradually add the milk, allowing the mixture to come to a simmer between additions. Cook, stirring, for 1–2 minutes, or until the mixture is smooth and thick.

Stir the cream, anchovies and salmon into the pan and season to taste with salt and pepper. Pour the mixture into a 1.5 litre (6 cup) capacity baking dish and scatter over the breadcrumbs. Dot the top with the remaining butter.

Bake for 20–30 minutes, or until golden and bubbling.

Auntie's Cakes

Mrs G Horgan, Nowra Branch

20 OCT

MAKES 12

375 g butter, softened
220 g (1 cup) caster sugar
4 eggs
2 teaspoons baking powder
500 g (4 cups) cornflour
finely grated zest of 3 lemons

Preheat oven to 180°C. Lightly grease a 12-hole flat-bottomed patty tin.

Using an electric beater, beat the butter and sugar in a bowl until light and creamy. Add the eggs, one at a time, beating well between each.

Sift the baking powder and cornflour into a bowl. Stir into the creamed mixture with the zest. Half-fill the patty tins with the batter.

Bake for 15–20 minutes, or until golden. Turn the cakes onto a wire rack to cool.

Calala Pudding

21 OCT

Mrs WH Keating, Quambone Branch

SERVES 8–10

500 g day-old bread (about 15 slices), soaked in water
500 g carrots, grated
500 g granny smith apples, grated
500 g pitted dates, finely chopped
500 g (2 cups) shredded suet (see note)
770 g (3½ cups) caster sugar
2 tablespoons golden syrup
2 teaspoons mixed spice
custard, to serve

Bring a large saucepan of water to the boil for steaming, placing a small heatproof plate upside down in the water to keep the pudding basin off the base of the pan. Grease and flour a 2.5 litre (10 cup) capacity pudding basin, or two 1.5 litre (6 cup) capacity basins.

Squeeze the bread dry. Combine the bread in a large bowl with the carrot, apple, dates, suet, sugar, syrup and spice.

Spoon the batter into the basin, cover tightly and lower it into the boiling water. Steam for 5 hours (4 hours if making two 1.5 litre puddings), or until cooked through, adding more water to the pan as required.

Serve hot, with custard.

Note: shredded suet is available as a packet mix at supermarkets, or fresh from your butcher.

Marmalade Pudding

22 OCT

Mrs Hanstock, Quandialla Branch

SERVES 6–8

125 g (½ cup) butter
75 g (⅓ cup) caster sugar
90 g (1½ cups, lightly packed) fresh breadcrumbs
2 eggs, well beaten
320 g (1 cup) marmalade, flavour of choice

Serve Marmalade Pudding topped with hot marmalade sauce.

Preheat oven to 180°C. Lightly grease and flour a 25 x 4 cm deep pie dish.

Using an electric beater, beat the butter and sugar in a bowl until light and creamy. Add the breadcrumbs, eggs and half the marmalade and beat well.

Spoon the mixture into the baking dish. Bake for 30 minutes, or until cooked through.

Heat the remaining marmalade in a saucepan with a little water over medium heat, stirring until the marmalade and water have combined to form a sauce. Simmer until ready to serve the pudding.

Sponge Custard

Mrs Andrew Heckendorf, Nyngan Branch

SERVES 6

600 ml milk
4 eggs, separated
110 g (½ cup) caster sugar
1 teaspoon vanilla essence
2½ teaspoons powdered
    gelatine
60 ml (¼ cup) water

Place the milk in a saucepan and bring just to a simmer. Whisk the egg yolks and 75 g (⅓ cup) of the sugar in a bowl. Pour the hot milk over the yolk mixture, add the vanilla and stir to combine well.

Return the mixture to a clean saucepan and cook over medium–low heat, stirring constantly with a wooden spoon, for 5–6 minutes, or until the mixture thickens enough to coat the back of a spoon – do not allow the mixture to overheat or the yolks will curdle. Remove from the heat.

Sprinkle the gelatine over the water in a small heatproof cup and stand for 5 minutes, or until the gelatine softens. Place the cup in a small saucepan with enough simmering water to come halfway up the side of the cup. Heat for 4–5 minutes, or until the gelatine dissolves.

Stir the gelatine into the custard and cool to room temperature. Stand until the mixture is just beginning to set.

Using an electric beater, whisk the egg whites in a bowl until firm peaks form. Gently fold the whites into the custard mixture.

Pour into a 1.5 litre (6 cup) capacity bowl and refrigerate for 3–4 hours, or until the custard is firm.

Cinnamon Biscuits

Mrs J Kinsella, Manildra Branch

MAKES ABOUT 40

125 g (½ cup) butter,
  softened
125 g caster sugar
1 tablespoon ground
  cinnamon
1 egg, well beaten
250 g (1⅓ cups) plain flour
¼ teaspoons baking powder
40 g (¼ cup) blanched
  almonds, split in half

Preheat oven to 180°C. Line two baking trays with baking paper.

Using an electric beater, beat the butter and sugar in a bowl until light and creamy. Add the cinnamon and egg and beat well.

Sift the flour and baking powder into a bowl, then stir it into the creamed mixture to form a coarse dough.

Turn the dough out onto a floured surface and knead lightly until smooth. Roll out to 5 mm thickness. Using a 4 cm round pastry cutter, cut pastry into rounds and re-rolling any scraps for more rounds.

Place the rounds on the trays and brush very lightly with water. Press an almond half lightly into the middle of each round.

Bake, one tray at a time, for 10–15 minutes, or until biscuits are light golden. Transfer to a wire rack to cool.

Merriwa Caramel Custard

25 OCT

Miss C Jennings, Merriwa Branch

SERVES 4–6

220 g (1 cup) caster sugar, plus 1 tablespoon, extra
juice of ½ lemon
125 ml (½ cup) water
600 ml milk
4 eggs, well beaten
1 teaspoon vanilla essence
boiling water, for baking

To serve, turn the chilled Merriwa Caramel Custard out onto a large plate.

Preheat oven to 150°C.

Combine the sugar, lemon juice and water in a saucepan. Bring slowly to a simmer then boil for 7–8 minutes, or until the mixture turns a deep caramel colour.

Pour the caramel into a 1.5 litre (6 cup) capacity baking dish, taking care as the mixture will be very hot.

Beat the milk, eggs and vanilla in a bowl, then strain the mixture into the baking dish. Cover the dish tightly with foil and place into a larger dish half-filled with boiling water.

Bake for 1½ hours, or until the custard is set. Cool to room temperature, then chill.

Coconut Shortbread

26 OCT

Mrs W Moore, Dungog Branch

MAKES ABOUT 16

150 g (1 cup) self-raising flour
110 g (½ cup) caster sugar
1 tablespoon butter, softened
1 egg, beaten
85 g (¼ cup) raspberry jam

Topping

1 egg, beaten
110 g (½ cup) caster sugar
90 g (1 cup) desiccated coconut
almond essence, as required

Preheat oven to 180°C. Grease and flour a 28 × 18 cm slice tin.

Combine the flour and sugar in a bowl and rub in the butter. Add the egg and mix to form a dough.

Turn the dough out onto a lightly floured surface and roll to fit the base of the tin. Line the tin with the dough and spread with jam.

For the topping, beat the egg with the sugar in a bowl, combining well. Stir in the coconut and a few drops of the essence. Scatter the topping over the jam.

Bake for 15–20 minutes, or until the pastry is cooked through and the topping is golden. Cool the shortbread in the tin, then cut into squares or fingers.

Raspberry Buns

Mrs C Gordon, Manildra Branch

MAKES 10

125 g (½ cup) lard or butter
110 g (½ cup) caster sugar
1 egg, separated
100 g (1 cup) ground rice
185 g (1¼ cups) plain flour
1 teaspoon baking powder
milk, as required
165 g (½ cup) raspberry
   jam

Preheat oven to 180°C. Line a baking tray with baking paper.

Using an electric beater, beat the lard and sugar in a bowl until light and creamy. Add the egg yolk and beat well.

Sift the ground rice, flour and baking powder into a bowl, then stir into the creamed mixture. Add a little milk, if required, to form a firm dough.

Divide the dough into 10 even-sized pieces and form each piece into a ball. Using your thumb, make a deep indentation in each ball. Spoon a little of the jam into each indentation. Bring the edges of the dough together to enclose the jam, pressing gently to seal, and place the dough balls on the tray. Lightly beat the egg white in a bowl and use to brush each ball.

Bake for 15–20 minutes, or until the buns are golden. Transfer to a wire rack to cool.

Walnut Cake

Mrs Arthur Martin, Wagga Branch

MAKES ONE 20 CM CAKE
175 g butter
165 g (¾ cup, firmly packed)
   brown sugar
115 g (⅓ cup) treacle
4 eggs
50 g (½ cup) ground rice
225 g (1½ cups) plain flour
1 teaspoon ground ginger
1 teaspoon ground cinnamon
1 teaspoon ground allspice
1 teaspoon baking powder
60 g (½ cup) chopped
   walnuts, for decorating

Caramel Icing
250 ml (1 cup) milk
370 g (2 cups, lightly
   packed) brown sugar
1 teaspoon butter
1 teaspoon vanilla essence

Preheat oven to 180°C. Lightly grease and flour a 20 cm round cake tin.

Using an electric beater, beat the butter and sugar in a bowl until light and creamy. Add treacle and beat well. Add 1 egg, beating to combine well.

Sift the ground rice, flour, spices and baking powder into a bowl and add the walnuts. Gradually stir the flour mixture into the creamed mixture, alternating with the eggs until all are added, stirring until the mixture is smooth. Spoon it into the tin, smoothing the top even.

Bake for about 40 minutes, or until a skewer inserted in the centre comes out clean. Cool the cake in the tin for 10 minutes, then turn it out onto a wire rack to cool completely.

For the caramel icing, combine the milk, sugar and butter in a small saucepan and bring to the boil. Cook over medium heat, stirring, for about 20 minutes, or until the mixture thickens. Remove from the heat and add the vanilla.

Pour the hot mixture over the cake, scatter with walnuts and stand until set.

Cheese Cakes

Mrs DM Broadhead, Bungonia Branch

MAKES 12

Pastry

185 g (1¼ cup) plain flour

1 teaspoon baking powder

60 g (¼ cup) chilled butter, chopped

1 tablespoon caster sugar

2 tablespoons iced water, or as required

Filling

50 g butter, softened

1 tablespoon caster sugar

5 teaspoons plain flour

1 egg

1 teaspoon baking powder

85 g (¼ cup) raspberry jam

Preheat oven to 180°C. Lightly grease the holes of a 12-hole round-bottomed patty tin.

For the pastry, sift the flour and baking powder into a bowl. Rub in the butter until the mixture resembles breadcrumbs. Stir in the sugar, then add about 2 tablespoons of iced water, or enough to form a firm dough.

Turn the dough out onto a lightly floured board and briefly knead until smooth. Roll the dough to 5 mm thickness, then use a 6 cm round pastry cutter to cut rounds.

Line the patty tin holes with the pastry rounds and place in the refrigerator while preparing the filling.

For the filling, using an electric beater, beat the butter and sugar in a bowl until light and creamy. Add 1 teaspoon of the flour and the egg and beat well. Sift the remaining flour and baking powder into a bowl then stir it into the creamed mixture.

Place 1 teaspoon of jam in each pastry case, then spoon the filling over.

Bake for 10–15 minutes, or until the pastry is cooked and the tops of the cakes are golden. Turn the cakes onto a wire rack to cool.

Stone Cream Pudding

Mrs DW Corney, Tenterfield Branch

SERVES 8

15 g powdered gelatine
60 ml (¼ cup) water
600 ml milk
75 g (⅓ cup) caster sugar
finely grated zest of
   1 lemon
165 g (½ cup) apricot jam
40 g (¼ cup) blanched
   almonds, to decorate

To decorate, press the blanched almonds into the top of the Stone Cream Pudding.

Sprinkle the gelatine over the water in a small heatproof cup and stand for 5 minutes, or until the gelatine softens. Place the cup in a small saucepan with enough simmering water to come halfway up the side of the cup. Heat for 4–5 minutes, or until the gelatine dissolves.

Combine the milk and sugar in a saucepan and warm, stirring, over medium–low heat for 4–5 minutes, or until the sugar has dissolved. Add the lemon zest, then stir in the gelatine mixture. Cool to room temperature.

Spread the jam over the base of a 1.5 litre (6 cup) capacity dish. Pour the milk mixture over. Refrigerate until set.

Crisp Biscuits

Mrs Nimmo, Narrandera Branch

MAKES ABOUT 25

125 g (½ cup) butter,
   softened
125 g caster sugar
1 egg
1 teaspoon vanilla essence
250 g (1⅔ cups) plain flour
1 teaspoon baking powder
60 g (⅓ cup) raisins
40 g (⅓ cup) chopped
   walnuts or almonds

Preheat oven to 175°C. Line two baking trays with baking paper.

Using an electric beater, beat the butter and sugar in a bowl until light and fluffy. Add the egg and vanilla and beat well. Sift the flour and baking powder into a bowl, then mix into the butter mixture with the raisins and walnuts until a dough forms.

Using your hands, roll tablespoons of the dough into balls. Place on the trays, leaving room between each and pressing with your hand to form rounds about 5 cm across.

Bake for 12–15 minutes, or until light golden. Transfer to a wire rack to cool.

❧ Family recipes ❧

_____

_____

_____

_____

_____

_____

_____

_____

_____

_____

_____

_____

_____

_____

_____

_____

_____

_____

		1	2	3
		Jellied Tomato and Chicken	Monday Pudding	Almond Jumbles
4	5	6	7	8
Chicken Croquettes	Coconut Tart	Madeira Cake	Eumungerie Brownie	Cream of Carrot Soup
9	10	11	12	13
Cream Cakes	Wreath Cake	Rainbow Cake No 2	Orange Onion Salad	Chocolate Hermits
14	15	16	17	18
Matrimony Tart	Shortbread No 2	Champagne Biscuits	Joy Pudding	Baked Fruit Pudding
19	20	21	22	23
Australian Omelette	Banana Cream	Paradise Pie	Apples in Red Jelly	Biscuits au Diable
24	25	26	27	28
Chocolate Soufflé	Oriental Sundae	Pan Pacific Fruit Salad	Banana Flan	Rice Coconut Pudding
29	30			
Orange Pie	Lemon Biscuits			

NOVEMBER

NOTE:
Time to start planning for Christmas!
See 20–25 December recipes for Christmas cake,
puddings and accompaniments.

Jellied Tomato and Chicken

Miss AE Robards, Nevertire Branch

SERVES 4–6

3 teaspoons powdered
   gelatine
80 ml (⅓ cup) water
500 ml (2 cups) chicken
   stock, preferably
   home-made
2 large firm, ripe tomatoes
500 g (3 cups) cooked
   chicken, finely chopped
2½ tablespoons finely
   chopped parsley

Sprinkle the gelatine over the water in a small heatproof cup and stand for 5 minutes, or until the gelatine softens. Place the cup in a small saucepan with enough simmering water to come halfway up the side of the cup. Heat for 4–5 minutes, or until the gelatine dissolves.

Heat the chicken stock in a saucepan until nearly simmering, then add the gelatine mixture and stir to combine well. Cool to room temperature.

Cut the tomatoes in half lengthways then thinly slice into half-moons. Use the slices to line the inside of a 1.5 litre (6 cup) capacity bowl, overlapping the slices where necessary – you will need two rows of tomatoes going up the bowl.

Place the chicken, parsley and plenty of salt and pepper in a bowl and toss to combine well. Spoon into the tomato-lined bowl then pour the stock mixture over.

Cover the bowl with plastic wrap and refrigerate for 4 hours or overnight, until set.

To serve, dip the bowl into hot water and turn the Jellied Tomato and Chicken onto a serving plate.

Coconut Tart

Mrs JM Wallace, Gunnedah Branch

MAKES ONE 22 CM TART
50 g butter, softened
50 g caster sugar
1 egg
1 egg yolk
80 ml (⅓ cup) milk, or as
  required
180 g (2 cups) desiccated
  coconut
165 g (½ cup) raspberry
  jam

Pastry
225 g (1½ cups) plain flour
½ teaspoon baking powder
125 g (½ cup) chilled butter,
  chopped
2 tablespoons cold milk,
  or as required

Preheat oven to 180°C.

For the pastry, sift the flour and baking powder into a bowl. Using your fingertips, rub in the butter until the mixture resembles breadcrumbs. Mix in the milk to form a firm dough, adding a little extra if required.

Roll the dough out on a lightly floured surface to 2.5 mm thickness. Line a 22 cm tart tin with the pastry. Reserve pastry scraps.

For the filling, using an electric beater, beat the butter and sugar until well combined. Beat in the egg and egg yolk, then stir in the milk and coconut.

Spread the jam over the pastry, then crumble the coconut mixture evenly over the top. Roll the pastry scraps out to form a rectangle about 22 × 16 cm and cut into strips about 1.5 cm wide. Place the strips neatly over the tart to form parallel lines, leaving room between each to show the filling.

Bake for 30–35 minutes, or until the tart is deep golden and pastry is cooked through.

Madeira Cake

MAKES ONE 18 CM CAKE
100 g butter
125 g caster sugar
3 eggs
grated zest of 1 lemon
grated zest of 1 orange
100 g (⅔ cup) plain flour
100 g (⅔ cup) self-raising
  flour
80 ml (⅓ cup) milk

Preheat oven to 170°C. Lightly grease and flour the side of an 18 cm cake tin and line the base with baking paper.

Using an electric beater, beat the butter and sugar in a bowl until light and creamy. Add the eggs, one at a time, beating well between each, then add the grated zest.

Sift the flours into a bowl, then stir into the creamed mixture with the milk. Spoon the batter into the tin, smoothing the top even.

Bake for about 45 minutes, or until a skewer inserted in the centre comes out clean.

Cool the cake in the tin for 15 minutes, then turn out onto a wire rack to cool completely.

Eumungerie Brownie

Mrs H Johnstone, Eumungerie Branch

MAKES ABOUT 24
440 g (2 cups, firmly packed)
  brown sugar
340 g (2 cups) sultanas
2 tablespoons butter
500 ml (2 cups) hot water
600 g (4 cups) plain flour
1 teaspoon bicarbonate
  of soda   -
2 teaspoons ground
  cinnamon
2 teaspoons mixed spice
1 teaspoon ground nutmeg

Preheat oven to 170°C. Grease and flour the sides of a 35 × 20 × 5 cm baking dish and line the base with baking paper.

Combine the sugar, sultanas, butter and hot water in a saucepan. Bring to the boil and cook for 5 minutes, then remove from heat and cool.

Sift the flour, soda and spices into a bowl. Add the boiled mixture and stir to combine well. Pour the batter into the dish.

Bake for about 1 hour 20 minutes, or until a skewer inserted in the centre comes out clean.

Cool in the dish, then cut into pieces about 5.5 cm square.

Cream of Carrot Soup

Mrs HJ Last, Cootamundra Branch

SERVES 4–6
60 g (¼ cup) butter
600 g carrots (about 4),
  peeled and thinly sliced
300 g desiree potatoes,
  peeled and finely chopped
1 onion, peeled and finely
  chopped
large pinch of sugar
1 litre (4 cups) chicken stock
100 ml pouring cream

Melt the butter in a large saucepan. Add the carrot, potato and onion and cook, covered and stirring often, for 25–30 minutes, or until the vegetables are very soft.

Add the sugar and chicken stock and bring to a simmer.

Place the mixture in a food processor (or use a stick blender) and purée until smooth.

Return the purée to the heat and bring it to a simmer. Add the cream, season to taste with salt and pepper and heat through.

Serve immediately.

Cream Cakes

Mrs Colless, Come-By-Chance Branch

MAKES 12
125 g (½ cup) butter,
  softened
220 g (1 cup) caster sugar
2 eggs
300 g (2 cups) plain flour
2 teaspoons baking powder
2½ tablespoons milk
250 ml (1 cup) thickened
  cream, whipped

Preheat oven to 180°C. Lightly grease and flour a 12-hole 125 ml (½ cup) capacity muffin tin (or line with cupcake cases).

Using an electric beater, beat the butter and sugar in a bowl until light and creamy. Add the eggs, one at a time, beating well between each addition.

Sift the flour and baking powder into a bowl, then stir into the butter mixture with a pinch of salt and the milk. Spoon the batter into the muffin holes.

Bake for 20–25 minutes, or until a skewer inserted in the centres comes out clean. Cool the cakes in the tin for 5 minutes, then turn out onto a wire rack to cool completely.

Cut the tops off the cakes, fill each with whipped cream, replace the tops then serve.

Wreath Cake

Mrs DG Munro, Nevertire Branch

MAKES ONE 22 CM CAKE

1 sachet dried instant yeast
60 ml (¼ cup) lukewarm water, plus 250 ml (1 cup) extra
600 g (4 cups) plain flour
1 teaspoon salt
165 g (¾ cup) caster sugar
2 teaspoons vanilla essence
2 eggs
100 g butter, softened
170 g (1 cup) sultanas
100 g (½ cup, lightly packed) brown sugar
1 teaspoon ground cinnamon

Lightly grease and flour an 18 cm, 2.5 litre (10 cup) capacity kuglehopf tin.

Sprinkle the yeast over the water in a large bowl with a pinch of sugar and stand for 5 minutes, or until foamy. Add the extra water with the flour, salt, sugar and vanilla and stir to form a rough dough.

Using a dough hook on an electric beater, beat in the eggs and 60 g of the butter. Knead until a smooth, elastic dough forms.

Place the dough in a large greased bowl, cover it with plastic wrap and leave to stand in a draught-free place for 1 hour, or until the dough has doubled in bulk.

Knock the dough back and turn it out onto a lightly floured surface. Roll out into a rectangle about 32 x 25 cm. Spread over the remaining butter and scatter over the sultanas, brown sugar and cinnamon. Roll up like a swiss roll, pinching the seam to seal. Place in the tin, seam side up.

Cover with a tea towel and stand in a draught-free place for 1 hour, or until the dough has risen to the top of the tin.

Preheat oven to 170°C.

Bake the cake for 50 minutes, or until a skewer inserted in the centre comes out clean. Turn the cake out onto a wire rack to cool.

Rainbow Cake No 2

Mrs Austin Seccombe, Wagga Branch

MAKES ONE 20 CM CAKE

500 g (2 cups) butter,
  softened
500 g caster sugar
6 eggs
500 g (3⅓ cups) plain flour
1 teaspoon bicarbonate
  of soda
2 teaspoons cream of
  tartar
250 ml (1 cup) milk
red food colouring
yellow food colouring
finely grated zest of
  1 lemon
1½ tablespoons cocoa
  powder, sifted
2½ tablespoons boiling
  water, or as required

Icing
440 g (2 cups) caster
  sugar
125 ml (½ cup) water
2 egg whites
90 g (1 cup) desiccated
  coconut

Preheat oven to 170°C. Grease and flour three 20 cm cake tins.

Using an electric beater, beat the butter and sugar in a bowl until light and creamy. Add the eggs, one at a time, beating well between each.

Sift the flour, soda and tartar into a bowl. Stir into the creamed mixture, alternating with the milk.

Spoon the mixture evenly into three bowls. Colour one portion pink with the red food colouring. Add the lemon zest and enough yellow food colouring to another to tint it deep yellow. Stir the cocoa in a cup with enough of the boiling water to form a smooth, thick paste, then stir it into the remaining bowl. Spoon each of the mixtures into a tin, smoothing the tops even.

Bake for about 35 minutes, or until a skewer inserted in the centres comes out clean. Cool the cakes in the tins for 10 minutes, then turn out onto wire racks to cool completely.

For the icing, combine the sugar with the water in a small saucepan and slowly bring to the boil. Cook for 7–8 minutes, or until the mixture reaches 115°C (soft ball stage) on a sugar thermometer.

Using an electric beater, whisk the egg whites in a bowl until firm peaks form. Whisking constantly, add the hot syrup in a thin, steady stream then whisk for 5–6 minutes, or until the mixture is very thick and glossy. Add the coconut and stir to combine well.

Spread each cooled cake with some of the icing, then stand for 10 minutes to allow icing to firm a little. Layer the cakes on top of each other, then spread with the remaining icing.

Orange Onion Salad

Miss DR Ripper, Narrabri Branch

SERVES 4–6
4 large oranges, peeled and
  all white pith removed
1 red onion, peeled
4–5 cups watercress sprigs

Dressing
1 tablespoon dijon mustard
2 tablespoons red wine
  vinegar, or to taste
large pinch of sugar
100 ml pouring cream

Thinly slice the oranges and onion into rings. Toss in a bowl with the watercress then place in a serving bowl or on a platter.

For the dressing, whisk the mustard, vinegar and sugar in a bowl until smooth. Slowly whisk in the cream and continue whisking until mixture thickens a little. Season well with salt and pepper.

Drizzle the dressing over the salad and serve immediately.

Chocolate Hermits

MAKES ABOUT 28
125 g (½ cup) butter, softened
220 g (1 cup, firmly packed)
  brown sugar
2 eggs, beaten well
300 g (2 cups) plain flour
2 teaspoons baking powder
1 teaspoon ground
  cinnamon
120 g (⅓ cup) raisins, plus
  extra, for decorating
60 g (½ cup) chopped
  walnuts
1½ tablespoons cocoa
  powder, sifted and
  dissolved in 2 tablespoons
  boiling water
white sugar, for sprinkling

Preheat oven to 180°C. Line two baking trays with baking paper.

Using an electric beater, beat the butter and sugar in a bowl until light and creamy. Add the eggs, one at a time, beating well between each.

Sift the flour, baking powder and cinnamon in a bowl. Add to the creamed mixture with the raisins and walnuts. Add the cocoa, stirring to combine well.

Drop heaped tablespoons of the mixture onto the trays, leaving room for spreading. Sprinkle with a little sugar and press a raisin into the top of each.

Bake for 15–16 minutes, or until firm. Transfer to a wire rack to cool.

Matrimony Tart

Mrs Austin Seccombe, Wagga Branch

MAKES ONE 36 × 12 CM TART
250 g (1⅔ cups) plain flour
1 teaspoon baking powder
125 g (½ cup) butter,
  chopped
380 g caster sugar
3 eggs, separated
80 ml (⅓ cup) lemon juice
grated zest of 2 lemons
custard, to serve

Preheat oven to 170°C.

Combine the flour and baking powder in a bowl. Using your fingertips, rub in the butter until the mixture resembles breadcrumbs. Stir in 2½ tablespoons of the sugar, add the egg yolks and mix to form a soft dough.

Roll the dough out on a well-floured surface, until large enough to line a 36 × 12 cm oblong tart tin. Line the tin with the pastry, trimming the edges even.

Using an electric beater, whisk the egg whites in a bowl until firm peaks form. Whisking constantly, slowly add the remaining sugar and whisk until the mixture is very stiff and glossy. Add the lemon juice and zest. Spoon the whites mixture into the pastry shell.

Bake for about 35 minutes, or until the topping is puffed and golden and the pastry is cooked through.

Turn the oven off and leave the tart to cool in the oven to 15–20 minutes.

Matrimony Tart can be served warm or at room temperature.

Shortbread No 2

MAKES 28
300 g butter, softened
125 g caster sugar
500 g (3⅓ cups) plain flour

Preheat oven to 170°C. Line a baking tray with baking paper.

Using an electric beater, beat the butter and sugar in a bowl until well combined. Add the flour then, using your hands, mix until a smooth, firm dough forms.

Knead the dough briefly on a lightly floured surface until smooth. Roll out to a 32 x 20 cm rectangle. Cut into 5 x 4.5 cm pieces then prick each piece two or three times with a fork. Place on the tray.

Bake for 20 minutes, or until firm – the shortbread should not colour. Cool on the tray for 5 minutes, then transfer to a wire rack to cool completely.

Champagne Biscuits

Miss Mary White, Armidale Branch

MAKES 22
150 g butter, softened
150 g (⅓ cup) caster sugar
4 egg yolks
300 g (2 cups) plain flour
½ teaspoon baking powder
1½ teaspoons vanilla essence
glacé cherries, halved, to
    decorate
egg white, beaten, for
    glazing

Preheat oven to 170°C. Line a baking tray with baking paper.

Using an electric beater, beat the butter and sugar in a bowl until light and creamy. Add the egg yolks and beat well. Combine the flour and baking powder in a bowl then add to the creamed mixture with the vanilla. Mix until smooth.

Spoon the mixture into a piping bag and pipe small 3 cm rounds onto the tray. (Or use your hands to roll tablespoons of mixture into balls.) Press a cherry piece gently into the top of each round and brush lightly with egg white.

Bake for 20 minutes, or until biscuits are light golden. Transfer to a wire rack to cool.

Joy Pudding

Mrs BF Cox, Mudgee Branch

17 NOV

SERVES 8

240 g (4 cups, lightly packed)
fresh breadcrumbs
100 g (⅔ cup) self-raising
flour
250 g (1 cup) shredded suet
(see note)
170 g (1 cup) raisins,
chopped
350 g (1 cup) treacle
250 ml (1 cup) milk
1 teaspoon bicarbonate
of soda
1 egg, beaten
custard or vanilla ice cream,
to serve

Bring a large saucepan of water to the boil for steaming, placing a small heatproof plate upside down in the water to keep the pudding basin off the base of the pan. Grease and flour a 2 litre (8 cup) capacity pudding basin.

Combine the crumbs, flour, suet and raisins in a bowl. In another bowl, mix the treacle and milk. Stir the soda into the milk mixture, then stir in the egg. Add to the crumb mixture and stir to combine well.

Spoon the batter into the basin, cover tightly and lower it into the boiling water. Steam for 3 hours, or until cooked through, adding more water to the pan as required.

Serve pudding hot with custard or ice cream.

Note: shredded suet is available as a packet mix at supermarkets, or fresh from your butcher.

Baked Fruit Pudding

Mrs G Harston, Kyogle Branch

18 NOV

SERVES 4–6

800 g black doris or omega
plums, stones removed,
and cut into slices
55 g (¼ cup) caster sugar

Topping
75 g butter, softened
75 g (⅓ cup) caster sugar
150 g (2½ cups, lightly packed)
fresh breadcrumbs
grated zest of 1 orange
2 tablespoons orange juice

Preheat oven to 180°C. Place the plums in a 1.5 litre (6 cup) capacity baking dish and sprinkle sugar over.

For the topping, using an electric beater, beat the butter and sugar in a bowl until light and creamy. Add the breadcrumbs, zest and juice.

Using your hands, scatter the topping evenly over the fruit.

Bake for 50 minutes, or until the fruit is bubbling and the topping is golden.

Australian Omelette

Miss LM Northcott, Mosman Branch

SERVES 4

60 g (1 cup, lightly packed)
  fresh breadcrumbs
185 ml (¾ cup) milk
1 tablespoon melted butter
1 tablespoon chopped
  parsley
3 French shallots, finely
  chopped
50 g (½ cup) finely grated
  parmesan
4 eggs, separated

Preheat oven to 180°C. Generously grease a 1.5 litre (6 cup) capacity baking dish.

Place the crumbs in a bowl. Heat the milk in a saucepan until nearly boiling, then pour over the crumbs. Add the butter, parsley, shallots and parmesan and season well with salt and pepper.

Beat the egg yolks in a small bowl. Stir into the crumb mixture.

Using an electric beater, whisk the egg whites in a bowl until firm peaks form. Fold the whites into the crumb mixture. Spoon the mixture into the baking dish.

Bake for 20 minutes, or until puffed and light golden.

Banana Cream

Mrs G Hadlow, Collector Branch

SERVES 6

2 teaspoons powdered
  gelatine
2 tablespoons water
3 large ripe bananas,
  chopped
75 g (⅓ cup) caster sugar
2 tablespoons brandy
300 ml pouring cream,
  whipped

Sprinkle the gelatine over the water in a small heatproof cup and stand for 5 minutes, or until the gelatine softens. Place the cup in a small saucepan of simmering water coming halfway up the side of the cup. Heat for 4–5 minutes, or until the gelatine dissolves.

Combine the bananas and sugar in a food processor and purée until smooth.

Spoon the banana mixture into a bowl. Stir in the gelatine and brandy. Refrigerate until the mixture starts to thicken. Fold in the whipped cream.

Spoon into six 200 ml glasses or serving bowls. Refrigerate until set.

Paradise Pie

Mrs Budden, Scone Branch

MAKES ONE 24 CM PIE
75 ml pouring cream
75 g milk
25 g butter, chopped
grated zest and juice of
    2 oranges
25 g caster sugar
150 g (1¼ cups) stale
    butter cake or sponge
    cake crumbs
2 eggs, separated

1 batch Marlborough Tart
    pastry (see January 25)

Preheat oven to 180°C.

Roll the pastry out into a circle to fit the base and side of a 24 cm round tart tin, trimming the side even. Line the pastry with baking paper then fill with baking beads or dried beans. Bake for 20 minutes.

Combine the cream, milk and butter in a small saucepan and heat until nearly simmering and butter has melted. Remove from heat.

Combine the juice, zest and sugar in a large bowl. Add the crumbs, egg yolks and milk mixture and stir to combine well.

Using an electric beater, whisk the egg whites until firm peaks form. Fold the whites into the crumbs mixture, then spoon into the pastry case.

Bake for 35 minutes, or until the filling is golden and set.

Apples in Red Jelly

Mrs Bennett, Junee Branch

22 NOV

SERVES 4–6

150 g (⅔ cups) caster
    sugar
600 ml water
thinly peeled rind of 1 lemon,
    white pith removed
6 cloves
6 granny smith apples,
    peeled, halved and cored
red food colouring
2½ teaspoons powdered
    gelatine
60 ml (¼ cup) of water

Combine the sugar in a large saucepan with the water and bring to the boil, stirring to dissolve the sugar. Add the rind, cloves and the apples and cook very gently for 15 minutes, or until the apples are tender but still holding their shape.

Transfer the apples to a large deep dish, placing them cut side down in a single layer. Strain the cooking liquid into a bowl and add enough red colouring to tint it pink.

Sprinkle the gelatine over the water in a small heatproof cup and stand for 5 minutes, or until the gelatine softens. Place the cup in a small saucepan of simmering water coming halfway up the side of the cup. Heat for 4–5 minutes, or until the gelatine dissolves. Stir the gelatine into the cooking liquid.

Pour the liquid over the apples in the dish. Refrigerate for 4 hours, or until the jelly is firm.

Biscuits au Diable

Mrs Kiley, Cootamundra Branch

23 NOV

MAKES 16

100 g (1 cup) grated cheddar
    cheese
1 tablespoon chutney
1 teaspoon mustard
pinch of cayenne pepper
1 tablespoon egg yolk
16 Captain's Table biscuits,
    or similar

Preheat oven to 180°C.

Place the cheese, chutney, mustard, cayenne and egg yolk in a bowl and stir to combine well.

Spread each biscuit thinly with the cheese mixture. Place on a baking tray and bake for 5–6 minutes, or until heated through.

Serve hot.

Chocolate Soufflé

Mrs WH Mackay, Scone Branch

SERVES 6

2 tablespoons cocoa
  powder, sifted
1 tablespoon plain flour
5 teaspoons powdered
  gelatine
220 g (1 cup) caster sugar
625 ml (2½ cups) cold water
150 ml pouring cream,
  whipped, plus extra,
  to serve
finely chopped dark
  chocolate, to serve

Place the cocoa, flour, gelatine and sugar in a bowl and whisk to combine well. Whisking constantly, add 125 ml (½ cup) of the water, mixing until a smooth paste forms. Add the remaining water and whisk until combined.

Pour the cocoa mixture into a saucepan and, whisking often to prevent lumps forming, bring the mixture to a simmer, Cook, stirring, for 3 minutes, then remove from the heat and cool to room temperature. Refrigerate until the mixture is beginning to set.

Transfer the mixture to a large bowl. Using an electric beater, whisk at high speed for 10–15 minutes, or until the mixture thickens and turns opaque. Fold in the whipped cream.

Spoon the soufflé into six 200 ml glasses and refrigerate for 2–3 hours, or until set.

Serve topped with whipped cream and sprinkled with chopped chocolate.

Oriental Sundae

25 NOV

Mrs WN West, Weetangera Branch

SERVES 6–8

2½ teaspoons powdered
    gelatine
80 ml (⅓ cup) water, plus
    500 ml (2 cups), extra
110 g (½ cup) caster sugar
juice of 2 lemons
red food colouring
250 g day-old sponge cake,
    cut into 2 cm pieces
3 bananas, sliced
300 ml pouring cream,
    whipped
pulp of 3 passionfruit

Sprinkle the gelatine over 80 ml (⅓ cup) of water in a small heatproof cup and stand for 5 minutes, or until the gelatine softens. Place the cup in a small saucepan of simmering water coming halfway up the side of the cup. Heat for 4–5 minutes, or until the gelatine dissolves.

Heat extra water in a pan and stir in the sugar and lemon juice. Remove from the heat. Combine with the gelatine and add enough food colouring to tint the liquid pink. Cool to room temperature.

Place the sponge in a 2 litre (8 cup) capacity bowl and pour the jelly mixture over. Refrigerate for 2–3 hours or until firm.

Place the bananas on the top. Spoon over the whipped cream and drizzle with the passionfruit.

Pan Pacific Fruit Salad

26 NOV

**Miss M Macdonald and Miss MEJ Yeo,
Delegates to Pan-Pacific Women's Conference**

SERVES 10–12

1 pineapple, trimmed, cored
    and eyes removed
1 small pawpaw, peeled
    and seeded
1.2 kg watermelon (about
    ⅓ watermelon), peeled
3 bananas, peeled and sliced
pulp of 12 passionfruit
110 g (½ cup) caster sugar
whipped cream or custard,
    to serve

Cut the pineapple, pawpaw and watermelon into 1.5 cm pieces. Layer all the fruits in a very large bowl, scattering each layer lightly with the sugar.

Cover the bowl with plastic wrap and refrigerate for 30 minutes, or until chilled. Serve with cream or custard.

Banana Flan

Mrs FD Smith, Crookwell Branch

SERVES 8

125 ml (½ cup) pouring
  cream
125 ml (½ cup) milk
150 g (⅔ cup) caster sugar
1 teaspoon vanilla essence
4 eggs, separated
2 large ripe, firm bananas

1 batch Marlborough Tart
  pastry (see January 25)

Preheat oven to 180°C.

Roll the pastry out on a floured surface into a circle just large enough to line a 24 x 2.5 cm deep tart tin, patching pastry as needed to cover base and side. Cover the pastry with baking paper and fill with baking beads or dried beans. Bake for 20 minutes. Remove from the oven and take off the paper and beads.

Heat the cream and milk in a small saucepan until nearly simmering. Remove from the heat, then stir in half the sugar and the vanilla.

Beat the egg yolks in a bowl, pour over the hot milk mixture and stir to combine well.

Slice the bananas and scatter evenly over the pastry shell. Pour the milk mixture over the bananas. Bake for 20 minutes, or until nearly set.

Using an electric beater, whisk the egg whites in a bowl until firm peaks form. Gradually add the remaining sugar, whisking until the mixture is stiff and glossy. Pile the whites over the banana mixture.

Bake for a further 15–20 minutes, or until the meringue is golden.

Rice Coconut Pudding

Mrs Percy Stacy, Singleton Branch

SERVES 6

75 g (⅓ cup) short-grain
   white rice
1 litre (4 cups) milk
1 teaspoon vanilla extract
150 g (⅔ cup) caster sugar
45 g (½ cup) desiccated
   coconut
4 eggs, separated

Combine the rice and milk in a saucepan, bring to a simmer then reduce heat to medium–low. Cook for 30–40 minutes, stirring often, or until rice is tender and mixture has thickened. Remove from the heat.

Preheat oven to 180°C. Generously grease a 26 x 18 x 5 cm baking dish.

Stir the vanilla, 30 g of the sugar and 30 g (⅓ cup) of the desiccated coconut into the rice. Whisk the eggs yolks in a bowl, pour a little of the hot rice mixture onto the yolks and stir to combine well. Add the stirred yolks into the hot rice mixture. Pour into the dish and bake for 20–25 minutes, or until nearly set.

Whisk the egg whites until firm peaks form. Whisking constantly, add the remaining sugar, 1 tablespoon at a time, until mixture is stiff and glossy.

Spoon the whites over the top of the pudding and scatter the remaining coconut over the top.

Bake for 20 minutes, or until the meringue is golden. Serve hot or warm.

Orange Pie

Mrs CA Barnes, Quambone Branch

SERVES 6

5 large oranges, peeled
and all white pith
removed
finely grated zest of
2 oranges
165 g (¾ cup) caster sugar
1 tablespoon cornflour
1½ tablespoons butter,
chopped
125 ml (½ cup) boiling
water

Pastry
185 g (1¼ cups) plain flour
½ teaspoon bicarbonate
of soda
1 teaspoon cream of
tartar
125 g (½ cup) chilled butter,
chopped
60 ml (¼ cup) cold milk,
or as required

Preheat oven to 180°C.

For the pastry, combine the flour, soda and tartar in a bowl. Using your fingertips, rub in the butter until the mixture resembles breadcrumbs. Add the milk and mix well, adding a little more milk if required to form a firm dough.

Turn the dough out onto a lightly floured surface and knead briefly until smooth. Roll the dough out until large enough to cover a 26 x 18 x 5 cm baking dish. Set aside.

Cut the oranges into 1.5 cm chunks and place in an even layer over the pastry. Combine the zest, sugar and cornflour in a bowl and scatter over the oranges with the butter. Pour the boiling water over the oranges.

Cover the dish with the pastry, trimming and crimping the edges.

Bake for 40 minutes, or until the pastry is golden and the orange mixture is bubbling and thickened.

Lemon Biscuits

Mrs Percy Stacy, Singleton Branch

MAKES ABOUT 22

125 g (½ cup) butter,
  softened
125 g caster sugar
2 eggs
finely grated zest of
  2 lemons
250 g (1⅔ cups) plain flour
1 teaspoon baking powder

Preheat oven to 170°C. Line two baking trays with baking paper.

Using an electric beater, beat the butter and sugar in a bowl until light and creamy. Add the eggs, one at a time, beating well between each. Stir in the zest.

Sift the flour and baking powder into a bowl, then stir into the creamed mixture to form a soft dough.

Roll the dough out on a well-floured surface to about 5 mm thickness, taking care as the mixture is very soft. Using a 6 mm round pastry cutter, cut rounds from the dough. Place on the trays, leaving room for spreading. Refrigerate for 30 minutes, or until firm.

Bake the biscuits for 12–15 minutes, or until firm. Transfer to a wire rack to cool.

Family recipes

		1	2	3
		Fruit Soup	Beef Stock	Fried Chicken Southern Style
4	5	6	7	8
Spanish Cream	Rice Pancakes	Cherry Cake	Glen Alice Savoury	Raw Vegetable Salad
9	10	11	12	13
Trifle	Chicken Salad	Sweet Mince Tart	Orange Relish	Narrandera Salad
14	15	16	17	18
Peach Salad	Tomato Paste	Apricot Whip	Marshmallow Pudding	Potato Puffs
19	20	21	22	23
Cheese Brittles	An Unrivalled Plum Pudding	Christmas Cake	Yass Plum Pudding	Hard Sauce
24	25	26	27	28
German Sauce	Boiled Custard	Pumpkin Scones	Walnut and Celery Sandwiches	Passionfruit Cake
29	30	31		
Mocha Cream	Sponge Sandwich No 2	Cauliflower Salad		

DECEMBER

Fruit Soup

Mrs JWC Beveridge, Junee Branch

SERVES 4

300 g pitted fresh or
  frozen cherries
500 ml (2 cups) water
75 g (⅓ cup) caster sugar
1 × 2 cm wide strip of
  lemon rind, white pith
  removed
1 stick of cinnamon
60 ml (¼ cup) white wine

Combine the cherries with the water, sugar, rind and cinnamon in a saucepan and bring to a simmer. Cook, covered, over medium–low heat for 25 minutes, or until the fruit is very soft. Remove the cinnamon stick and rind.

Place the cooked fruit in a food processor and purée until smooth. Push the purée through a sieve into a bowl, discarding the solids. Stir in the wine and cool to room temperature.

Refrigerate for 3 hours, or until chilled. Serve in small cups or glasses.

Beef Stock

Mrs Hoskings, Binnaway Branch

MAKES 3 LITRES (12 CUPS)

2.5 kg beef bones
1 carrot, peeled and
  coarsely chopped
1 turnip, peeled and
  coarsely chopped
1 onion, peeled and
  coarsely chopped
2 large stalks celery,
  coarsely chopped
small handful of thyme
  and parsley sprigs
12 black peppercorns
4–5 cloves
1 blade of mace
3 litres (12 cups) water,
  or as required

Place all the ingredients in a large stock pot then add the water, adding more if required to cover the bones and vegetables.

Bring to a simmer, skimming off any scum that rises to the top. Simmer over low heat for 4–5 hours, adding a little extra water as required to keep bones just covered.

Strain the stock, discarding the solids, and cool to room temperature. Skim off any fat and refrigerate for later use. (Stock can also be frozen.)

Fried Chicken Southern Style

Mrs RH Dangar, Coolah Branch

SERVES 4

1 x 1.5 kg chicken, or
   chicken pieces
plain flour, for dusting,
   plus extra, for cooking
100 g butter
vegetable oil, for shallow-
   frying
125 ml (½ cup) pouring
   cream
125 ml (½ cup) milk,
   or as required

Cut the chicken into 8 pieces through the bone. Season each piece with salt and pepper, then dust well with flour, shaking off the excess.

Melt the butter in a large, deep frying pan over medium heat, adding enough oil to shallow-fry the chicken (the oil mixture should come about 3 cm up the side of the pan).

When the oil is hot, add the chicken and cook, turning occasionally, for 25 minutes, or until the chicken is deep golden and cooked through.

Remove the chicken to a plate lined with paper towels to drain off the excess oil, then cover loosely with foil to keep warm.

Pour all but 2 tablespoons of the fat from the pan, add 1 tablespoon of flour and stir to combine well. Stirring or whisking constantly to prevent lumps forming, add the cream and milk and bring to the boil. Cook for 2–3 minutes, or until the mixture has boiled and thickened, adding a little more milk as required if the gravy is too thick.

Serve chicken with gravy poured over.

Spanish Cream

Mrs F Hylton Kelly, Crookwell Branch

SERVES 6–8

900 ml milk

5 teaspoons powdered
    gelatine

110 g (½ cup) caster sugar

3 eggs, separated

2 teaspoons vanilla essence

Place 1 cup (250 ml) of the milk in a small heatproof bowl and sprinkle over the gelatine. Stand for 5–6 minutes, or until the gelatine has softened. Place the bowl in a small saucepan of simmering water and heat for 4–5 minutes, or until the gelatine dissolves.

Bring the remaining milk to a simmer in a larger saucepan. Remove from the heat, add the gelatine mixture and sugar and stir well.

Pour a little of the hot milk into the egg yolks in a bowl and mix well. Stir into the hot milk mixture in the pan. Cool to room temperature.

Using an electric beater, whisk the egg whites in a bowl until firm peaks form. Gently stir the whites into the milk mixture. Pour the cream into a wet 2 litre (8 cup) capacity mould. Refrigerate for 5 hours or overnight, until set.

To serve, dip the mould in hot water and turn the Spanish Cream out onto a serving plate.

Rice Pancakes

Mrs Waugh, Bathurst Branch

MAKES 12

110 g (½ cup) medium-grain
   white rice
150 g (1 cup) self-raising
   flour
2½ tablespoons caster
   sugar
1 egg, well beaten
200 ml milk
butter, for cooking
honey, to serve

Cook the rice in plenty of boiling water for 12–15 minutes, or until tender. Drain well and set aside to cool.

Preheat oven to 120°C.

Combine the flour and sugar in a bowl, making a well in the centre. In another bowl whisk the egg and milk then add to the well in the flour mixture. Gradually work the flour mixture into the milk mixture, whisking until smooth. Stir in the rice and a large pinch of salt.

Melt 1 tablespoon of butter in a large, non-stick frying pan over medium heat. Spoon the batter into the pan, in batches, forming pancakes 8–9 cm across. Cook the pancakes for about 3 minutes, or until bubbles appear on the surface, adding more butter as required. Turn over and cook for a further 2–3 minutes.

Transfer the cooked pancakes to a plate, cover with foil, and keep warm in the oven while the remaining pancakes cook.

Serve warm pancakes drizzled with honey.

Cherry Cake

Mrs Evans, Wagga Branch

MAKES ONE 18 CM CAKE
200 g butter, softened
165 g (¾ cup) caster sugar
3 eggs
½ teaspoon almond essence
200 g (1⅓ cups) plain flour
25 g cornflour
2 teaspoons baking powder
120 g (½ cup) glacé cherries,
　halved
2 tablespoons milk
35 g (⅓ cup) flaked almonds

Preheat oven to 170°C. Grease and flour the side of an 18 cm cake tin and line the base with baking paper.

Using an electric beater, beat the butter and sugar in a bowl until light and creamy. Add the eggs, one at a time, beating well between each. Add the essence.

Sift the flour, cornflour and baking powder into a bowl. Stir into the butter mixture with the cherries and milk. Spoon the batter into the tin, smoothing the top even, and sprinkle over the almonds.

Bake for 1½ hours, or until a skewer inserted in the centre comes out clean – cover the cake with foil if it browns too quickly.

Cool the cake in the tin for 10 minutes, then turn out onto a wire rack to cool completely.

Glen Alice Savoury

Miss Georgina Baker, Glen Alice Branch

SERVES 4
1 x 105 g tin sardines
　in oil, well drained
2 hard-boiled egg yolks,
　finely chopped
2 tablespoons butter,
　softened
2–3 teaspoons lemon juice,
　or as required
1 tablespoon finely
　chopped parsley
4 slices hot buttered toast

Using a fork, mash the sardines in a bowl until a chunky purée forms. Add the yolks, butter, juice and parsley and stir to combine well.

Season to taste with salt and pepper, adding a little extra lemon juice if required.

Serve spread on hot buttered toast.

Raw Vegetable Salad

Mrs Frank Dixon, West Maitland Branch

SERVES 6–8

2 large carrots, peeled
  and cut into thin batons
1 large kohlrabi, peeled
  and cut into thin batons
3 spring onions, trimmed
  and finely sliced
2 Lebanese cucumbers,
  thinly sliced
4 cups watercress sprigs
2 large tomatoes, cut into
  wedges
1 stalk celery, trimmed
  and finely sliced
1 large pink lady apple, cut
  into wedges and sliced
1 small red cabbage heart,
  finely sliced
1 small handful of parsley,
  chopped

Dressing
1 egg yolk
1 tablespoon mustard
80 ml (⅓ cup) white vinegar
250 ml (1 cup) olive oil

For the dressing, whisk the egg yolk and mustard in a large bowl. Add the vinegar and combine well. Whisking constantly, add the oil in a slow, steady stream until a thick, smooth dressing forms. Season well with salt and pepper.

Toss all the vegetables in a bowl then arrange on a large platter. Drizzle the vegetables with the dressing, sprinkle with the parsley and serve.

Trifle

Mrs Bennett, Aylmerton Branch

SERVES 8
250 g day-old sponge cake
2 bananas, sliced
8 fresh apricots, or
    16 drained apricot
    halves, coarsely chopped
1 packet orange jelly
125 ml (½ cup) sweet sherry
1 egg white
300 ml pouring cream,
    whipped
18 glacé cherries, to
    decorate
coloured sugar, to decorate

Cut the cake into 2.5 cm squares. Place alternating layers of fruit and cake in a 2.5 litre (10 cup) capacity serving bowl.

Make the jelly according to the packet directions. Stir in the sherry.

Pour the jelly mixture over the cake and fruit in the bowl. Cool to room temperature then refrigerate for 4 hours, or until set.

Using an electric beater, whisk the egg white in a bowl until firm peaks form. Fold the egg white into the whipped cream. Spoon the cream mixture over the trifle.

Decorate the trifle with the cherries and coloured sugar.

Chicken Salad

Mrs Jack Quilter, Gundagai Branch

SERVES 6–8
1 butter lettuce, leaves
    washed and dried
80 ml (⅓ cup) olive oil
2½ tablespoons white
    wine vinegar
450 g kipfler potatoes,
    boiled and cooled
3 large ripe tomatoes,
    cut into wedges
1 cold, cooked chicken,
    flesh coarsely shredded
mayonnaise, for drizzling
120 g (⅓ cup) stuffed green olives
3 hard-boiled eggs, peeled
    and cut into wedges

Place the lettuce in a large bowl and sprinkle with the oil and vinegar.

Slice the potatoes, then scatter over the lettuce with the tomato. Place the chicken on top. Drizzle the salad with mayonnaise to taste and scatter over the olives and eggs.

Season well with salt and pepper and serve.

Sweet Mince Tart

Miss Jean Lamont, Younger Set, Wagga Branch

SERVES 8

250 g (1⅔ cups) plain flour
½ teaspoon baking powder
125 g (½ cup) butter,
  chopped
iced water, as required
2 large granny smith apples,
  peeled, cored and finely
  chopped
55 g (¼ cup) caster sugar
185 g (1 cup) mixed dried
  fruit
milk, for brushing
sugar, for sprinkling

Preheat oven to 180°C.

Combine the flour and baking powder in a bowl. Using your fingertips, rub in the butter until the mixture resembles coarse breadcrumbs. Gradually add enough iced water to form a firm dough.

Turn the dough out on a floured surface. Remove a third of the dough and set aside. Roll the larger piece of dough into a circle large enough to line a 24 × 5 cm deep tart tin. Line the tin and trim the edges, reserving any pastry scraps.

Scatter the apples, sugar and dried fruit over the base of the tart. Roll out the remaining pastry and scraps into a circle large enough to cover the tart. Place the pastry over the tart and press edges to seal. Brush the top of the tart with a little milk and sprinkle over a little sugar.

Bake for 45 minutes, or until the pastry is golden.

Orange Relish

Miss IM Tubman, Gosford Branch

SERVES 6

2 oranges, peeled and
  thinly sliced
1 tablespoon Worcestershire
  sauce
1 teaspoon salt

Remove any seeds from the orange slices and place in a bowl. Drizzle over the Worcestershire sauce and scatter over the salt.

Leave to stand for 10 minutes before serving. This relish is delicious with cold meat or ham.

Narrandera Salad

Mrs Bratton, Narrandera Branch

SERVES 4

85 g (½ cup) raisins,
  chopped
300 g ham, in one piece,
  cut into 1 cm pieces
1 Lebanese cucumber,
  sliced
75 g (½ cup) gherkins,
  thinly sliced
mayonnaise, to bind
lettuce leaves, for serving

Combine the raisins, ham, cucumber and gherkins in a bowl and stir in enough mayonnaise to bind the mixture well. Season well with salt and pepper to taste.

Spoon the mixture onto lettuce leaves and serve.

Peach Salad

Mrs Jas. Rawsthorne, Forbes Branch

SERVES 4

2–3 ripe yellow-fleshed
  peaches, sliced
1 butter lettuce, leaves
  washed and dried
1½ tablespoons chopped
  chives

Widgee Salad Dressing
1 teaspoon mustard
  powder
½ teaspoon sugar
1 tablespoon white wine
  vinegar, or to taste
125 ml (½ cup) pouring
  cream

Scatter the peach slices over the lettuce leaves on a platter and sprinkle the chives over the top. Season well with salt and pepper.

For the dressing, combine the mustard, sugar, vinegar and cream in a bowl. Season well and add a little more vinegar to taste, if required.

Drizzle the dressing over the salad and serve.

Tomato Paste

Mrs MB Crozier, Albury Branch

SERVES 4

3 large ripe tomatoes,
   finely chopped
50 g butter
1 onion, finely chopped
50 g fresh breadcrumbs
50 g (½ cup) grated
   cheddar cheese
large pinch of cayenne
   pepper
2 eggs, well beaten
hot buttered toast, to serve

Combine the tomato, butter and onion in a saucepan and bring to a simmer. Cook, stirring often, over medium heat for 6–7 minutes, or until the onion is very soft.

Add the crumbs, cheese, cayenne and eggs and cook, stirring constantly, for about 3 minutes, or until the mixture has thickened slightly – do not allow it to boil or the eggs will scramble.

Season well with salt and pepper and serve on buttered toast.

Apricot Whip

Mrs Tom Lindsay, Trangie Branch

SERVES 4–6

1 x 410 g tin apricots in
   juice
1 packet orange jelly
   crystals
8 savoiardi (lady finger)
   biscuits
whipped cream, to serve

Drain the apricots, reserving 125 ml (½ cup) of the juice. Place the apricots in a food processor and purée until smooth. Combine the purée with the juice in a bowl.

Make the jelly according to the packet directions and cool to room temperature. Refrigerate until it starts to set.

Using an electric beater, whisk the jelly and apricot mixture in a bowl until foamy and holding its shape. Place the biscuits in the base of a 1.5 litre (6 cup) capacity bowl and spoon the mixture over.

Refrigerate for 3–4 hours or until firm. Serve with whipped cream.

Marshmallow Pudding

Mrs FE Bassingthwait, Cootamundra Branch

SERVES 6–8

1 tablespoon powdered
  gelatine
125 ml (½ cup) water, plus
  125 ml (½ cup) extra, cold
3 egg whites
220 g (1 cup) caster sugar
1 teaspoon vanilla essence
red food colouring

Sprinkle the gelatine over the water in a small heatproof cup and stand for 5 minutes, or until the gelatine softens. Place the cup in a small saucepan of simmering water coming halfway up the side of the cup. Heat for 4–5 minutes, or until the gelatine dissolves.

Remove the gelatine from the heat, combine with the cold water and stand until cooled to room temperature.

Using an electric beater, whisk the egg whites until firm peaks form. Gradually add the sugar, whisking constantly, until mixture is thick and glossy. Whisk in the gelatine mixture and the essence. Stand for 5–10 minutes, or until the mixture starts to firm a little.

Spoon half the mixture into small serving glasses. Using a couple of drops of food colouring, tint the remaining half pink. Spoon the pink mixture over the top of the white mixture.

Refrigerate until firm then serve.

Potato Puffs

Mrs PS Bowman, Glen Innes Branch

SERVES 6
flour, for dusting
900 g (about 3 large)
   desiree potatoes,
   peeled and chopped
2 tablespoons butter,
   softened
90 ml cream
2 eggs, separated

Preheat oven to 180°C. Generously grease a 6-hole 250 ml (1 cup) capacity giant muffin tin with butter. Dust with flour.

Boil the potatoes in boiling salted water for 15 minutes, or until very soft. Drain, place in a bowl and mash well. Add the butter, cream and egg yolks and stir to combine. Season to taste with salt and pepper.

Using an electric beater, whisk the egg whites in a bowl until firm peaks form. Fold the whites into the potato mixture. Spoon the potato mixture into the muffin holes.

Bake for about 30 minutes, or until golden. Serve hot as a side dish.

Cheese Brittles

Mrs WJ Keast, Junee Branch

MAKES 16
4 thin slices of bread,
   crusts removed
butter, for spreading
30 g (⅓ cup) grated
   parmesan cheese

Preheat oven to 170°C.

Butter the bread lightly and cut into quarters to form triangles. Place the bread on a baking tray. Sprinkle over the cheese, then season with salt and pepper.

Bake for 30 minutes, or until dry and crisp. Serve hot or cold.

An Unrivalled Plum Pudding

20 DEC

Miss Ivy Quinton, Maitland Branch

MAKES TWO 18 CM PUDDINGS

400 g (2⅓ cups) raisins
400 g (3½ cups) currants
500 g sultanas
100 g mixed peel
50 g (⅓ cup) almonds, finely
  chopped
500 g (2 cups) shredded suet
  (see note)
250 g fresh breadcrumbs
250 g (1⅔ cups) self-raising
  flour
pinch of bicarbonate
  of soda
2 teaspoons freshly grated
  nutmeg
8 eggs, beaten well
160 ml (⅓ cup) brandy

Bring two large saucepans of water for steaming to the boil, placing a small heatproof plate upside down in the water in each pan to keep the pudding basin off the base. Grease and flour two 18 cm, 2.25 litre (9 cup) capacity pudding basins (see note below).

Combine the dried fruits, almonds, suet and crumbs in a very large bowl. Sift the flour, soda and nutmeg into a bowl, add to the fruit mix and stir to combine well. Combine the eggs and the brandy then pour over the mixture in the bowl and stir to combine well.

Spoon the batter into the basins, cover tightly and lower them into the boiling water. Steam for 6 hours, or until cooked through, adding more water to the pan as required.

To store, wrap the puddings in plastic wrap, then in several layers of foil. Store in an airtight container in a pantry cupboard, or refrigerate if preferred. These puddings also freeze well.

Notes: shredded suet is available as a packet mix at supermarkets, or fresh from your butcher.

This recipe makes a large quantity of pudding mixture. You may prefer to make one very large or several small puddings — select your basin sizes accordingly. The recipe can also be halved.

This pudding may be made 6–8 weeks in advance and stored for later use.

Christmas Cake

Mrs J Connell, Yass Branch

MAKES THREE 18 CM CAKES

500 g (2 cups) butter,
    softened
500 g caster sugar
8 eggs
500 g raisins
500 g sultanas
500 g currants
250 g mixed peel
125 g almonds, finely
    chopped
750 g (2½ cups) plain flour
1 tablespoon mixed spice
1 teaspoon baking powder
125 ml (½ cup) brandy

Preheat oven to 150°C. Line three 18 cm cake tins (see note below) with several layers of baking paper.

Using a stand mixer, beat the butter and sugar in a bowl for 10 minutes, or until very pale and creamy. Add the eggs, one at a time, beating well between each.

Combine the fruit and almonds in a large bowl. Add 110 g (¾ cup) of the flour to lightly coat.

Combine the fruit mixture and the creamed mixture in a very large bowl. Sift the remaining flour, mixed spice and baking powder, then stir into the mixture in the bowl. Stir in the brandy. Spoon the batter into the cake tins, smoothing the tops even.

Bake for 2 hours, or until a skewer inserted in the centres comes out clean — cover the top of the cakes with foil if they brown too quickly.

Cool the cakes in the tins. To store, remove from tins, wrap the cakes in plastic wrap and then in several layers of foil. Store in an airtight container in a dark, cook place, or refrigerate if preferred.

Note: this recipe makes a very large quantity of cake mixture. You may prefer to make one large or several small cakes — select your cake tin sizes accordingly.

This cake may be made 6–8 weeks in advance and stored for later use.

Yass Plum Pudding

Mrs J Connell, Yass Branch

22 DEC

SERVES 10–12

250 g brown sugar
250 g (1 cup) butter, softened
4 eggs
2 teaspoons vanilla essence
½ teaspoon almond essence
finely grated zest of 1 orange
finely grated zest of 1 lemon
250 g currants
250 g sultanas
250 g raisins
125 g almonds, finely chopped
125 g plain flour
2 teaspoons ground cinnamon
½ teaspoon ground nutmeg
½ teaspoon ground cloves
125 g fresh breadcrumbs
80 g (½ cup, firmly packed)
   finely grated carrot
150 ml brandy

This pudding may be made 6–8 weeks in advance and stored for later use.

Bring a large saucepan of water to the boil for steaming, placing a small heatproof plate upside down in the water to keep the pudding basin off the base of the pan. Grease and flour a 2.25 litre (9 cup) capacity pudding basin.

Using an electric beater, beat the sugar and butter in a bowl until light and creamy. Add the eggs, one at a time, beating well between each. Add the essences and citrus zest.

Place the currants, sultanas, raisins and almonds in a bowl. Combine the flour, spices and breadcrumbs in another bowl and mix well. Add the fruit and flour mixtures to the creamed mixture alternately, stirring to combine well. Add the grated carrot and stir in the brandy.

Spoon the batter into the basin, cover tightly and lower it into the boiling water. Steam for 4½ hours, or until cooked through, adding more water to the pan as required.

To store, wrap the pudding in plastic wrap, then in several layers of foil. Store in an airtight container in a pantry cupboard, or refrigerate if preferred. This pudding also freezes well.

Hard Sauce

23 DEC

MAKES ABOUT 1½ CUPS

125 g (½ cup) butter, softened
125 g (1 cup) icing sugar
2 tablespoons brandy
pinch of freshly grated
   nutmeg

Using an electric beater, beat the butter and icing sugar in a bowl until very pale and creamy. Beat in the brandy and nutmeg. Transfer to a serving bowl. Keep at a cool room temperature until ready to serve with Christmas pudding, or any other rich, steamed fruit pudding.

German Sauce

Mrs H Moore Sims, Moree Branch

SERVES 6

6 egg yolks
75 g (⅓ cup) caster sugar
125 ml (½ cup) brandy
125 ml (½ cup) medium-
    sweet sherry

Bring a saucepan of water to the simmer.

In a large bowl that will fit snugly over the top of the saucepan, whisk the egg yolks, sugar, brandy and sherry.

Whisking constantly with a balloon whisk or an electric beater, whisk the egg mixture over the simmering water for 5 minutes, or until thickened and foamy – do not stop whisking or allow the mixture to overheat or it will scramble.

Remove the bowl from the heat and continue to whisk until it has cooled a little.

Serve warm on puddings or desserts.

Boiled Custard

SERVES 4–6

2 eggs, beaten well
1 tablespoon cornflour
1 teaspoon vanilla essence
600 ml milk
1 tablespoon butter
75 g (⅓ cup) caster sugar

Whisk the eggs in a large bowl. Place the cornflour in a small bowl, whisking in a little of the egg to form a smooth paste. Mix the paste into the egg in the bowl and add the vanilla.

Heat the milk, butter and sugar in a small saucepan, stirring to dissolve the sugar. When nearly boiling, pour the milk mixture onto the egg mixture, stirring to combine well. Take the pan off the heat.

Working carefully, pour the mixture between the pan and the bowl several times until the custard thickens.

Serve warm on puddings or desserts.

Pumpkin Scones

Mrs C Gordon, Manildra Branch

MAKES 10

410 g (2¾ cups) self-raising
  flour
165 g (¾ cup) caster sugar
½ teaspoon salt
50 g butter, chopped
250 g (1 cup) cold, mashed
  pumpkin
1 tablespoon milk, or as
  required

Preheat oven to 200°C. Line a baking tray with baking paper.

Combine the flour, sugar and salt in a bowl. Using your fingertips, rub in the butter until the mixture resembles breadcrumbs. Mix in the pumpkin and enough milk to form a soft dough.

Using your hands, pat out the dough on a floured surface to 2 cm thickness. Using a 6 cm round pastry cutter, cut rounds from the dough, patting out the scraps for more rounds. Place on the trays.

Bake for 20 minutes, or until golden and cooked through. Transfer scones to a wire rack to cool.

Walnut and Celery Sandwiches

Mrs Waddell, Merriwa Branch

MAKES 9 FINGER SANDWICHES

2 large celery stalks,
  trimmed
80 g (⅔ cup) walnuts, very
  finely chopped
2 tablespoons mayonnaise
2 tablespoons whipped
  thickened cream
1 tablespoon chopped
  parsley
6 slices buttered brown
  sandwich bread

Using a potato peeler, peel the tough fibres from the celery stalks, then very finely chop the celery.

Combine the celery in a bowl with the walnuts, mayonnaise, whipped cream and parsley. Season well with salt and pepper.

Spoon the mixture onto three of the bread slices, spreading evenly to cover. Place remaining bread slices on top. Trim the crusts and cut each sandwich into three fingers.

Serve immediately.

Passionfruit Cake

Mrs Fraser, Dungog Branch

MAKES ONE 18 CM CAKE

125 g (½ cup) butter,
   softened
125 g caster sugar
2 eggs
250 g plain flour
1 teaspoon baking powder
125 g (½ cup) passionfruit
   pulp (about 6 passionfruit)

Filling
1 egg white
185 g (1½ cups) icing sugar,
   or as required
60 g (¼ cup) butter,
   softened
pulp of 4 passionfruit

Preheat oven to 175°C. Grease and flour the sides of two 18 cm cake tins and line the bases with baking paper.

Using an electric beater, beat the butter and sugar in a bowl until light and creamy. Add the eggs, one at a time, beating well between each.

Sift the flour and baking powder into a bowl. Add to the creamed mixture with the passionfruit pulp, stirring to combine well. Spoon the batter into the tins, smoothing the tops even.

Bake for about 30 minutes, or until a skewer inserted in the centres comes out clean. Cool the cakes in the tins for 10 minutes, then turn out onto a wire rack to cool completely.

For the filling, using an electric beater, whisk the egg white in a bowl until firm peaks form. Gradually add 125 g (1 cup) of the icing sugar, whisking constantly, until the mixture is firm and glossy. Add the butter and half the passionfruit pulp, then whisk in enough of the remaining icing sugar to form a very thick, creamy icing.

Spread half the icing mixture over one cake and layer with the other cake. Cover the top of the cake with the remaining icing, and drizzle over the remaining passionfruit pulp.

Mocha Cream

Mrs JC Dowling, Manildra Branch

SERVES 6

600 ml milk
1 tablespoon coffee essence
1½ teaspoons vanilla essence
110 g (½ cup) caster sugar
3 eggs, separated
2½ teaspoons powered gelatine
60 ml (¼ cup) water
whipped cream, to serve
grated chocolate, to serve

Combine the milk, essences and sugar in a saucepan and bring to a simmer, stirring to dissolve the sugar.

Beat the egg yolks in a bowl. Pour a cup or so of the hot milk mixture over the yolks and stir to combine well. Stir the yolk mixture into the rest of the milk mixture in the pan. Stirring constantly with a wooden spoon, cook over medium–low heat for 5 minutes, or until the mixture thickens slightly.

Sprinkle the gelatine over the water in a small heatproof cup and stand for 5 minutes, or until the gelatine softens. Place the cup in a small saucepan of simmering water coming halfway up the side of the cup. Heat for 4–5 minutes, or until the gelatine dissolves.

Add the gelatine to the milk mixture and stir to mix well. Cool to room temperature, then refrigerate until the mixture begins to thicken.

Using an electric beater, whisk the egg whites in a bowl until firm peaks form. Fold the whites into the milk mixture.

Spoon the cream into six wet 300 ml capacity glasses or dishes and refrigerate for 4 hours or overnight, until firm.

To serve, top with whipped cream and grated chocolate.

Sponge Sandwich No 2

Mrs GT Hindmarsh, Parkes Branch

MAKES ONE 18 CM CAKE

6 eggs, separated
300 g caster sugar
125 g plain flour
125 g cornflour
2 teaspoon baking powder
1 teaspoon vanilla essence
jam of choice, for spreading
whipped cream, for filling
icing sugar, for decorating

Preheat oven to 170°C. Lightly grease and flour the sides of two 18 cm cake tins and line the bases with baking paper.

Using an electric beater, whisk the egg yolks and sugar in a bowl on high speed for 10 minutes, or until thick and pale and the mixture leaves a trail when the beaters are lifted up.

Sift the flour, cornflour and baking powder into a bowl three times. Using clean beaters, whisk the egg whites in a bowl until firm peaks form. Fold the flour mixture into the yolk mixture just until combined, then carefully fold in the whites. Spoon the batter into the tins.

Bake for 30–35 minutes, or until a skewer inserted in the centres comes out clean. Cool cakes in the tins for 10 minutes, then carefully turn out onto wire racks to cool.

When cool, spread one cake with jam then top with whipped cream and layer with the other cake. Dust with icing sugar and serve.

Cauliflower Salad

Miss Helen Sandilands, Uralla Branch

SERVES 6

1 cauliflower, cut into florets
1 butter lettuce, leaves
    washed and dried
6 hard-boiled eggs, sliced
chopped chives or parsley,
    to sprinkle

Dressing

2 hard-boiled egg yolks
1 tablespoon dijon mustard
160 ml (⅔ cup) sweetened
    condensed milk
160 ml (⅔ cup) malt vinegar

For the dressing, push the boiled egg yolks through a sieve and combine in a bowl with the mustard. Mix with the condensed milk, then whisk in the malt vinegar until smooth. Season well with salt and pepper.

Cook the cauliflower in a large saucepan of boiling water for 3–4 minutes, or until cooked but still a little firm. Drain well and stand until cool.

Place the lettuce leaves on a platter then scatter over the cauliflower and egg. Drizzle with the dressing, sprinkle with chives and serve.

Family recipes

INDEX